# AT THE TURN

# At the Turn

*How Two Electrifying Years Changed Golf Forever*

# Steve Eubanks

*Crown Publishers* **©** NEW YORK

Copyright © 2001 by Steve Eubanks

Published by Crown Publishers, New York, New York.
Member of the Crown Publishing Group.

Random House, Inc. New York, Toronto, London, Sydney, Auckland
www.randomhouse.com

CROWN is a trademark and the Crown colophon is a registered trademark of
Random House, Inc.

Printed in the United States of America

Library of Congress Cataloging-in-Publication Data
Eubanks, Steve, 1962–
     At the turn / by Steve Eubanks.—1st ed.
     1. Golf—Tournaments.   2. Golfers.   3. PGA Tour (Association).   I. Title.
GV970.E83 2001
796.352—dc21                                                      00-035854

ISBN 0-609-60743-X

10  9  8  7  6  5  4  3  2  1

First Edition

*To my wife, Debbie.*

# CONTENTS

# AT THE TURN

*One*

# A QUESTION OF LIFE AND DEATH

THE LATE OCTOBER AIR was crisp, not cold, even though the first snowfall was less than a month away and residents of Geneva were hurriedly preparing for the winter ski season. Rain and fog had draped the city in gray for most of the day, but skies cleared by late afternoon and a few remaining clouds bumped lightly against the snow-capped Alps as dusk settled. Flickering lights from a ferry bound for Montrose shimmered against Lake Leman providing the perfect backdrop for a quiet dinner.

A small battery of patrons littered the restaurant: bankers mostly, dressed in dark suits and French-cuffed Egyptian-cotton shirts with all the accoutrements required for status in the Swiss financier community. It was somewhat prejudiced to assume every professionally dressed man or woman in Geneva was a banker, but with only 180,000 residents, and over 450 banks, it was also a pretty safe bet. Locals could always pick out the bankers, distinguishing them with relative ease from the government emissaries, artists, importers, and International Red Cross executives who worked and lived in the city. Of course tourists remained the easiest group to spot. Late October was a transition period for tourism as the weather had become a bit too nippy for waterskiing and day trips to the botanical gardens, but skiers wouldn't arrive for another month or so. It was also a Monday, which meant the Parisians who had been in town for the weekend had returned home, and the cathedral of Saint Pierre, a sprawling structure showcasing architectural and artistic history from Roman rule through the Reformation, was closed. All that remained (in this popular dining establishment at least) were a handful of casually dressed visitors seated silently at two tables in the corner. The bankers were relatively subdued as well. All in all, it was a peaceful night for dining out, exactly the kind of relaxing experience Jean Van de Velde and his wife Brigitte needed.

To the rest of the diners they were a mystery couple: obviously local from their demeanor and familiarity with the restaurant staff, but not a pair you could neatly place in the rigidly enforced Geneva hierarchy. Jean was certainly not a banker; the tan and weathered skin said tourist. The Rolex hinted that he might be an investor from Monaco, but his clothes and demeanor didn't fit that mold. He was young (33 to be exact) and strikingly handsome. With his thick black hair combed back he bore an uncanny resemblance to a young Gregory Peck. He certainly could have passed as France's latest film export, or fashion model. Even when reading a menu or prattling on about the relative virtues of tonight's roast pheasant special his eyes sparkled and his expressions showed an unaffected air of self-assurance and *joie de vivre*. Several of the patrons stared a moment too long assuming he must be someone they should recognize, but no one did.

Brigitte, on the other hand, was a strawberry blonde with just enough tiny wrinkles to confirm she was about his age. Were it not politically incorrect, she would have been described as cute—not ravishing or striking, but attractive in a deeper sense, with high cheekbones, soft skin, a pixie smile, and an engaging stare that confirmed her complete adoration for her husband. She had known Jean since they were 5-year-old children attending grade school in Mont-de-Marsan, a town of 40,000 in the southwest corner of France where the Van de Veldes were well-known industrialists. Jean's father, Jean Marcel Van de Velde, owned one of the largest commercial engine factories in the region, but Jean, the slightly awkward youngest of five brothers, wasn't cut out to sell combine engines to French farmers. Brigitte recognized his spark, and the two became steady sweethearts at age 15. "He's a good person to spend time with," she would say to anyone who asked, quite an admission after spending most of her childhood and all her adult life with only one man. "He never complains, never gets too demanding. He's very good company."

He was also quite popular these days. While no one in the restaurant recognized him (and in Geneva, where privacy is a sacred right, they would have left him alone even if they had) Jean Van de Velde was a professional, a golfer who, after 11 journeyman years on the European PGA Tour where he had posted only one victory and 31 top-ten finishes in 292 tournaments, had been thrust into semi-stardom in late July of 1999. It wasn't the kind of attention Jean or Brigitte wanted, and certainly they wished the circumstances surrounding their newfound fame had been different. But in typical *que será, será* fashion, they accepted their fate and fortune with smiling equanimity.

"So many more people want to know me, want my time, but that's exciting, you know," Jean openly admitted. There was a genuineness to his speech, as if no question was too inane, no subject taboo for him. His English, while good, was laced with a silky French accent, enough to confirm his status as a marketable celebrity—a "hunk" as they would say in the trashy tabloids, or a candidate for "Sexiest Man Alive" in some of the more sensational glossy weeklies.

"It's nice to have people wanting to know what you think and who you are," he continued. "But by the same time it's a bit heavy on your shoulders. There are a certain number of hours in the day, and when the demand is very big you need to sometimes sound like a bad guy and say you can't do that thing someone wants."

It obviously wounded him to be thought of as a bad guy, even by those who were so brash as to make unreasonable requests of his time. He had always been open and available, willing to answer questions anyone might have or sign autographs anyone might want. He even poked fun at his own accent, mimicking Peter Sellers's Inspector Clouseau perfectly. "Does your dog bite?" he would say, cocking an eyebrow just so. Even though he oozed savoir faire, there had never been an overwhelming demand for his impressionistic comedy, or his signature, or his time, during his decade on the European PGA Tour. There were the standard occasions when a voice would shout, "May I have your autograph?" followed by a cap or a folded program being thrust in his direction. "Sure," Jean would always answer, scrawling his name across the item with a black Sharpie. Then the inevitable question would come: "By the way, who are you?" Politely and without hesitation he would answer, "I am Jean Van de Velde." That was usually followed by an "Oh, well, thanks," and off the fan would go in search of Montgomerie or Westwood or any one of the many other players with more name recognition than Jean What's His Name.

But all that had changed. "The last half of the [1999] season I haven't practiced as much as maybe I should have, but that's the way it is, you know," Jean said with only a slight hint of guilt in his voice. "Since the Open it has been very hectic."

"The Open" Monsieur Van de Velde spoke of was the 1999 Open Championship, or the British Open, as it's referred to in America. The third of golf's four major championships played each year, the Open was the only world golf championship that existed in 1860, so there was no reason for the Brits to qualify it as the British Open. According to many imperialist Anglophiles "British Open" remains redundant today, since in many minds there is no other golf event worthy of comparison with the one, true, Open Championship. The U.S. Open, the only other major to qualify as an "open" contest, where anyone with an entry fee and a dream can conceivably work his way into the field, is a mere babe by comparison. First contested in 1895, the U.S. Open was a second-tier event dominated by British players until 1913, and even after it gained momentum and prominence it never fully penetrated the fabric of American culture the way the Open Championship did in Britain. Schoolchildren in Sussex know the Open champion by name as surely as they know their Queen. Unless he wore his trademark knickers, American kids wouldn't have known Payne Stewart (the 1999 U.S. Open Champion) if he stood in front of their classroom and gave an hour-long clinic.

British golf fans are some of the most knowledgeable and avid in the world. Even though the Open Championship is staged in July, the weather at some of the courses can range from testy to downright miserable. St. Andrews, located on the eastern coast of Scotland and considered the birthplace of golf, is on the same latitude as Siberia, and while the weather isn't quite arctic, it can be windy, wet, and frighteningly cold. But the fans come anyway, usually between 30,000 and 40,000 a day braving the elements to watch the world's greatest golfers test their mettle on golf courses that wouldn't fetch a five-dollar greens fee in America.

They are called "links" courses because they sit on land that supposedly links the inland to the sea, and they are unlike any other courses in the world. Some of the oldest and most storied courses in America are links; places like Shinnecock and National Golf Links on Long Island are considered American masterpieces. But as wonderful as those golf courses are, they don't come close to capturing the essence of links golf. For that you have to visit places like St. Andrews, Turnberry, and Muirfield in Scotland; Portmarnock, Ballybunion, and Royal County Down in Ireland; and Birkdale near Liverpool in England. God was the chief architect of these courses, with rising and receding tides routing the holes and centuries of relentless winds shaping the features.

Trees are a rarity on links layouts while blind shots, bad bounces, and hidden bunkers are all common. "It's different," Tiger Woods said of the links game, one of his more understated appraisals. Links golf is nothing like the golf played by most players in America. Whereas players in the United States spend years learning to hit the ball high with lots of spin, links courses require low shots that bore into the wind, then bounce and run along the undulating terrain. Downwind five-iron shots that travel 270 yards are common, while well-struck drivers into the wind often carry no farther than 160 yards.

"I hated it," five-time British Open champion Tom Watson said of his early experiences with links golf. "I said, 'This isn't golf.' It wasn't until I had been over here several times that it occurred to me that this was golf, not what we played. This was the way the game was meant to be played."

And the Open Championship was the ultimate test of the way the game was supposed to be played. The first 12 Opens were contested at a links course called Prestwick on the coast of Scotland. Eight of those times two men named Tom Morris won; Tom Morris, Sr., known as "Old Tom" long before he reached today's Social Security age, won four times and had two runner-up finishes between 1860 and 1867. His son, Tom Morris, Jr., nicknamed "Young Tom" by those creative Scots, won the Open four times in a row between 1867 and 1872. In 1873 the members at Prestwick ran into a little financial trouble, so the Royal and Ancient golfers of St. Andrews stepped in and joined the party, hosting the Open at the Old Course that year, and at Musselburgh the next. That began the tradition of an "Open rotation," whereby the tournament was rotated among links courses. St. Andrews, Musselburgh, and Prestwick ran the rota for 20 years until 1892, when Muirfield was added.

By the 1890s the U.S. Open was getting on its feet, and the game had become a bit more popular both in the states and in Great Britain, so the Open Championship was extended from a 54-hole to a 72-hole contest. Rather than run the event into the weekend, the championship committee decided it should still begin on Wednesday and end with 36 holes on Friday so golf pros could be back in their shops selling featheries, repairing cleeks, and steppin' and fetchin' to their members' needs come Saturday morning. Old traditions die hard, and even though the role of professional golfers changed over the years, the traditions of the Open did not. It wasn't until 1980, when Mark McCormack—Arnold Palmer's longtime agent and founder of the world's largest sports management company, International Management Group—broke out his pocket calculator and showed executives at the Royal and Ancient how much money they were losing in weekend U.S. television fees that the event was finally moved to the standard Thursday through Sunday format professional golfers and golf fans have grown to expect. By then Palmer had won the Open twice, Nicklaus had won it three times, Lee Trevino had won it two times in a row (1971 and 1972), and Watson was in the process of picking up the third of his five victories.

That is not to say that Americans had taken over the Open. A fair number of players over the years have chosen not to make the trip across the pond for various reasons ranging from weather to scheduling conflicts to a genuine dislike for links golf. Sam Snead made his first trip to the Open in 1946, the first contest after a six-year hiatus while the Allies beat back fascism and freed the world from Hitler. Snead won handily, beating Bobby Locke and Johnny Bulla by four shots at St. Andrews, but when the first-place prize money didn't cover Snead's travel and lodging expenses he vowed never to return. "They asked me if I was going to go back, and I said, 'Are you kidding?'" Snead said.

Ben Hogan also made only one trip to the Open. In 1953, after winning the Masters and U.S. Open, Hogan traveled by ship to Scotland where he spent two weeks traipsing around Carnoustie, a small village of 10,000 residents, one marmalade and chocolate factory, and 54 holes of golf, 18 of which were considered the toughest in Britain. Hogan didn't socialize much during his stay. In fact he checked out of the Bruce Hotel (the only one in town at the time) and moved into a rented house 10 miles away in Dundee after the first night. Hogan needed to soak his legs regularly in warm water after a 1949 auto accident, and the only hotel in the town hosting the Open Championship didn't have tubs.

Every day Hogan would take a chauffeur-driven car to the golf course, where he mapped out every nook and cranny of the Medal Course in preparation for his only Open appearance and only Open win. This was during the time when the final 36 was played on Friday (so all those pros could get back to work behind the counters of their shops) and many wondered if Hogan's legs would hold up. They did, and despite a few distractions, like the small band of squealers who discovered Frank Sinatra in his gallery, Hogan shot 70–68 on Friday and won by four. According to former CBS commentator and author Ben Wright, who was also in the gallery that day, "To see this perfectly tailored gentleman in his perfectly pressed pants and sparkling shoes was eminently impressive and equally breathtaking. Hogan looked like he was King." He also never returned to the Open.

Others have passed as well, much to the chagrin of traditionalists who think that skipping a major, especially when you're exempt, is stupid. "Hard to win a major if you don't play in it," Tom Kite pointed out.

Fred Couples chose to pass in 1999, citing a bad back and difficulty traveling long distances on airplanes. Even the most ardent British Open supporters accept legitimate medical excuses. It's those without a doctor's note who get chastised. One player who has drawn particularly harsh criticism for skipping the Open and for his general comments on links golf is Scott Hoch. Even though he had 14 worldwide victories before his 45th birthday, Hoch was best known for the one that got away: the 2-foot par putt he missed on the first playoff hole that would have won the 1989 Masters. Nick Faldo beat Hoch with a birdie on the second extra hole to win the first of his three green jackets. Unfortunately for Hoch his name rhymes with "choke" and tour galleries over the years have been replete with lyricists who have never let him forget that missed opportunity at the Masters. Few cynics know about all the time, effort, and money Hoch and his wife Sally put into supporting the Arnold Palmer Children's Hospital in Orlando. The same year he missed the short putt at the Masters, Hoch won the Las Vegas Invitational and donated his entire $100,000 winner's check to the hospital. Every year he coordinates at least two local pro-ams in Orlando to benefit charities, and he is a visible figure at most of the celebrity fund-raisers in the area. But at least once a year Hoch draws the ire of golfers and fans around the world when he passes on the British Open. In 1997, Brad Faxon, a well-liked player who would later be on the Ryder Cup team with Hoch, said, "Anyone who is exempt and doesn't come over here to play shouldn't be allowed to be on the Ryder Cup or Presidents Cup teams." As if that comment weren't pointed enough, Faxon went on to mention Hoch by name, a comment that cost Faxon $500 for breaking the PGA Tour rule against speaking ill of a fellow player.

Hoch is unrepentant, and will continue to miss the Open. "I don't like the weather or the golf courses," he said. "It's as simple as that. I also like to support our tour, so I play in Mississippi (at the Southern Farm Bureau Classic) the week of the British Open. Sally's family is from Mississippi and I feel that, rather than going to an event I don't like, I should support a PGA Tour event in that community."

While Hoch's opinions might draw criticism from American pros like Faxon, Kite, and Davis Love III, the men who run the R&A couldn't care less. In their view the Open is the ultimate worldwide test of golf, and if players don't like coming—for whatever reasons—they jolly well best stay home.

So sure are the British that their Open is the one true test of golf, the secretary of the Royal and Ancient (British golf's ruling body) stands before the assembled masses after the tournament's conclusion and introduces the winner as "the champion golfer of the year"; not the "British Open champion," or the "Open champion" but "THE champion golfer," an absurdly magniloquent title handed down with such quiet authority it presumes the matter is no longer open for debate. The Open champion is the champion golfer of the year, period. If you object, you are simply wrong.

After that modest introduction, the secretary (Sir Michael Bonallack until his retirement in early 2000, now Peter Dawson) hands the champion golfer of the year the coveted Claret Jug, a two-foot-high ornate silver pitcher with the winners' names inscribed at the base. The first trophy was a Moroccan-leather belt (similar to a prizefighting belt), but when "Young" Tom Morris won his third Open in a row, he was allowed to keep the belt and a new trophy had to be created. The jug idea came from the Honourable Company of Edinburgh Golfers, who thought it marvelously clever for a Claret Jug to be entrusted to the Open winner for the year of his reign, so he could ostensibly drink claret from it in celebration of being the champion golfer of the year.

That's exactly what Ian Baker-Finch did after his Open Championship win in 1991. A few days after the championship Mark O'Meara drove to the Baker-Finches' home in the Torrey Pines subdivision of suburban Orlando to offer congratulations. Baker-Finch heartily accepted O'Meara's good wishes, then invited his neighbor and fellow tour player inside, where the two took a couple of stiff drinks from the Claret Jug, just as the honorable golfers of the 1870s had envisioned.

But the old men in wool probably rolled over in their graves at the little impromptu party Alissa Herron threw with the Claret Jug in the summer of 1996. Tom Lehman, the champion golfer of that year, hosted a charity dinner and auction in his hometown of Minneapolis and took the Claret Jug as a centerpiece for the head table. The dinner dragged on until after midnight, with Tom shaking hands and signing autographs long past his normal bedtime, so no one seemed too shocked when the champion forgot to pick up the trophy. A friend of the Lehmans handed the Claret Jug to Tom's wife, Melissa, who was also busy glad-handing with guests. Melissa relinquished custody of the jug to Alissa Herron, an exceptional amateur golfer and sister of PGA Tour player Tim Herron. Alissa worked for Tom's brother Jim at Signature Sports, a sports management agency that handled the business affairs for Lehman, Herron, Larry Mize, David Ogrin, and Scott Simpson, among others, so Melissa Lehman had no problem entrusting golf's oldest trophy to the young Ms. Herron. At 2:00 A.M. the following morning Tom was awakened from a deep and much-needed R.E.M. sleep by a blasting telephone. It was the Minneapolis police reporting that a young woman had been detained in a local bar for questioning after she and a number of friends were found drinking draft beer out of the British Open trophy.

"Does the suspect have blond hair, big dimples?" Lehman asked.

"That's affirmative," the cop said.

Lehman paused for a moment, wondering if he should leave Alissa to the mercy of Minneapolis's finest. Then he asked, "Is her name Alissa Herron?"

Once Alissa was given a reprieve the cops posed for photos with the Claret Jug, and the party wound down without further incident.

One hundred and eighteen times between 1872 and 1999 the Claret Jug was presented to the Open champion after being returned to the championship committee by the previous year's winner. Sometimes, as was the case when the Lehman children took it off the mantel and played with it in their living room, there were nicks and dings that had to be repaired, but for the most part the Claret Jug survived relatively unscathed for 122 years. Each year the previous champion golfer would ceremoniously return the jug, and after the final putt of the tournament fell, the secretary would hand it out again to the newly crowned "champion golfer of the year."

With each passing year the ceremony became more refined, and in recent years the British Open winner has been expected to offer some profound and reverent remarks, accompanied, it is hoped, by a single tear, only moments after signing his final scorecard. Blubbering is untoward and un-British and thus frowned upon by the tweed-clad purveyors of the Open Championship, but emotion in such a lofty moment is fine as long as it is demonstrated with proper decorum. A perfect example was the acceptance speech American Justin Leonard proffered only moments after he became the champion golfer of 1997. After praising everyone from runners-up Jesper Parnevik and Darren Clarke to the fans and volunteers, Leonard began to speak about what the Open Championship meant to him, a mere 25-year-old mortal from Texas. But the words would not come. Leonard's voice cracked, his eyes turned downward, and the corners of his mouth twitched ever so slightly. "Pardon me," he said as he stepped away from the microphone. After an acceptably quiet moment in which he regained his composure, Leonard gave simple but eloquent thanks to the championship committee and the people of Great Britain, then he hoisted the Claret Jug above his shoulder and smiled for the cameras and the crowd.

What a moment! That, the men of the R&A thought, was what an acceptance speech by the champion golfer of the year should be. It had been perfect in every detail, right down to the tear and silent moment. Justin Leonard was the kind of winner the Open Championship loved in 1997, and the kind it desperately needed again in 1999 as the Open returned to Carnoustie for the first time in 24 years amid the biggest controversy in recent championship memory.

It's a commonly held misconception that professional golfers are spoiled by the conditions under which they compete. Just go to any municipal golf course in America on any summer Sunday afternoon and you'll likely hear the same mantra from pot-bellied 18-handicappers settling their bets over pitchers of beer while the weekly professional golf tournament glows from big-screen televisions. "Dadgum, them fairways look like greens," one would no doubt offer, following almost automatically by, "Yeah, those guys are spoiled. They ought to have to play out here a few times and they'd quit their bellyaching." Different regions of the country might present different interpretations and dialects, but the gist of the conversation is as universal as it is inaccurate.

Professional golfers, particularly those on the U.S. PGA Tour, make their living playing the toughest golf courses under the toughest conditions week in and week out—a fact that often escapes the weekend player who constantly wants to compare his course to PGA Tour venues and his game to that of his favorite tour pro. A typical example of this came in mid-summer 1998, when former PGA Championship winner Mark Brooks spent a late afternoon on the range practicing his middle irons. As Brooks worked, a fan from the bleachers carped, "What are you hitting?"

"A six-iron," Brooks responded.

After two more swings where Brooks's shots sailed 155 yards with a slight fade, the spectator chided, "Jeez, I can hit it that far!" At which point Brooks turned and gave the man an incredulous stare before saying, "We do this for money!" He might as well have finished the sentence by calling the man a moron, but Brooks had too much class for that. The point had been made, but there were thousands of others just like Mr. "Jeez, I can hit it that far" who didn't get it.

Every swing on the PGA Tour represents thousands if not hundreds of thousands of dollars. Sure, the courses are nice, the clubhouses impeccable, the courtesy cars clean, and the range balls new and shiny, but the greens are the hardest and fastest in the world, the roughs are the highest and toughest, and the fairways, while pristine and immaculate, are narrower than at any other time throughout the year. As Brad Faxon once noted, "The good club players and good amateurs don't understand the difference. Good players who I play with when I'm home say, 'You know, I hit it as far as you, and as close as you a lot of the time. I must be close.' They might shoot even-par and I might shoot one-under when we're out playing a casual round at home, but they don't realize how different it is out there. They can't imagine hitting a perfect nine-iron from a perfect lie and having the ball bounce over the back of the green, or hitting what they think is a perfect putt and having it roll off the green and into a bunker. Those are the conditions we find every week on tour."

Some weeks the courses are harder than others. Bermuda Dunes and Indian Wells, two of the courses that host the Bob Hope Chrysler Classic, are layouts where most of the celebrity amateurs in the field have a good time, play to their handicaps, and get around without embarrassment. They also produce some of the lowest scores of the year. On the other hand, the Tournament Players Club (TPC) at Sawgrass, host site of the Players Championship, rarely gives up as many birdies as bogeys or double-bogeys, and the tournament is always one of the highest-scoring events of the season.

The USGA is notorious for growing high rough around narrow fairways and starving greens until they are brick-hard. Every year players bemoan the conditions at the U.S. Open, and every year a certain percentage of spectators sneer at the "spoiled" pro golfers who cry about a little too much grass. Rarely, if ever, do amateurs play under U.S. Open conditions, and even on the rare occasions when they do, it isn't with the pressure of a major championship on the line. Even some of the players enjoy hearing the complaints. Jack Nicklaus used to love trolling the locker room for negative comments about a particularly hard course setup. "I knew I was going to beat those guys," Nicklaus said of the perpetual bitchers.

On the toughest setups, opinions are usually mixed: players who score well think the courses are tough but fair, and players who post high numbers think the person who set the pins or grew the rough should be drawn and quartered in the town square before sundown. No matter how seemingly unreasonable the setup, there is always one player who digs out the most worn cliché in the game: "We all have to play the same golf course." While technically accurate, the truth is that the same golf course can seem very different depending on circumstances. Time of day, wind, weather, number of players in the field, and amount of alcohol consumed by the fans in attendance can dramatically change the makeup, playability, and enjoyment of a golf course. Players know it, but they also know it's good PR to say things like "tough but fair," and "we all have to play the same course." For anyone to say, "It was okay at eight this morning, but by 3:00 it was unplayable" would be professional suicide.

So it was somewhat surprising that from July 17 through July 23 of 1999 professional golfers were virtually united in their condemnation of any given golf course setup. But never in the annals of professional golf had there been an event like the 128th Open Championship.

The warning signals had come almost a month earlier, in June at the U.S. Open in Pinehurst. Speaking about the Open Championship's triumphant return to historic Carnoustie after a two-decade hiatus, Sir Michael Bonallack said, "Some of [the fairways] were just too narrow to the point where there was rough on the fairway side of the bunkers. We want balls to run into the sand, so the long grass has been removed."

That was news to Sandy Lyle, the champion golfer of 1985 and a man who played quite a few rounds at Carnoustie. "The course is as tight as a duck's behind," he said. "From what I've seen it won't matter what the weather is like in the run-up to the championship. The rough is going to be terrible. You can be in an awful lie just a few feet off the fairway. If you're going to miss from the tee, you're better to miss by at least ten yards."

Bonallack, who had finished as low amateur in the 1968 Open at Carnoustie, said of the course, "When the wind blows it's probably the toughest golf course in Britain, and when it's not blowing, it's still the toughest." Those comments were uttered long before the fairways were narrowed to 9 yards in spots and before the rough was grown knee-high off the edges of the fairways, so it shouldn't have been a shock to Bonallack and the other members of the R&A when golfers took exception to the setup at Carnoustie.

When they arrived for the practice rounds, the greatest golfers in the world were shocked by what they found. Phil Mickelson could do nothing but laugh as he trudged through the rough expecting to scare up a bevy of quail with each step. On Wednesday, up to his knees in waving grass, Mickelson put his hands on his thighs, hunched over, and found his golf ball in an impossible lie three paces off the 6 fairway. Across the fairway a maintenance worker with a Weedwacker trimmed brush in an area none of the players were likely to find during the week. "Hey, over here!" Mickelson shouted to the worker, but to no avail. The man simply nodded, waved, and went back to his work.

So evidently silly had it become by Wednesday that Mickelson, Mark Calcavecchia, and Billy Mayfair each put up $2,000 for whoever among them could play Wednesday's round without a bogey. "I made it through ten holes," Calcavecchia said. "Then I made about six after that."

By the time Ivor Robson, the primly dressed gray-haired official starter for the Open, announced the first group Thursday morning, the course had been nicknamed "Carnasty," and comments grew louder as the world's greatest players (circa 1999) were embarrassed, humiliated, and angered by what they collectively perceived as the stupidest golf course setup in major championship history. "Terribly unfortunate," Nick Price, who is unanimously recognized as the nicest man in golf, said of what they had done to Carnoustie. "If I were in the gallery, I would ask for my money back." For Price to criticize any golf course under any circumstances was big news. This was a man who was too polite to shoo away a club salesman who wanted to give him a few putting tips, even though Price had 39 tournament wins (including three majors) at the time.

Colin Montgomerie, Europe's number-one player for a record six consecutive years who was well on his way to making it a seventh, said, "Some of the shots that have to be hit can't be."

"It's like trying to hit a driver into my hotel room," Greg Norman said. "That's about the width we've got to hit into."

These weren't your average, every-year, badmouthing also-rans who could always be counted on to complain; these were the guys who rarely complained, and they were the guys who loved hard courses. The harder the better! A harder course meant the toughest competitor, the player with the most heart, the most patience, the most tenacity, and the strongest endurance would win, and the group of players who were now complaining fit that mold.

Mickelson said, "I wish I hadn't come. There isn't an individual in the R&A who could break one hundred on this course," while U.S. Open champion Payne Stewart said, "I've never been so happy to walk off a golf course in my life. I think 'over the top' is being kind." Stewart, one of the men who consistently prevailed on tough courses, continued by saying, "[In America] we don't call these fairways; we call them walkways. This could actually be a place where people wished they would miss the cut. If [the R&A] does this to St. Andrews [in 2000] it's not going to be any fun at all. Maybe they've learned a lesson this week. We'll have to wait and see. My attitude hasn't changed on the Open, though. I'm disappointed in the course setup, but my view of the British Open hasn't changed. I love the tournament and I think it is the foremost golf tournament in the world. It's always been that way to me, even being an American and having won two U.S. Opens. I've always held the British Open dear to my heart and it would really complete my career to win one. This week, though, the hardest thing to do was to try not to hurt myself."

Fred Funk did hurt himself, injuring his wrist while trying to hack his ball from the rough en route to an opening-round 83. His playing partner, Sandy Lyle, who shot a first-round 85, said, "When someone like Fred Funk, who's known for accurate play and hitting fairways all the time, shoots eighty-three, you know it's impossible."

This from an Open champion, the champion golfer of 1985, and a loyal Scot at that! If Lyle's and Stewart's comments weren't bad enough, Tom Watson, one of the most beloved Open champions and the last man to win an Open at Carnoustie, joined the party. "Giving golfers a fairway that is fifteen yards wide is below the minimum by quite a bit," Watson said. "The USGA's minimum is twenty-three yards. We have several fairways here close to fifteen yards wide or less. That's unfair." In fact, some of the fairways were 10 yards wide, and the sixth measured nine yards wide in the landing area, but that was beside the point: this was Tom Watson, Payne Stewart, Greg Norman, Phil Mickelson, and Sandy Lyle complaining!

It was all too much for the Angus residents and those who lived around the Firth of Tay, an inlet of the North Sea with Carnoustie on its north shore and St. Andrews nestled on its southern banks. Golf was more than a recreational pursuit for these people: golf was life itself. Carnoustie's courses belonged to the town's residents and were managed by the Carnoustie Links Council, which, as far as the citizenry is concerned, was a far more important body than the Angus District Council. They might work in the local pubs or the newly constructed Carnoustie Hotel, or at Mackays, the local factory that made chocolate golf balls filled with hazelnut truffle, but these people lived for their golf, and Open week was the culmination of two decades of tenacious work. When the R&A said the Open had outgrown the roads and infrastructure of the tiny town, residents set out to work to rectify the problems, widening roads and building the new hotel. They improved the conditioning of their course to attract events like the 1992 British Amateur, and eventually worked their way back into the Open rotation. This was their shining moment in the sun, and now they were being criticized!

The players' comments weren't personal, but that didn't matter to the people of Angus. Ian Salmond, the irrigation specialist for the Carnoustie Links, had named his two sons Ben and Tom after Hogan and Watson, two of the Open champions from Carnoustie. Now Salmond's course was coming under fire from his son's namesake, among others. It was more than many could bear.

But the players had a point. On the scorecard par was 71, but the average score in the opening round was over 78, and even after the 36-hole cut, the average round for the week was more than five-over-par. Defending golfer of the year Mark O'Meara shot 83 on Thursday, while opening-round leader Rodney Pampling shot 86 on Friday and became the first player in the 128-year history of the Open to miss the cut after leading at the end of round one. The only light moment of the week came on Thursday when a 20-year-old "dancer" named Yvonne

Robb, who displayed her craft at an Aberdeen club called Private Eyes, sprinted onto the 18th green in thong panties and a lacy bra to lay a big wet kiss on Tiger Woods. That brought a smile from Woods and a hearty laugh from his playing partner, Ian Woosnam, but that fun and frivolity was fleeting. Once the tournament resumed the dour frustration returned.

"I think they've introduced luck into it," David Duval said. "It looks to me like we're being asked to play target golf on a links layout. We all know what it's going to be like. It's going to be hard." Duval, who called Carnoustie "a good course spoiled," stopped practicing after Tuesday even though the tournament didn't start until Thursday, saying, "There are only so many punches you can take on the chin. The U.S. Open was very difficult but it was enjoyable. It shouldn't be stress free, but if you can't enjoy an event like this, then you've got to question what's going on." Then after opening the tournament with a 79, Duval added, "It was about what I expected. I hit a couple of good shots I thought were perfect and they ended up terrible. If the average player had to play out there he'd probably quit the game, and a lot of pros, too. The R&A says it's an out-of-control greenkeeper. I don't know what they're trying to accomplish." Later in the week Duval did his best to put a positive spin on those comments by meeting with Mr. Hugh Campbell, the chairman of the championship committee, but everyone still agreed the entire week was a hapless mockery of championship golf.

The out-of-control greenkeeper theory wasn't a bad defense. John Philp, the much-heralded superintendent who came to Carnoustie from St. Andrews in 1985, was the man responsible for narrowing the fairways and growing hayfield-high rough everywhere else. Brash and unapologetic, Philp sounded like a Scottish version of the beer-bellied 18-handicapper watching "them spoiled golfers" on Sunday afternoon. "Golf has gone soft," he said. "Players are pampered nowadays. They have their gurus all helping them, and they get their courtesy cars taking them everywhere. There is an ego problem here. They want a good payday with as little hassle as possible. Well, sorry, Jimmy. This is the Open, the big exam. They have psychologists and titanium, but I have what God gave me, nature."

God and nature won. Even Gary Player, who won the Open at Carnoustie in 1968, and a man who once chantilly called an abysmal condo-laden course in the swamps of central Florida "the most unique layout of its kind," couldn't muster a single positive accolade for this rendition of golf's oldest championship. "It's the toughest course I've seen in forty-five years of championship golf," Player said in as neutral a tone as he could muster.

A far more impetuous Sergio Garcia, who shot 89–83 and finished dead last among those who didn't withdraw, said, "For the first time in ten years I won't watch the British Open on television because I don't think it deserves it. I don't care. Not this week. I would care if it came on a different type of course under different conditions, but I don't think this tournament deserves to be remembered."

But remembered it would most certainly be, for the 1999 Open Championship would be the coming-out party for France's most visible golf export, Jean Van de Velde, the man who one British tabloid cruelly dubbed "The Frog That Croaked." The Open Championship at Carnoustie ended as a tragic comedy, with Van de Velde at the center of both the tears and the punch lines. *Golf World* magazine labeled him a "French Dip," one of the kinder *entendres* given to Van de Velde after his antics in the final round. During the height of the debauchery one of Britain's more prolific sports journalists watched events unfold on the BBC from the comfort of the press tent with a cup of tea propped precariously on his expansive midsection. By way of explanation for the events that had just unfurled, he said, "There's a reason the French haven't won a war this century." At the time it was as good a rationale as any.

Even the PGA European Tour piled on. The first two sentences of the tour's "official" bio on Van de Velde read, "Will always be remembered as the man who nearly won the Open Championship. He led by three shots playing the 72nd hole only to take triple bogey and then lose a playoff to Paul Lawrie."

The explanation was just that simple: ranked 152nd in the world at the beginning of the week, Jean Van de Velde led the Open by five shots after 54 holes and by three shots after 71 holes. At that point everyone assumed it was mercifully and finally over. The 18th was a par-four measuring 487 yards guarded on all quadrants by the "Barry Burn," a meandering ditch about 10 feet wide with a stream of water about mid-shin deep. It was certainly a tough hole, averaging 4.45 for the week, but 4.45 was all Van de Velde needed. He would have taken 6.45 if such a thing had been allowed under the rules. It still would have been good enough for the win. Certainly a man who had negotiated 71 of the most demanding holes in tournament golf history could get down in six or less on the final par-four. If all else failed he could hit his seven-iron three times and three-putt for the win. Even Brooks's admonition, "We do this for money," didn't apply. The Open Championship, by all rights, should have been over.

Instead the unimaginable happened. With his name already engraved on the Claret Jug (by an overanxious engraver named Alec Harvey who was trying to save time in the interest of television) Van de Velde stepped onto the 18th tee and took out his driver. "That is not a smart play," ABC commentator Curtis Strange said of the decision. "He doesn't need to hit driver." Indeed, all Van de Velde needed was to find the fairway and avoid the Barry Burn. A two-iron would have worked, or a three-, or even a four-iron. But Van de Velde never considered those options. The world's largest Rolex clock, mounted on the south wall of the new Carnoustie Hotel, was the perfect target for him, and he had been driving the ball well. It was driver all the way.

"I stood there and there is no easy tee shot, I think," Van de Velde said of his decision making, or lack thereof. "Even being three ahead, what do you do? Do you hit five-iron down the left, or do you hit something down the right, or do you try to go as far up as you can? I took that option, and I didn't hit a good shot."

In fact, he hit a poor shot, a dead-right push that sent groans through the assembled gallery. But fate seemed to be shining on Van de Velde. His ball, apparently destined for the water when it left the club, miraculously stopped on a small peninsula near the 17th fairway. It was one of golf's miracles, no less amazing than Fred Couples's gravity-defying shot that somehow stayed dry on the banks of the 12th hole at Augusta National when Freddie won the 1992 Masters. Van de Velde's decision to hit driver off the tee hadn't cost him. The ball had found a thumb of dry land from which he could advance his next shot.

Unfortunately for Van de Velde, the lie on his island oasis was perfect. Had he been nestled in the rough, or submerged in a divot, he would have had no option but to play a wedge shot back to the fairway. From there he could hit another short iron onto the green, two-putt or three-putt, hoist the Claret Jug, say some nice words, shed one tear, and be on his way. But the lie wasn't just good; it was perfect. "I could not have placed the ball any better," he said. "The only thing I had was 189 yards to carry the burn, which wasn't very demanding."

His caddie, Christophe Angiolini, could have counseled him in the relative merits of laying up, but instead Angiolini said, "Perfect lie. So try for the green."

"The only thing I didn't want to do was hit it left into the out of bounds," Van de Velde continued to explain. "So the option was to hit a wedge down the left and pitch on and two-putt or three-putt or whatever, or try to move forward. The ball was lying so good and I took my two-iron and thought, 'You're going to hit it down there, and either be on the green or just on the right in the bunker.' I didn't feel comfortable hitting a wedge. To me, it was against the spirit of the game. I'm going to hit wedge, then another wedge, and then what? Three-putt from thirty feet to win by one?

"Okay, fair enough, I would win by one, but what a way to finish!"

Curtis Strange called Van de Velde's decision to hit two-iron "the stupidest thing I've ever seen," while Ian Baker-Finch (champion golfer of 1991) said Van de Velde had gone "from dumb to dumb and dumber." Strange's comments seemed to come from genuine befuddlement at what he was seeing, but Baker-Finch's sounded a bit too rehearsed and far too glib from a man who had virtually given up the game. The low point of Baker-Finch's career came at St. Andrews in 1995, when he took a vicious swing on the first tee of the championship (knocking his hat off) and became the first man in Open history to hook a ball out of bounds on the first hole of St. Andrews. The shot was over 100 yards offline. Shortly after the event, Baker-Finch officially retired from competitive golf. Now he was criticizing Jean Van de Velde, a bit of irony that wasn't lost on those who knew their Open history.

Not that Jean didn't deserve a little criticism. The 18th green was guarded by the Barry Burn, a bunker on the right, and an out-of-bounds fence only a few yards long and left. From the angle he had, Jean's shot was only slightly easier than Norman's "driver through the hotel room," and under the circumstances it seemed an unnecessary risk. Perhaps the best reason anyone gave for Jean's decision to go for the green came from Brigitte, who said afterward, "Every time he lays up, he goes in the shit."

This time he went for it, and he ended up in deeper shit than he could have ever imagined. Mere moments after pushing his tee shot (a sure sign that his swing wasn't up to the kind of miraculous shot he was attempting) Van de Velde pushed his second shot into the grandstand right of the green. The ball ricocheted backwards off a railing in the stands, hopped off the masonry wall of the Barry Burn, and finished waist high in John Philp's God-and-nature-loving gorse.

"I have hit maybe a million two-irons in my life," Van de Velde would say later. "Some of them turn out bad and some of them turn out good. I didn't think it was a stupid shot; I didn't go for anything special. I didn't go for glory. I just went for a golf shot I know I'm capable of hitting every day of the year, every day of my life, and it just turned out to be a terrible break. It's a distance of a four-iron to clear the water, and I'm hitting a two-iron. I'm not going to think about the water. That would be silly. I would have been better off in the burn, because then I would have had somewhere to drop. But, no, it came back and I had a dramatic lie. I couldn't go backwards; I don't think I could have gone anywhere."

The drama continued as Van de Velde considered the options for his third shot, none of which was very good. The out-of-bounds fence loomed to the left of the fairway and over the green. He turned to Angiolini and said, "If I play sideways I might not make the fairway."

Angiolini said nothing.

"If I stay in the rough, is that any gain?" Van de Velde asked rhetorically. "No," he answered himself. The decision was made. Van de Velde would once again take his best shot at the green.

Gorse flew like Kansas wheat in a spring storm, but the golf ball traveled only 20 yards, dropping with a resounding splat into the Barry Burn. If Van de Velde was shocked by this turn of events he never showed it. He and Angiolini examined the situation with the same dispassionate thoroughness they had displayed throughout the week when Jean played the 18th with a par and two birdies. Now they were staring headlong at a seven or possibly an eight. It was shaping up to be the most spectacular collapse in major championship history.

"We went to one of those scoring trailers in the back and the first thing I see is Jean hitting the ball in the creek," Justin Leonard said. Leonard, a champion who would have lent great credibility to this slow disaster, had finished with a bogey at the 18th to shoot six-over-par for the week—good enough for third or maybe a tie for second, he thought. Never could he have imagined it would be good enough to win. But with Van de Velde in the water on his third shot, the three-shot advantage he had carried to the final tee was gone. After a drop, Van de Velde would have to get the ball up and down to win. A pitch and two putts meant playoff, and Leonard wasn't ready. He quickly grabbed his caddie, Bob Reifke, and headed to the practice ground for a swing or two just in case.

Paul Lawrie, the other man who had finished at six-over-par courtesy of a final-round 67, was already on the putting green with his coach, Adam Hunter, former PGA European Tour player. "Adam did a great job of keeping me focused," Lawrie said. "He was the only one who believed six-over-par would win, or at worst get into a playoff."

Meanwhile Jean had decided to take a closer look at his ball. As casually as he might have disrobed in his own bathroom, he sat on the top row of bricks at the edge of the burn, took off both shoes, then removed his dark socks before rolling up his pants as if he were about to take a summer afternoon stroll on the beach. At the exact moment Jean climbed down the wall and into the water, droplets of rain began to pepper the Barry Burn like tears of laughter from above.

There he stood, Gregory Peck in a royal-blue Disneyland shirt, ankle deep in a creekbed with his trousers pulled above his knees. It was a picture that would don the cover of magazines and newspapers around the world the following day and for days to come.

"I don't give a shit about what people think," he said, although not bitterly. He was in no way embarrassed by the utterly farcical scene he was creating. If he could play the shot from the water and win the tournament, he would look like a hero. Instead, the little dip in the burn was all for naught. "As I started to climb down I could see the ball sinking," he said. "It was two or three inches underneath the water so there was no hope. It was telling me, 'Hey you, silly man. Not for you.'"

Craig Parry, the other member of the final twosome who had stood as the closest witness to this surreal moment, added a little levity when he said to Jean, "You should wait a few minutes. The tide's going out."

Even Jean had to laugh at that one. He laughed even harder after he climbed out of the ditch, got dressed, and looked at his drop options. It was back to the gorse. "After I dropped, I knew I couldn't get it on the green from there," he said. In fact, he stood a good chance of dumping the ball back into the water. But after another thrash that sent grass flying, Jean's ball made it over the burn and into the bunker. From there he blasted a routine sand shot to within 6 feet, and calmly made the putt for triple-bogey. He hadn't lost, but he hadn't won. To their surprise Leonard and Lawrie were in a playoff with Van de Velde for the Open Championship.

The committee gave Jean 15 minutes to change clothes and get himself together for the playoff, a break he didn't need. Even though he went to his hotel room, changed his shirt, and put on a sweater, the quarter-hour was just long enough for him to come down from the emotional roller-coaster he had just ridden for the last half-hour, but it was not enough time for him to absorb the enormity of what had happened. It was also enough time for his joints to stiffen, and for him to realize how cold his feet were after his little romp in the water on 18. The break took him out of his rhythm, and broke what semblance of concentration he had remaining.

A quarter-hour later, stiff and a little out of sorts, Jean arrived at the 15th tee for the playoff and immediately began joking, telling Leonard, Lawrie, and the gallery members what a surprise it was to see them. Most who saw this assumed he was in shock. There was no way a man could self-destruct in such grand fashion only to joke about it 15 minutes later. When Jean hooked his tee shot into the bushes left of the 15th fairway, everyone knew it was over.

An hour later, Paul Lawrie, who came into the championship ranked 159th and who was considered a slightly bigger underdog than Van de Velde, calmly made a 4-foot birdie putt on the final hole to win the playoff and become "the champion golfer of 1999." It was only then that Jean Van de Velde sat down at a scorer's table, put his head in his hands, and cried.

Within minutes, though, he was answering reporters' questions, head held high. "You know, I made plenty of friends because a Scottish man won," he joked. "Maybe I wasn't humble enough. I didn't need to go for glory. Maybe I should have laid up. But there are worse things in life. I read the newspapers like you and some terrible things are happening to other people. It is a golf tournament. A game! I gave it my best shot." With a shrug and a smile, he put it all into perspective when, with a greatly exaggerated French accent, he said, "Hey, ziss better than a kick in zee ass."

For months following the Open, Jean Van de Velde was cheered as he played the rest of his European tour schedule. "Who is that?" novice spectators would continue to ask. "That's Jean Van de Velde, the man who blew the Open Championship," would come the answer. American galleries at the Ryder Cup matches in Brookline had waved and shouted, "Go get 'em Jean," to which Jean politely had returned the wave and politely thanked them, just as he had done for over a decade when nobody cared. In an odd way, Van de Velde had become the hero of Carnoustie, not the goat. He would have certainly been emotional and charismatic in victory, but instead he had shown the world how to be equally charismatic in defeat. Only moments after losing the biggest golf tournament of his life, he was reminding everyone that it was just a golf tournament. A game! No governments were toppled, and no lives were destroyed. The sun came up on Monday morning, the rest of the world went back to work, and life moved on. In a year when every round of golf had been televised and professional golfers took on rock-star celebrity status; when jingoism and provocative rhetoric had reached an all-time high; and when many of the gentlemanly aspects of the gentle-man's game were being questioned, it took a man who had crashed and burned in a major championship to remind everyone that it was just a game.

"There have been a lot of people who wrote that I should feel very proud of what I did, that my attitude was exceptional, and that people should learn from it," he said several months after the Open. "One guy wrote me a few weeks later and said, 'Thanks for reminding me it's a game, because since then, I'm playing better and enjoying it more.' It's not a question of life and death."

That night in Geneva, Jean paid for dinner and slipped on his coat as Brigitte gathered her purse. He had returned home from Belgium the night before, and the following morning he would leave for Spain where he would spend the last two weeks of the season playing in the Volvo Masters and the WGC American Express Championship at Valderrama, a course he didn't particularly like, but one he knew how to play. He felt good about his year, and his family, and his life. Geneva was a gem of a city. After the first of November he would be home with Brigitte and the girls. He would take their oldest, Alexandra, to school, then hit the slopes for a few hours before returning to rue Robert de Traz at 2:00 to spend the afternoons with his family. The 35 museums in the city Jean-Jacques Rousseau and John Calvin had once called home would also be on his winter agenda, as would a few visits to the Greenwich Village for shopping and a drink or two with friends.

He knew he would forever be known as the man who blew the 1999 British Open, but it could not be changed, and it should not be dwelled upon. No one remembered that he had also made a seven in the final round of the 1993 Roma Masters to fall into a playoff with Greg Turner. Jean won that playoff on the third extra hole for his only victory as a professional, but the Roma Masters was not the British Open. He knew he would be considered a choker, someone who didn't have the heart to close a win. Two weeks after the Open a spectator in the gallery pointed to Jean and said, "There's the man who has 'Idiot' painted on his chest." But those who said such things had never seen him play right center and stand off for *L'Etoile Sportive* Rugby Club, where his grit and tenacity were legendary. At first the world had considered him a flake. Later, though, thoughtful fans of golf accepted him, seeing a little of themselves in Jean Van de Velde. He typified the temporary insanity everyone experiences at some point in professional life, personal life, and especially in golf. Perhaps he was more of a role model than he or anyone else ever realized.

When they returned to their apartment, Jean removed his coat and checked the phone messages while Brigitte tended to the girls. Although only 7 years old, Alexandra already had her father's striking good looks and mesmerizing eyes. Brigitte knew she would break many hearts and give her father many gray hairs. God, she loved her husband. Win or lose, he was the genuine article, and she felt happy to have married him.

Jean came around the corner from the telephone, and Brigitte immediately knew there was trouble. She couldn't imagine what might have caused him to go so pale. "What's wrong?" she asked.

After he told her, they spent the rest of the evening watching live Euro News coverage of a privately chartered Learjet streaking through the skies over the American Midwest. According to the early reports, all on board were presumed dead. As the news unfolded in front of them, Jean and Brigitte Van de Velde silently moved closer, and the silly game of golf seemed all the more trivial.

# Two

# THE INCIDENT

NEWS OF THE "INCIDENT" spread throughout the golf community over an informal network of cell phones that began ringing a little after 11:00 A.M. on Monday, October 25. Because of their travel schedules almost all professional golfers carry digital cell phones with nationwide paging, and while all the numbers are unlisted, fellow pros and their wives share contact numbers with each other so dinners can be arranged, schedules can be coordinated, and play-dates with the kids confirmed. On the morning of the incident, the wives were the ones making most of the calls. Conversations were short and frantic. "Julie, this is Katie. Have you heard about the plane?" It was the kind of preamble that made a tour wife's heart sink, and the kind of greeting most of the wives received from their friends that morning. "Debbie, it's Tammy, have you heard? There's a problem on a plane." "Problem" was the only way they knew to describe it since details were sketchy. The only thing they knew for certain was that someone they knew had perished aboard an aircraft, and it was up to the wives to get the word out to friends before the media did.

None of the wives said the word "incident," which was the official term FAA employees assigned to the streaking Learjet as experts attempted to predict where and when it would come down. Air traffic controllers were given only a few labeling options: the first was to call it a NORDO, which was a contrived acronym for "No Radio." NORDO indicated a loss in radio contact between an aircraft and the controllers. While not a regular occurrence, NORDOs weren't highly unusual, either. Mechanical trouble with an aircraft's radio or microwave interruptions on the frequency could cause a plane to lose contact with controllers, at which point procedure dictated that the pilots continue on their assigned heading and altitude, allowing controllers to arrange traffic around them. The NORDO label didn't apply in this case, nor did calling it a "deviant aircraft" seem appropriate. That title was normally reserved for low-flying, unmarked prop planes inbound from Mexico or the Caribbean, usually carrying contraband and trying to elude detection. This was a high-flying chartered jet every control center in the country had on their scopes. There was nothing deviant about it. The other two options were to label it a "crash" or an "incident" and since, for four hours, the plane was still in the air, "crash" seemed too macabre, even though everyone from the FAA's chief administrator to the guy who swept the floor in the air traffic control center knew a crash was inevitable. But until such time as it went down, calling it a crash was inaccurate and inappropriate. Therefore, it was called an "incident," a sterile, understated description for an aircraft catastrophe that hadn't happened yet, but one that couldn't be stopped.

Those nuances of language were lost on all the tour wives who spent much of that Monday morning trying to find their husbands. Each call sent a deeper sense of panic throughout the close-knit community. It was an unspoken fear among the wives who watched their husbands board planes for the next tour stop every week, many of them logging more time in the sky than some commercial pilots. The spouses, who went out on the weekends and in the summer when the kids were out of school, knew all the statistics: flying was the safest form of travel. Tour players, like all business travelers, were more likely to be killed driving to the corner grocery store than flying to and from work. Statistics never alleviated the anxiety, though. Now their worst fears were unfolding with every chirp, ping, or cute musical ditty springing forth from their cell phones, bringing news that one of their own might be on a doomed flight. It was a sickening feeling. Even though the passenger manifest wouldn't be confirmed for some time, everyone felt the sense of impending tragedy no matter who was on board. As Jim Furyk said, "The bad part was you knew somebody was on that plane. Even if it wasn't your buddy, and for a while we weren't sure who it was, somebody with a family was up there."

Furyk had been standing on the driving range at the Champions Club in Houston when he heard the news. The Tour Championship, an elite event of the PGA Tour's top 30 money winners and (until 1999) the official grand finale of the season, was back in Houston for the second time in three years, and Furyk (number 12 on the money list at the time) had arrived a day earlier than usual to get in a little extra practice.

As was normally the case during practice rounds, there were as many equipment reps and sports agents on the driving range as there were players. On Mondays, Tuesdays, and Wednesdays driving ranges on tour looked like manufacturers' expos, with tour reps showing their wares and phoning custom orders back to the plants, while overdressed agents pressed the flesh with sponsors. The Tour Championship was no different. Thursday through Sunday the range was a workplace for players, caddies, and coaches, but early in the week it was a carnival and convention center with a smattering of practice on the side.

Just like players, all manufacturers' reps had digital cell phones, and it was from one of those phones that word of the tragedy first arrived on the range in Houston. "Holy shit! You're kidding," one of the reps said into his phone. Even though they were a demonstrative bunch, that sort of reaction from a club seller was unusual, especially with spectators sitting in bleachers behind the range. "You're not going to believe this," the rep said to Furyk and the handful of players who were practicing beside him. "There's a Learjet flying around on autopilot. The crew and passengers are dead. It isn't confirmed, but they think Payne Stewart is on board."

Everything stopped. There was a moment of stunned silence as everyone tried to grasp the magnitude of what had been said. Then players huddled and tried, without showing too much anxiety, to discern fact from speculation. Furyk didn't want to jump to any conclusions, but if Payne's name was already being batted about this freely, there was a better than average chance it was true. After another couple of swings Furyk took off his glove and handed the club to his caddie, Mike "Fluff" Cowan. Practice was over.

Within minutes Sid Wilson and Mike Starks from the PGA Tour walked onto the range and confirmed the earlier report. An unspecified problem had incapacitated the crew and passengers of a Learjet. They were presumed dead, but the plane was continuing to fly on autopilot over the Midwest. No one had confirmation, but U.S. Open champion Payne Stewart was probably one of the passengers.

Furyk felt a dull sickness nestle into his stomach as the news sank in. He had known Payne since 1994, but only in the sense that all competitors on tour knew each other. They were friends, but not bosom buddies. Then, only five weeks earlier after five years together on tour,

Furyk got to know Payne as a Ryder Cup teammate, an emotional leader and a man who openly shared his feelings and shed his tears with 11 brothers in combat. During the Saturday-night team meeting, after an emotionally and physically draining week in Boston, Payne Stewart bared his soul in front of his Ryder Cup brethren and their wives, recalling the memory of his late father and what the Ryder Cup meant to him. Those were the memories running through Jim Furyk's mind as he walked off the range and into the locker room. His instincts were telling him that his Ryder Cup teammate, a man who had been a pillar of courage and character, was gone.

Radio talk show host Rush Limbaugh, an avid golfer and friend of many tour players, was one of the first with the news. Rush called Tom Watson and informed him of the details, sketchy though they were. Watson's wife, Hillary, then called Sally Hoch at home in Orlando. The Hochs were neighbors and close friends with the Stewarts, and Sally was one of the most respected and well organized of the tour wives. If anybody would know what to do and whom to call, it was Sally. Hillary wasn't quite sure how to break the news, so she chatted with Sally for a moment then said, "I've got something I have to tell you."

"What is it?" Sally asked.

"There's a plane that has depressurized and is flying on autopilot. Everyone is gone." Hillary paused for what couldn't have been more than a beat or two, but it seemed like an eternity. "One of them is Payne."

Sally went into shock. Moments later she watched as CNN and FOX News broke in with "Special Reports" on the runaway Learjet. It couldn't be real. The news anchors were saying what Hillary had said: the plane was on autopilot and all passengers and crew were presumed dead. Within minutes CNN had aviation experts on the air confirming that if, indeed, reports of ice on the windows were accurate, then the cabin had depressurized, and at the hostile environment of 40,000 feet everyone aboard had fallen unconscious in a matter of seconds and had died within minutes. FOX was the first to utter Payne's name.

By that point Sally Hoch was a wreck. She called Bev Janzen, wife of 1998 U.S. Open champion Lee Janzen. The Janzens lived two doors down from the Hochs in a gated community on the Butler chain of lakes, and Sally and Bev were close friends. When Bev answered the phone she barely recognized the voice on the other end. "Get over here!" Sally screamed.

By the time Bev Janzen arrived, speculation among the television intelligentsia had run amok. It could have been rapid depressurization, a blown window or door that had rendered everyone unconscious. There could have been a problem with the oxygen flow, or with the air-conditioning, or the plane might never have pressurized at all and the passengers simply experienced a euphoric giddiness before falling asleep. There was plenty of speculation, but few, if any, facts. When someone labeled "aviation expert" openly speculated that the military might have to shoot the Learjet down if its path took it near a densely populated area, Sally couldn't believe it. What was poor Tracey Stewart doing? Surely someone was with her by now. Surely she wasn't hearing this on television like the rest of them.

Unfortunately, Tracey Stewart, Payne's Australian-born wife, was watching events unfold on television just like the rest of the world. It had been only four hours since she had kissed her husband goodbye. Now she was hearing people on television tell her the man she loved was dead in the seat of an airplane, and that the plane might have to be blown out of the sky! After prefacing everything with such disclaimers as "We are guessing at this stage," and "This is one of several possibilities," the experts speculated on the various ways in which Payne Stewart might have perished, while Tracey sat transfixed in their Orlando home frantically dialing Payne's cell phone number.

"You've reached Payne Stewart's phone," Payne's recorded voice said in his distinct and ever-jovial Ozark twang. "He's not with it right now, so leave him a message and I'll tell him you called and he'll get back to you. Thank you."

As time dragged on, Tracey realized the reports must be true. If Payne were alive, he would have called, and he would have raised teetotal Cain with whoever had scared his family like this. But he didn't call, and slowly she realized he wouldn't call. All she had at the moment was his voice on the end of the cell phone. "He's not with it right now, so leave him a message . . ."

It was supposed to be the first step in a new career path, a source of alternative income that would keep him in the game he loved but give him the flexibility to pare down his playing schedule at some point in the future. Payne Stewart had seen many of his peers on the PGA Tour design golf courses, some with great success, others without much luck, but all with an eye toward creating a business that would outlast their playing careers. Arnold Palmer and Jack Nicklaus had been designing courses for years. In Nicklaus's case, the design business was not only a way to remain in the forefront of the game long after he had stopped winning major titles but also a legacy he could leave for his family. Jack's sons Jackie and Michael both worked in the family business, as did his son-in-law Bill O'Leary. That appealed to Payne. While the Stewart children were only 14 and 10, it was never too early to plan for their futures as well as his own. At 42, Payne was winding up the best year of his 20-year professional career, and there was no reason to think he wouldn't continue to play well for years to come, but he also had a family to consider, soccer and football games to attend, school plays, trips to Disney, and all the things a financially secure father in his forties would want to do with his life. David Fay, executive director of the USGA and a man Payne had got to know reasonably well over the years, had recently pulled him aside and said he thought Payne was a "late bloomer, not unlike Ben Hogan," who had his greatest successes after his 40th birthday. That was quite a compliment, but Hogan never had children, nor were the extracurricular demands on tour players as consuming in the 1950s as they are today. Payne's success was a dual-edged sword: his 1999 U.S. Open win and his victory at the AT&T Pebble Beach Pro-Am made him a shoo-in for "Comeback Player of the Year," and he had more earning opportunities than ever before, but all those opportunities had costs, the biggest being time away from Tracey, Chelsea, and Aaron. It was a struggle, but it was also a good problem to have. Perhaps course design was the answer. Ben Crenshaw had successfully transitioned from major championship winner to noted architect without losing touch with his two young daughters. There was no reason Payne Stewart couldn't do the same thing.

He wanted to be careful about this opportunity, though. The last thing he wanted was a repeat of what happened after his 1991 U.S. Open win when, in his words, he had "chased the almighty dollar," traveling around the globe in an attempt to cash in. He made gobs of money during that period, but his game had all but tanked. In 1994 he finished 123rd on the money list, and he picked up only one win (the 1995 Shell Houston Open) between his first U.S. Open win and his comeback in

1999. He had been forced to watch from home as his friend and neighbor Mark O'Meara won the 1998 Masters, and although he and Tracey celebrated Mark's victory with a bottle of wine in their bedroom, Payne felt a slight twinge as he watched Nick Faldo slip the green jacket onto O'Meara's shoulders. He knew he should have been there. He was too good a player not to qualify for a major.

When he came, literally, within inches of winning the 1998 U.S. Open in San Francisco he proved to himself and to the rest of the golf world that he did belong back on top. It hadn't happened at the Olympic Club, but Payne and everyone else knew it would happen soon. The two wins in 1999 and the spot on the Ryder Cup team weren't a big surprise to Payne. He had worked long and hard to get back where he belonged, and now it was time to take a break, to reassess, and to map out the goals for the year 2000 and beyond. He had called his sports psychologist and friend Dick Coop the night before, and they had chatted about Aaron's football and Chelsea's upcoming basketball schedule. It would be good to be home. Two more weeks, and he would have the entire holiday season with his family. Christmas was right around the corner, and then the biggest New Year's Eve of their lives. The Hochs and Stewarts had already planned a big Y2K party with friends from Isleworth (another gated golf community in suburban Orlando where the O'Mearas and Tiger Woods lived) and Payne couldn't wait for the celebration.

This meeting in Dallas might be the start of a signature course design career, or it could end up being a waste of time. Payne had one course design under his belt, Coyote Hills in Fullerton, California, and his agents, Van Ardan and Robert Fraley, had been diligent in researching other prospective sites, looking in spots like Nashville and North Florida, but they had been very selective. As long as he was playing Payne didn't want more than two design jobs a year, if that. "I don't think it would be fair to my family or to my golf game," he told anyone who asked.

Dallas had potential, however. Developer Jeff Blackland had found a 700-acre site in Frisco, just north of FM720 off the Dallas North Tollway, and close to Payne's alma mater, Southern Methodist University. Payne loved the idea of designing a signature golf course within shouting distance of SMU, but deals of this type were complicated. Blackland planned for Payne to meet with a fellow named Jeff Mundy, managing director of Olympus Real Estate, about the site. Mundy worked for an investor named Tom Hicks who owned the Texas Rangers and who had invested in Blackland's properties in the past. The prospect of a Payne Stewart signature golf course on this site might clinch the necessary funding to get the project rolling.

Originally Blackland had considered coming to Orlando, but that didn't make sense. Payne was heading to the Tour Championship in Houston anyway, and, besides, how was he supposed to talk intelligently about designing a golf course if he had never seen the site? He had spoken to Blackland on the phone over the weekend and they had worked out the details. Payne would fly into Dallas with Arden, Fraley, and an architect named Bruce Borland who worked with Nicklaus Design. They would meet at Casa Dominguez, Payne's favorite Mexican restaurant in Dallas, at 11:30 central time. It was convenient to downtown (just across the street from the Crescent Hotel) and a good rendezvous spot. From there they would meet with Mundy and go to the site where Payne would put on boots and blue jeans and kick some dirt while getting a feel for the land.

At the time he spoke with Blackland Payne wasn't sure if he would be flying commercially or chartering a jet. He was part owner of a Learjet 45, but he wouldn't be taking that plane. His "fractional ownership" arrangement was through Flexjet, a glorified jet-time-sharing company out of Montreal and a subsidiary of Bombardier Aerospace. It was a common program among tour players. For about $400,000 anyone interested in jet ownership could purchase a one-sixteenth share in a Learjet. Then for a monthly maintenance fee of about $5,000 and an hourly rate of $1,300, a jet would be available when and where the owner needed it. It was a pricey way to travel, but for most tour players the benefits of being home on Sunday nights, and the hassle-free environment a private plane provided, were more than worth it. Nick Price estimated he played in five more events a year after purchasing his jet, and Davis Love III (who was a fractional owner of a Hawker through Executive Jet, another prominent jet-time-share company owned by billionaire Warren Buffett), said he spent an additional 25 days a year at home with his family because of his plane. That extra time at home was priceless for Payne. But like most time-sharing arrangements, Payne had an allotted number of flying hours every year, and his 1999 allotment was close to being maxed out. Blackland was picking up the tab for the trip to Dallas, so there was no reason to use up precious time in his own jet when he could lease another plane on someone else's nickel.

Van Ardan, one of the principals in Leader Enterprises, the group that represented Payne, Paul Azinger, major league pitcher Oral Hershiser and NFL coach Bill Parcells, arranged for Sunjet Aviation, a charter operation out of Sanford, Florida, to have a Learjet 35 waiting in Orlando on Monday morning. Sunjet was a small operation with six jets, and Payne knew the owner, James Watkins, reasonably well. The Learjet 35 was a slightly smaller and much older plane than the one Payne owned, but it was a fine alternative on short notice. The pilots would meet them at Orlando International a little after 9:00 A.M. They would fly to Dallas, meet, greet, and walk around the proposed development site, then fly to Houston where Payne would play in the Tour Championship.

As excited as he was about the prospects of designing this golf course, Payne felt bad about what he was going to miss because of the trip. He had committed to play in the Champions for Children charity outing, one of the many events Scott and Sally Hoch supported, at Bay Hill on Monday. Scott had seemed a little peeved when Payne told him he couldn't play, but Payne explained the opportunity and told his friend that Monday was the only time everyone could meet. Scott said he understood, which he did. It had happened to every tour player at some point, even Hoch. Time was precious when you traveled as much as they did, and sometimes scheduling conflicts arose that couldn't be helped. This was simply one of those times.

Payne was lucky that Monday worked for everybody. Getting Blackland, Mundy, Fraley, Ardan, and Payne in the same city at the same time was a cosmic event. Bruce Borland was icing on the cake. Borland was a 40-year-old architect who had been with Jack Nicklaus since 1990 and had worked with Jack on 12 signature courses including Colleton River Plantation on Hilton Head Island, which had won a boatload of national awards. He was also a devout Christian with a strong sense of family, two things Payne looked for now in partners. Borland had four children, ranging in age from 8 to 13, and, like Payne, he had a 10-year-old son who was into all the things 10-year-old boys enjoyed. If the deal in Dallas worked out, Borland was the perfect design associate to put Payne's ideas on paper and work through the mechanics of the design process.

Borland had approached Nicklaus the week before with the idea of doing a design job with Payne and Jack had said, "Sure. I knew it would be a great opportunity for Bruce, and it would be a good experience for him to work with another golfer for a different perspective." Such arrangements weren't uncommon. Most tour player-architects designed a couple of courses a year. They had neither the expertise nor the infrastructure to draft routing plans, estimate yards of dirt, calculate irrigation and drainage requirements, or put together a budget. Tour players knew the game and they had general ideas about how a course should look and play, but they didn't know backwater runoff from backspin on a six-iron. For that they needed design experts, and Nicklaus employed more of those than anybody else. If things worked out, Borland would join a long list of Nicklaus Design associates who had worked with other tour players under the Nicklaus Design banner. For Borland and Payne this was a "get to know each other" trip. They could chat on the plane about design philosophies, holes they liked, courses they liked, and what they could expect to find off the Dallas North Tollway, while each got a better feel for the personality of the other.

With the travel arrangements still up in the air on the weekend, Borland was a late addition to the trip. He left his home in Jupiter in the wee hours of Monday morning to drive to Orlando where he was to meet Payne, Fraley, and Ardan at Aircraft Service International Group general aviation, a fixed-based operator (FBO) at Orlando International. They would fly to Dallas, take Payne to Houston, then return to Orlando. Payne would take the tour's charter to Spain for the year-end World Golf Championship event.

Steve Smart, the manager of Aircraft Service International, greeted Borland when he arrived and the two chatted briefly. Borland couldn't help noticing the large "Congratulations Payne Stewart" banner in the lobby, a holdover from Payne's 1999 U.S. Open victory. He was obviously a regular at this FBO.

Moments later, Michael Kling, the 43-year-old pilot of the Learjet 35, called Smart to say they were on their way from Sanford. It was 8:55, so the plane should be outside on the tarmac in no more than 10 minutes.

Kling, a former Air Force officer and high-altitude instructor, had moved to Florida in 1989 after becoming an ordained minister. His goal was to start a church in the area and fly missionaries to different mission fields. With the support of his wife, Donna, and his three stepsons, Kling had founded Eagle Wings International, a small Christian mission that, in his words, "delivered food and the gospel to developing countries." He was a focused man with 4,000 hours of flight time in jet aircraft.

His co-pilot, Stephanie Bellagarigue, was a 27-year-old former college swimmer who never met a party she didn't like. She was the anti-Kling—a single, free-spirited Salvadoran immigrant who moved with her family to Maryland at age 2 and settled in Winter Haven, Florida, in 1983. Those who knew her best described her as someone who "liked going against the grain," but who was "passionate about flying." Much like the famous golfer she would be transporting, Bellegarigue lived life to the max, always being the most rambunctious female at any event she attended, and never shying away from a challenge. She had spent the previous weekend in Daytona Beach with her best friend, Helena Reidemar, where the two had enjoyed Biketoberfest, the annual ride-in attracting Harley-Davidson owners from around the world. She played hard and worked hard, having been employed by Sunjet for a year. Even though flying was her passion, the rigidity and hierarchy of the airlines didn't fit her lifestyle. Right seat in a corporate jet was exactly where she needed to be, and with someone like Kling beside her, Bellegarigue knew she could learn a lot and gain the experience she needed to transition to captain.

The hop from Sanford to Orlando International hardly seemed worth the fuel. Once on the ground outside the FBO, Kling cut the engines, opened the cabin door, locked the folding stairway into place, and unlocked the baggage compartment in the rear of the aircraft. If everyone was on time, they should be airborne and bound for Dallas in no more than 15 or 20 minutes.

Payne and the others arrived 5 minutes later. Bruce Borland shook hands with everyone and, without meandering too long, they all walked underneath the "Congratulations" banner, through the rear door, and onto the tarmac where Kling waited to help them on board. Because he flew in and out of Orlando almost every week, Payne knew Steve Smart reasonably well, so as he walked outside he turned to Smart and said, "I'll see you next week." Actually he wouldn't see him for two weeks, but who was counting.

Those were the last words Payne Stewart would utter to anyone other than those who boarded the plane with him. It was an encounter that would haunt Steve Smart for months to come.

• • •

"Orlando tower, November-four-seven-bravo-alpha ready for departure, left runway three-six," Kling radioed to the tower controller at 9:16 A.M.

"Roger, four-seven-bravo-alpha, taxi to position and hold runway three-six left." David Johnson, the tower controller at Orlando International, tried not to yawn. It was a slow Monday in Mickeyville, and Johnson never thought twice about the routine takeoff request crackling over his headset. He didn't know the passengers included a famous golfer, a renowned course architect, and a couple of heavy-hitting power brokers from the sports world, but even if he had it wouldn't have changed the way he worked the plane. When the pattern cleared, Johnson cued his mike and said, "Four-seven-bravo-alpha clear for takeoff runway three-six left."

"Roger, four-seven-bravo-alpha rolling," Kling answered. It was 9:19 A.M. when the wheels lifted off and the gear retracted.

Johnson's last contact with the plane came as it climbed out of the tower control space. "November-four-seven-bravo-alpha, contact departure one-two-zero-point-one-five," he said. Routine all the way.

"Roger," Kling said. "Going to departure. Good day."

Eight minutes later, Orlando departure controllers handed the Learjet off to the Jacksonville Air Traffic Control Center, known as Jax Center in the jargon of the air. In addition to a business and vacation mecca, Florida was a tax haven for wealthy athletes and executives who could avoid state income tax by declaring the Sunshine State as their primary residence. Since most people rich enough to troll the skies in private jets have beach or golf course homes anyway, Florida was now a hotbed of jet-setting commuters, and a Lear 35 from Orlando to Dallas on a Monday morning was as common as a fishing boat on the Intercoastal. When the Jax controller contacted Kling at 9:44 A.M. there was nothing unusual about the flight or the demeanor of the pilot.

"November-four-seven-bravo-alpha climb and maintain flight level three-nine-zero," the controller said.

"Roger," Kling said. "Up to three-nine-zero."

Ten minutes later, as the Learjet passed over Gainesville, Florida, Kling should have turned west for Dallas. That was the flight plan, and that was what Jax had cleared them for, but Kling never made the turn.

"November-four-seven-bravo-alpha, Jax," the controller said.

No response.

"Four-seven-bravo-alpha, Jax," he said again.

After realizing the pilot was not responding, the Jacksonville controller declared November-four-seven-bravo-alpha a NORDO. Within minutes, however, he realized there was a much bigger problem with the Learjet 35 than a malfunctioning radio.

Joe Hambrite, a supervisor at the Atlanta Air Traffic Control Center, had just come down from his office and plugged into the Display System Replacement (DSR) sector console for his required monthly time when the call came over. Every supervisor had to spend eight hours a month working planes through the system to remain current, and even though Hambrite hadn't been an active controller since 1987 he still enjoyed his time on the control room floor, even though he caught endless grief for his attire. There was no dress code, so it wasn't unusual for air traffic controllers to wear dirty jeans and T-shirts while working, but Hambrite, a tall African American with a well-groomed beard and a distinct baritone voice, always dressed to the nines in dark double-breasted suits, silk shirts, and stylish ties. Today was no different. With his freshly polished black Italian loafers and his perfectly pressed black suit, Hambrite ignored the snickers coming from other controllers as he worked his sector. He would do his time on the floor and be back in his office by mid-afternoon. When he took the call from Jacksonville, all those plans changed.

Jax Center called the "incident" into Hambrite over a landline. "We've got a Lear 35 that's NORDO, last assigned altitude three-nine-zero," the Jacksonville controller said. "I tried to turn him on course, but no response, so show him NORDO. I'll put something in the machine to get you a strip." Since the Learjet was never supposed to enter Atlanta Center's control space, Hambrite had no information on the plane. A "strip" was an identifier for the controllers. It would show the type of plane and the flight plan. It would not, however, tell them who was on board.

Hambrite's heart beat faster. Failure to turn on course indicated the plane was probably on autopilot. Throw in the fact that the flight had been NORDO for over five minutes and it didn't take a NASA scientist to figure out something was terribly wrong. Pilots and passengers could be in distress. Hambrite consciously slowed his breathing as he found the Learjet on his scope. He paused before speaking, thinking through what he would say and do over the next few minutes. Every word was being taped, Hambrite knew, and in addition to being the flashiest dresser in the control center, he was also the king of the malapropism, inventing such words as "circulosity" to describe the spherical nature of an object, and "unthoughtedly" for bone-headed behavior, as in, "He did that unthoughtedly." Now he knew everything he said would be taped, reviewed, transcribed, and copied to people in FAA offices from Seattle, Washington, to Washington, D.C. The last thing he needed was a screw-up.

The first order of business was to get all other traffic out of November-four-seven-bravo-alpha's path. One problem was enough. Having a "deal" (controller lingo for two planes encroaching too close to each other) would only exacerbate the situation. Hambrite informed the other controllers and supervisors of the situation, then he tried to reach the Learjet by radio. When that failed, he knew he needed help.

"Uh-oh," said John Riley, a controller who was working the floor next to Hambrite.

"What?" Hambrite asked.

"Orlando to Dallas Learjet. That's got to be a golfer," Riley, a single-digit handicap, said. "The tour was at Disney World last week and the Tour Championship is in Houston this week. Those two cities . . . it's got to be a golfer."

No one said anything for a couple of seconds. Then Hambrite called in reinforcements.

At 10:08 A.M. Hambrite contacted Air Force Staff Sergeant James Hicks, a controller at Eglin Air Force Base in Destin, Florida. "We have a Learjet that's NORDO and has failed to turn on course," Hambrite told Hicks. "We're pretty sure it's in distress. Do you have any fighters that can help?" By then the plane was north of Tallahassee and continuing to fly on a northwesterly heading.

Sergeant Hicks had an F-16 airborne on maneuvers, and he quickly radioed the pilot, Captain Chris Hamilton. Within a matter of seconds, Hamilton broke away from his maneuvers and headed north where he rendezvoused with an airborne tanker. After refueling, Hamilton throttled up the F-16, climbing from 15,000 to 44,000 feet and reaching 600 miles an hour as he tried to catch the wayward jet before it reached Memphis, a city of 600,000 people.

Two F-15s were scrambled out of Tyndall Air Force Base in Panama City, along with an A-10 Warthog from Eglin, but Captain Hamilton was the first to make visual contact with the plane at 11:09 A.M. just north of Memphis. What he saw surprised him.

"It was flying straight and level," Hamilton said. "It didn't seem like anyone was at the controls. The entire time I was trailing the aircraft, nothing had changed. That's very unusual."

Hamilton moved into formation beside the Learjet and his heart sank when he saw ice and fog on the cockpit windshield and windows. He checked the right side first, dropped beneath it, then pulled up on its left to try to detect movement. There was none. He attempted to make radio contact, to no avail. By then he knew. Ice on the windows could only mean one thing: the cabin had depressurized. Everyone on board that plane was dead.

"I was very disheartened," Hamilton said. "At that point I realized it was going to continue on that heading until it ran out of fuel."

Controllers throughout the Midwest were alerted, as were officials at the Pentagon and the White House. Despite speculative reports, no one seriously considered shooting the plane down, since no one had any idea when and where it would run out of fuel. The Midwest was a big and sparsely populated region. Everyone prayed the plane would crash in a cornfield or other open area. For those on board, it was already too late.

Hamilton and the F-15s shadowed the Learjet as it passed eerily close to Springfield, Missouri, Stewart's hometown. By the time they hit the Nebraska state line Hamilton had to break off because of fuel, but two more F-16s from the Tulsa, Oklahoma, Air National Guard joined the flight at 11:59 and followed the plane into South Dakota. More F-16s were scrambled out of Fargo at 12:50, but by then the Learjet was obviously running low on fuel. As the fuel level dropped and the plane became lighter it began to climb, cresting at above 50,000 feet at one point, 5,000 feet above the maximum cruise altitude for a Learjet 35. After that, the plane began porpoising (rapidly descending and ascending) between 35,000 and 50,000 feet. Those in pursuit and those watching from their scopes on the ground knew it would be over soon.

• • •

Mary Kamm, a lifelong resident of Mina, South Dakota, a small community 12 miles north-northwest of Aberdeen, was on her front porch repotting plants when she heard the fighter jets fly over. "They sure are low," Mary said to herself, but she assumed it was the Air National Guard on maneuvers. Mina was in one of their regular training patterns, so it wasn't terribly unusual to have F-16s overhead. After they passed Mary went back to work, packing soil around the edges of the pots with a small spade and preparing to take the plants inside before winter. Then two trucks raced down the narrow road in front of Mary's house. At first she thought it was those darned pheasant hunters in "way too big a hurry" to get a jump on the season, but when another truck, and another, then car after car after car poured down the road at breakneck speeds, Mary knew something was amiss. A few seconds later she heard a dull rumble coming from over near Jon Hoffman's pasture, followed by what sounded like a thousand sirens. Mary stood and wiped the potting soil from her hands before going inside to turn on the television. Whatever had happened in Mina, it was big enough to be on the local news.

At 1:16 P.M. EDT, 12:16 local time, the squadron commander from the F-16 fighter group dispatched from Fargo radioed that the Learjet was spiraling downward. Mina was the contact point. When the call came over, Lieutenant Bob Marler of the South Dakota Highway Patrol walked out to the parking lot of the district office just west of Aberdeen on Highway 12 and gazed skyward. The office had become a makeshift command center for police and rescue personnel. Spotters were all over the county, with fire and rescue vehicles on standby. Marler heard the planes before he saw them, but once he spotted them there was no question what was happening. Sergeant Jim Sutton and Sergeant Scott Wherry joined Marler in the parking lot to witness the doomed Learjet's final moments.

"We watched it for a very short time before it started a very rapid descent," Marler said. "We started spotting approximate positions where it might land. We already had spotters north and west of Huron and Aberdeen all the way to the North Dakota border, so we knew we'd have somebody on the scene immediately."

That somebody turned out to be Sergeant Jim Sutton, who hopped in his car when he saw the plane start its descent. "We were on the scene in five minutes," he said. "We were actually there before we even had a call reporting it." What Sutton found was a small debris field and a pile of indistinguishable rubble. Had he not known it was a jet, he would have never guessed the wreckage was anything larger than a pickup truck. It had hit the ground at over 600 miles an hour, compressing the plane into the dirt like an accordion and sending debris as deep as 30 feet underground.

Although they had been dead for hours, it was hard for Sutton to comprehend that this pasture in Mina was the resting place for six vibrant people who had bid their families goodbye that morning and taken off from Orlando on this mysterious and tragic flight. Sutton didn't know that the pile of smoldering scrap metal meant 10 young children were now fatherless, and five loving wives were now widowed. He didn't know a young woman in the prime of her life had been snatched away before her 28th birthday, and he couldn't have known the national grief this crash would cause. All he knew was that Payne Stewart, the professional golfer who wore knickers and an old-style touring cap, was one of the passengers Sutton now had to help recover and identify. It was a sad day to be a state trooper.

Fifteen minutes after the Learjet plowed into the field in Mina, Chelsea and Aaron Stewart were pulled out of class at First Academy (their private Christian school at the First Baptist Church) and told there was a "problem" with their dad's plane. "They were taken home and told at home," Steve Smith, an administrator at the school, said. The Stewart children were, perhaps, the only two people within site of a television or earshot of a radio who had been spared the agonizing blow-by-blow details of the plane's final hours.

At first, news organizations would only say, "It is believed that someone involved with the PGA Tour is on board." That announcement had a ripple effect in the golf community, as everyone who knew anyone who had anything to do with the tour scrambled for telephones. A dozen of the top-30 money winners owned or partially owned private jets, and many more players were regular passengers on chartered aircraft. Nicklaus, Palmer, Greg Norman, Hale Irwin, and Ray Floyd all owned jets, and Norman even owned his own helicopter; the PGA Tour owned an Astra, a 10-seat jet that carted tour officials to and from meetings and events around the country; and as the early reports were coming in no one seemed certain what kind of aircraft was involved.

Richard Combs, father of Bob Combs, the tour's director of communications, phoned his son's office in Ponte Vedra, Florida, the instant he heard the reports. "May I speak to Bob?" Richard asked, leery of the answer he might get.

"I'm sorry, he's on the phone right now," Combs's secretary said. "Do you want me to interrupt him and tell him you're on the line?"

"No, thanks," the senior Combs said. "You just answered my question."

Combs wasn't the only concerned father scrambling to find his son that Monday. Jim Cook, father of tour player John Cook, frantically tried to reach John and his wife, Jan. "I got a call from California about a runaway jet and there were supposed to be three tour players aboard," Jim Cook said. "You never know when those guys are flying together." Jan Cook called her father-in-law back within 15 minutes and told him John was with their 13-year-old son, Jason, at a school golf match.

For Jan Cook the news came especially hard. The Cooks had recently moved to Orlando from California, and Payne and Tracey Stewart had gone out of their way to make them feel welcome. Payne was a member at Isleworth, where he and John played and practiced together regularly. They went to baseball games together, boated along the Butler chain together, grilled out (with Payne doing most of the grilling), and did all the things good friends and neighbors did together. "One of the main reasons we moved to Isleworth was because of Mark [O'Meara] and Payne being here," John said. The O'Mearas lived right down the street, and the Stewarts owned a lot 150 yards away where they planned to build once they sold their $6 million mansion. Their kids were close enough in age to get along well together, and the Cooks and Stewarts were constantly comparing Pop Warner football, and recreation league soccer stories. Only yesterday morning Jan had been playing tennis with Tracey Stewart and Alicia O'Meara, and now, in an instant, Payne was dead. Jan felt sick and numb by it all. Then she did what the rest of the wives did that morning: she started working the phones.

When Sally Hoch finally reached Scott he had just walked off the 15th green at Bay Hill. He and his amateur partners were having a great time, and while the money hadn't been tabulated yet, Scott Hoch felt reasonably sure the Champions for Children outing had been a financial success. They couldn't have asked for better weather, and the people he had seen all seemed to be enjoying their day. Even Arnold Palmer had flown in for the event. Palmer hadn't spent much time at Bay Hill since his tournament, the Bay Hill Invitational in March, because of his wife's losing battle with cancer. Since returning to Latrobe for the summer, Palmer had stayed at Winnie's side almost full-time. He had played in events where he was committed, but that was it. It said a lot about him that he had flown back to Orlando for this one round of golf. In all, Hoch thought, it would have been tough for the day to be much better.

Then his cell phone rang. It was Sally, and Hoch's perfect day came to an end. "At first I thought it had to be a mistake," Hoch said. "Sally said they were speculating that they might have to shoot the plane down!"

Hoch put the phone down and walked around in a daze for a moment. Then he hit his tee shot on the 16th hole, and thought, "What am I doing?" He turned to the men in his group, gave them the news Sally had just given him, and said, "Guys, I'm sorry. I can't play." The other men in his group understood completely.

Hoch rode around the course relaying the news to as many of his fellow pros as he could find. "Arnold was visibly shaken" by the news, Hoch said. By then the media knew, and Bay Hill was being swarmed by camera trucks, still photographers, and eager reporters, notebooks firmly in hand. Hoch said something to one or two of them—he couldn't remember exactly what—before getting in his car and speeding toward home.

All the memories were flooding through his mind. The two practice rounds they had played together at Pinehurst, and the meticulous way Payne had gone over every nook and cranny of the golf course. Hoch had grown up in Raleigh, so Pinehurst No. 2 was like a home course for him, and, like everyone, he wanted to play well in the U.S. Open, but Payne took it to extremes. Then there were the encouraging admonitions Payne had given Hoch as Ryder Cup qualifying came down to the wire. "Come on," Payne had said. "You've got to get on the stick and get on the team with me! We would be great partners." Payne would have made a great captain, too, Hoch thought. He always had a way of loosening people up, motivating them, inspiring them, and making them want to do more. Payne would have worn the flag on his shoulders and his heart on his sleeve as captain of the U.S. squad. Hoch had played on only one Ryder Cup team and he thought it was one of the most overrated events he had ever seen. But Payne's team . . . that would have been different. THAT was a team Hoch would have wanted to make.

Other players immediately thought about the Ryder Cup when they heard the news as well. Hal Sutton, the 41-year-old veteran who had been heralded as the Hero of Brookline in the 1999 Ryder Cup, was having lunch in Shreveport, Louisiana, with his father, Howard, a wealthy Louisiana oil man, when Hal's sister called. "She said she had just heard it on the news and that a prominent golfer from Orlando was on the plane," Sutton recalled. "I felt like it was Payne going to Dallas. I knew it was either him or Scott Hoch. I called my wife [Ashley] and told her to turn on the TV. Then I left and went straight home."

Like everyone else Sutton watched events of the incident unfold live, his mind running back to that Sunday evening in Massachusetts when 12 Americans made history in the Ryder Cup Matches. After the celebration, when the champagne baths had dried into a sticky paste on their clothes and their voices had become hoarse from all the off-key renditions of "The Star-Spangled Banner," Hal and Ashley Sutton had crawled into a van in the parking lot of The Country Club along with Davis and Robin Love, Jim Furyk and his girlfriend Tabitha Skartved, and Payne and Tracey Stewart. In the back of that van, as Brookline became Boston and the lights of downtown shone through the windshield, Payne had looked at Hal and said, "You know, the only thing I regret about this Ryder Cup is that you and I didn't get to play together as partners. I would have liked that." Later on, in the team room at the Four Seasons as the celebration extended into night, Payne found Hal again and said, "You know, I'm going to be a captain someday, and you're going to be on my team in some way, either as a player or as an assistant captain. You've got the spirit. You and me, we share the same passion for the Ryder Cup, and I would want you on my team one way or the other. You've got what it takes."

The bond between Payne Stewart and Hal Sutton had been an evolutionary one—a slow-growth relationship that matured over the years, stemming, in large part, from the fact that their names were so close alphabetically they were usually assigned side-by-side lockers and adjacent parking spaces at tournament sites. Nothing forged a relationship like watching a man put on a "clown suit," as Sutton had called Stewart's knickers over the years. But even though they had been competitors for the better part of 22 seasons, Sutton and Stewart had grown accustomed to each other, working through each other's idiosyncrasies to become like brothers. "Early in our careers, Payne was so aggressive and self-confident that it was almost intimidating to some degree," Sutton said. "When he would sign a cap, for example, he'd sign all the way across the bill (leaving no room for any other signatures). That would aggravate me. I'd kid him, saying, 'They need to make hats bigger for you so you can sign your name.' But as we grew out here and we matured out here together, that never bothered me anymore. I knew Payne and he knew Hal."

By all rights if anyone had cause to be arrogant in the early days of their careers it was Sutton, who arrived on tour richer than most long-time veterans and who was being touted as the "Next Nicklaus" from the time he won the Walt Disney World Classic in his rookie year. "Prince Hal," he was dubbed, and for a while it looked as though Sutton would live up to the hype. He won the Players Championship and the PGA Championship in his second season, finishing first on the money list with a whopping $427,000, a staggering sum at the time. Sutton couldn't help but smile at the thought of that now. In 1999 he won once, the Bell Canadian Open, and his highest finish in a major was a tie for seventh in the U.S. Open, but his official earnings were $2,127,578, more than his combined earnings from his first eight years on tour back when that "Next Nicklaus" thing was being bantered about a little too freely for Sutton's liking.

He never lived up to expectations, but it wasn't because of arrogance or attitude. When Sutton was winning the money title and major championships he spoke with a courtly respect worthy of his southern roots, saying, "Yes, sir," and "No, sir" to his playing partners and tour officials, just like his mamma and daddy had taught him back in Shreveport. Some in the media thought he was a bit too back-behind-the-barn-door for someone with such a silver-spoon upbringing, but Howard Sutton, while indulging his son's golf, had also taught him the value of down-home humility, a lesson Hal carried with him through the good years and bad years on tour. It was no wonder Sutton found the dogmatic Stewart somewhat off-putting in the early going.

"Payne was able to get away with what a lot of other guys were not able to get away with because he always had that twinkle in his eye and that smile," Sutton said in his straightforward, down-home, Huey Long–Louisiana style. Sutton's voice was captivating. Even though the words might be less than spectacular, even simple in transcript form, it was his understated, magnetic delivery that made Hal such a dominating force. Each word had a certain punch coming from this burly, yet gentlemanly, figure. In describing his relationship with Payne Stewart, Sutton oozed passion with purpose, bringing each recollection of his friend back to life, and capturing the complexity of Stewart with simple stories that cut to the heart of the man being remembered, and to the character of the man doing the remembering.

"Payne might say something a little brash," Sutton continued. "Something that if somebody else had said it, you might have thought it was a little too much, but because Payne said it, you knew he didn't mean it; and even if he did, you overlooked it. He'd wink and smile and you'd forget it. Payne had his own style, his own way. I don't have to explain that to everybody. Everybody knew Payne's style. We will miss him. I almost feel like I've lost a family member.

"As tragic as this is, I think it makes us all evaluate what we are going through in our lives. We are a lot more of a family out here [on tour] than everybody has always made us out to be, and in a tragic situation like this, you find out how much more of a family you really are.

"Payne and I shared a lot of moments together. In the last year or so, I guess you might say we took some pride in the fact that we were coming back at the age we were both at. He'd say to me, 'Let's win one for the old guys' or things like that. Although I don't want to admit we're older."

There was little question in Sutton's mind that Payne was, indeed, bound for a Ryder Cup captaincy sooner rather than later. "[PGA of America CEO] Jim Awtrey asked me who I thought should be the next captain and the first person out of my mouth was Payne. Jim said, 'It might be a little too early for Payne, because he might qualify for the next Ryder Cup.' Curtis [Strange] completely slipped my mind, but I'm glad he got it. Curtis'll make a great one. He's callused enough that nothing will bother him. Payne would have been a great one, too. He had what it takes."

•     •     •

Monday, October 25 was supposed to be the day another U.S. Open champion dominated the golf news. At 10:00 A.M., about the time Joe Hambrite was requesting military assistance in visually contacting Stewart's wayward jet, PGA of America president Will Mann stood at a podium in the conference room of the association's Palm Beach Gardens headquarters and announced, to the surprise of absolutely no one, that Curtis Strange, winner of back-to-back U.S. Opens in 1988 and 1989, would lead a U.S. team to the Belfry in 2001 to defend the Ryder Cup Matches. Looking a bit more uncomfortable in his new role than he did in the broadcast booth at ABC, Strange thanked the PGA of America, then waxed on for several minutes about what an honor it was to be selected to represent his country.

After successfully fielding a few questions and getting one hearty laugh out of the assembled media when he said the uniforms for the 2001 team would be "six pair of khakis and a dozen white shirts, and I told Tiger if he plays good I'll give him a red shirt for Sunday," Strange thanked everyone and stood. That was when the "scrum" started, a nickname given to the mad rush by reporters to speak to the interviewee after the formal interview concluded. Print reporters knew that all the good sound bites from the "official" news conference would be old news by the time their papers hit doorsteps the next morning. If they were to get any fresh news to their readers it would have to come from the questions they asked *after* the cameras were turned off and the court reporter stopped taking notes. Al Tays from the *Palm Beach Post* and Tim Rosaforte from *Golf World* magazine cornered Strange for a half-hour afterward, then the reporters meandered off to the buffet lunch the PGA had prepared.

Moments later a staff member pulled Julius Mason, the director of communications for the PGA of America, aside and whispered the news in his ear. Within minutes, Strange, Mason, Mann, and Awtrey were huddled around a television watching in stunned disbelief as their "news of the day" became totally irrelevant.

Like everyone else in the early moments, Strange's concerns were for the Stewart family, but like many that day he hoped and prayed no other player had caught a ride with Payne.

From 10:00 A.M. to 2:00 P.M. rumors ran rampant. Alastair Johnston, vice president and head of the golf division of IMG, was pulled out of his weekly golf staff meeting when the news broke. Stewart wasn't an IMG client, but Stuart Appleby was, and for over an hour the Cleveland staff of the world's largest sports management company went on a manhunt to locate Appleby. No one knew if he had hitched a ride, but no one could rule out that he hadn't, which sent the company into a Monday-morning tizzy. Appleby had lost his wife, Renay, in a freak accident outside London's Heathrow Airport after the 1998 British Open, and now he was rumored to be aboard the flight with Payne. It wasn't until Appleby answered his cell phone as he walked off the 10th green at the Champions Club that everyone realized he was fine.

Another preliminary report said that Justin Leonard, another Ryder Cup teammate of Stewart's, had planned on meeting the plane in Dallas and riding with Stewart to Houston late Monday afternoon. At the time Leonard was at a ribbon-cutting ceremony for the newly renovated Ben Hogan Company plant in Fort Worth. While he was shaken by the news and had to excuse himself from the ceremony, Leonard said he didn't even know Payne was coming to Dallas.

Perhaps the eeriest incident concerning the news of the tragedy occurred in Far Hills, New Jersey, at the headquarters for the United States Golf Association. USGA executive director David Fay was in his office sorting mail that Monday morning when he noticed a letter postmarked and dated September 30, but the stamp the USGA mailroom places on every incoming piece of mail the day it arrives was dated October 25. When he opened the letter he saw that it was from Payne Stewart, the reigning U.S. Open champion. It was a request by Payne that his home club in Missouri be allowed to display a replica of the U.S. Open trophy. Fay didn't think that would be a problem. The USGA had accommodated similar requests in the past. There would be an executive committee meeting that weekend, and he would kick it around with a few of the officers before officially responding to the request. After all, it had taken a month for the post office to get the letter to his office. Another five days wouldn't matter.

Just as he was about to put the letter aside, Fay's secretary walked into his office and delivered the news. "It was unbelievable," Fay said. "As I'm hearing the news that Payne is dead, I'm looking down in front of me at his signature on this letter that had arrived that very morning." It was sad, and a little spooky, but like everyone else, Fay quickly turned his concerns to Tracey and the kids.

Fortunately the family had plenty of support. Bev Janzen, Alicia O'Meara, Sally Hoch, and a total of 11 friends were at the Stewart house when the plane made its final descent. The husbands followed shortly behind. Mark O'Meara went from Bay Hill to his Isleworth home, where he waited long enough to confirm that it was, indeed, Payne on board. Then O'Meara drove his boat across the lake to the Stewarts' dock, where he found Norm Ferguson, Tracey's father, standing on the end of the dock, gazing out over the calm waters of Pocket Lake. O'Meara had seen Ferguson in that same location many times in the past, having a beer, laughing, and chatting with his son-in-law. Now, all O'Meara could do was offer a consoling hug and a weak but heartfelt "I'm sorry."

After a silent moment, Ferguson cleared his throat and said, "Payne was my son-in-law, but he was much more than that. He was like my son."

Before the following week was over, that would be the sentiment of every golf fan in America.

*Three*

# ONE FOR PAYNE
# AND ONE FOR THE AGES

BY MID-AFTERNOON ON MONDAY, one of the volunteers at the Tour Championship had attached a blue ribbon to Payne Stewart's nameplate in the players' parking lot, and within minutes the flags in front of the clubhouse—American Stars and Stripes, and the Lone Star banner of Texas—were lowered to half staff in honor of the fallen champion. Women in neatly pressed uniformed golf shirts openly wept, while meaty Texas men stared at their shoes and wore hard, sorrowful frowns. Texans had a habit of adopting anyone who had ever spent more than a month in their state as one of their own, and Payne, while being a native of Missouri and a resident of Florida, had attended SMU in Dallas. As far as Texas was concerned, Payne was a Texan and a Mustang to boot. They weren't just grieving the loss of a national champion; they were mourning the loss of an adopted son. The ladies working the registration desk were red-eyed and weary, tired of checking in the world's most famous golfers and sick of thinking about the tournament they were preparing to host. Marshals on the driving range, normally some of the most outgoing of tour volunteers, didn't analyze swings or chat about how "galdarned far those boys hit that ball." Even the hard-nosed Harris County sheriff's deputies had pools in their eyes. It was a grim opening to what everyone agreed was the grimmest week in PGA Tour memory. For a while those who had poured their hearts and souls into preparing for the Tour Championship in Houston weren't sure the tournament would be played, nor were they sure it should be.

The decision on whether or not to proceed, not only with the Tour Championship (which would now comprise 29 players) but also with the Southern Farm Bureau Classic in Madison, Mississippi (the tournament for the rest of the PGA Tour members), and the Pacific Bell Classic, the Senior tour event in California, belonged to commissioner Tim Finchem, a pragmatic 52-year-old former White House official who was as politically savvy as any sports commissioner since Peter

Ueberroth ran baseball in the early 1980s. Finchem was also as qualified and capable of handling a crisis as anyone else in sports. In 1979, Finchem had been behind his desk in the Old Executive Office Building, a nine-iron-shot away from the West Wing and the Oval Office, when he received word that Iranian fundamentalists had stormed the U.S. Embassy and taken 52 hostages, and for 444 days he had watched as the president of the United States . . . his President! . . . managed and often bungled the crisis. Finchem had learned from those long, dreadful days. Almost 20 years to the day later, Finchem was also in his office in Ponte Vedra, Florida, concluding a media conference call where he had announced that Buy.com—an Internet retail company that, like most dot-com companies in the late '90s, enjoyed an IPO jump in its stock price of 300 percent while the company was losing over $100 million— had taken over title sponsorship of the Nike tour. After hanging up with reporters (none of whom had any idea what was happening in the skies over the Midwest) Finchem listened as Bob Combs filled him in on the stunning news.

"I knew you didn't file a flight roster with the FAA, and if the information that it was Payne was coming from the FAA it was secondhand information," Finchem said. "I kept telling people, 'I don't believe this until we get some sort of confirmation.' Unfortunately that is what the family was going through at the same time." After the crash, Finchem called South Dakota governor William Janklow, and he remained in contact with the National Transportation Safety Board from the moment they moved into Mina and cordoned off the crash site. Being politically plugged-in didn't hurt when it came to getting in touch with people, but, like everyone else, Finchem got few answers. There simply weren't many answers out there. "We were struggling to organize and say something coherent, but I think everybody was in shock," he said.

Within minutes of the crash, Finchem came out with a coherent but less than eloquent written statement and a hastily developed but properly reverent video by PGA Tour Productions. Finchem then traveled to Orlando to be with Tracey Stewart. While he would be the ultimate decision maker on what the tour's official response would be, he had learned over the years, from his White House days through his time as Deane Beman's kinder, gentler right-hand man at the PGA Tour, that this was a time for listening, consoling, grieving, and consensus building.

The first question was whether or not to play the tournaments. That was answered fairly quickly. Everyone agreed Payne would have jumped up and down and thrown a hissy fit if the tour had canceled its penultimate events of the year because of him. "Payne would have said, 'Boys, you gotta play,'" Tom Lehman said. Scott Hoch, who knew Payne as well as anyone, agreed. "Those who said we shouldn't play are not athletes," Hoch said. "Payne wouldn't have had it any other way."

But if they were going to play, Finchem had to make sure the proper respect was given and the family's wishes were honored. That was where Tracey came in. After conferring with a number of people, including his player advisors and the corporate executives who sat on the tour board, Finchem developed the best scenario anyone could imagine under the circumstances. The senior event would go ahead as scheduled. Since they were in California, the logistics of shuttling everyone from L.A. to Orlando and back just wouldn't work. That angered several of the senior players who thought their place was with the family in Florida, but most understood. The funeral was Friday, so Mississippi would be shortened to 54 holes. The tour would charter an airliner to transport players from Madison to Orlando for the service, then back to Mississippi for the conclusion of play. Houston would be handled differently. Since it was a small field and daylight wouldn't be a problem, Finchem decided that 27 holes would be played on Thursday. Friday, the players would travel to Orlando for the funeral on a fleet of corporate jets Finchem had coordinated; then another 27 holes would follow on Saturday. Sunday would be a normal 18-hole final round, even though Finchem understood that nothing about the week would be normal. He had asked his staff in Houston to coordinate a memorial service for Thursday morning, and he asked Tom Lehman, one of the more devout Christians on tour, to give a brief eulogy. No one knew how things would play out as the week progressed, but Finchem could do no more than he was doing. The balancing act between reverence and competition was a tightrope he would walk all week.

Nothing like this had ever happened before, so no one was exactly sure how to respond. Payne's death had done more than change the week or the year: it had changed professional golf. Stewart had been a master showman and marketer, wearing colorful knickers and caps on the golf course and jeans and T-shirts off of it. He had always been a pied piper, attracting cheers from fans during his good years and his lean years because of his distinct attire, but when he changed into khakis and put on a baseball cap he could eat lunch in a grillroom full of weekend golfers without being recognized. People assumed they knew him because of his celebrity and the bizarre "live on CNN" way in which he had died, and even though most had never met him, his death sparked a national sense of mourning. It was golf's equivalent of Princess Diana's death.

Players were affected differently, however. The transitory nature of the tour had long ago turned players and tour officials into an extended family, traveling together, eating out together, staying in the same hotels, hitching rides, and generally supporting each other on the road. Payne was one of them in every respect. He was always asking how the other players were doing, always offering support and providing a measure of comic relief in the locker rooms each week. He was also someone to whom other players could easily relate. Payne had played well for several years, and he had played poorly for a number of years before playing well again, just like many of them. He had gone through a maturing process, alienating most reporters and a lot of his peers in the early years with his self-absorbed cockiness, but he had softened with age. Humility still wasn't his strongest suit, but Payne had learned to make friends and get along, a lesson all professional golfers learned to some degree if they spent any time on tour. He was also a family man who balanced career opportunities with time at home, just like most of the players over 30 years old on tour. But the one thing that linked Payne to everyone else in professional golf was the manner in which he died. They all flew. Whether it was on chartered planes, planes they owned, or planes they borrowed, every week, to every event, corporate outing, course design site, and charity dinner, they climbed aboard airplanes with no more thought given to the unnaturalness of it all than the average commuter has when he pulls out onto the freeway. So frequently did they fly that many golfers knew as much about the latest advancements in aviation radar as they knew about the newest golf clubs and balls being developed. Now one of their own had died on a chartered plane, and they all knew it could have just as easily been one of them. It was a sobering thought for everyone.

"I think about how many times we have all flown on private airplanes and how many times we have gotten in planes we didn't know anything about or anything about the pilots," Hal Sutton said when he arrived in Houston. "I think about how many times I have put my family in a situation like that. It is just tragic that Payne had to be an example for us. We are reminded how short life really is, and we are just passing through. So all the people you haven't told you love lately, you better tell them. And you better live your days like you mean it."

They all took the news hard, but few took it harder than Davis Love III, and with good reason: in the thirty-odd years since professional golfers started traveling in private planes, only one active PGA Tour player had died in a plane crash. "Champagne" Tony Lema was two years removed from his first major victory, the 1964 British Open, when he and his wife Betty were killed along with two pilots in a plane they had chartered to go from Akron, Ohio, to an outing in Chicago. Lema was 32 years old when he died in July of 1966. The only other golf-related air tragedy occurred on November 13, 1988, when a single-engine Piper Cherokee, a piston-driven nonpressurized puddle jumper, crashed in a swamp a few miles shy of the runway at Jacksonville International. Four men died, including the pilot and three golf instructors from Sea Island, Georgia: John Popa, Jimmy Hodges, and Davis Love, Jr., husband of Penta and father of Mark and Davis III.

There is no script for how you should receive the news your father has been killed in a plane crash, but in Love's case, the process was particularly awkward. He was supposed to be on a working vacation on Maui, although the vacation was mostly for his wife, Robin. Davis's idea of a vacation was dressing in a camouflage jumpsuit and sitting in the woods with a rifle or a bow. One hundred ten players listed hunting, fishing, or both as hobbies in the tour's media guide, but none was more serious about those pursuits than Love. When he wasn't on the golf course Davis III bow-hunted in bow season, shot quail in bird season, hunted deer in deer season, scouted turkey whenever he could find time; and when he wasn't in the woods tracking wildlife, he was on the water, fishing in lakes, ponds, and on the open seas whenever he could get away. So the trip to Hawaii, while wonderful in every respect, wasn't Davis's dream vacation. When the golf course was your office, a golf resort was the last place you wanted to spend your down time. But Robin had given birth to their first child, Alexia, six months prior, and this venture to Maui was to be her first substantial trip away from the baby. Davis would play in the Kapalua Invitational, one of his favorite events in the postseason (or "silly-season," as it was commonly called because of the less than serious competition and the large purses and appearance fees), while Robin enjoyed the sandy beaches and the road to Hana. Love's friend Mark Rolfing ran the silly-season event at Kapalua, and given how he had played in 1998, Love felt fortunate to be invited. Seventy-fifth on the money list didn't normally earn you invitations to special events, but Love's prodigious length and quiet demeanor always drew a crowd. It would be a quiet, relaxing week for the two of them. Lexie, the nickname they had given Alexia, would be fine on Sea Island with Davis's parents.

In their first full day on the island the Loves ran into a friend of Davis's parents from Atlanta, and they talked briefly about having dinner one night during the week. Later that afternoon, Davis phoned his mom back in Georgia to check on Lexie and to tell her about running into her friend. It was already 10:00 P.M. on the East Coast so the baby should be asleep, but Penta Love would be awake and waiting to hear from everyone. When his mom answered the phone, Davis knew something was wrong.

She told him his father's plane had "fallen off the radar," a nice way of tiptoeing around what they both knew: the plane had crashed. As Love would later write in his book, *Every Shot I Take,* a memoir of life with his father where he devoted 16 pages to a chapter entitled "The Crash," "Planes don't just disappear off radars. You can't roam the air in a plane the way you can roam the streets in a car. But I wanted to do everything I could to minimize my mother's worry before confirmation came."

The six-hour flight from Hawaii to San Francisco was agonizingly long. They couldn't call anyone, couldn't speak to anyone, or radio anyone for up-to-the-minute information. The airline had been accommodating in getting them off the island, and Davis had called a friend in Monterey to organize a private jet for the flight from California to Sea Island, but throughout the flight he couldn't stop worrying about his mother, and he couldn't shake the thoughts of the last meaningful conversation he had with his father.

They had been driving from Sea Island to Waycross, Georgia, so young Davis could buy a new Johnson engine for his fishing boat. They always talked about golf on these little forays, but this time, Davis Jr. had surprised his son by broadening the discussion, questioning whether or not the then-24-year-old still loved the game the way he once had, and whether "Trey," a common nickname for people with III behind their names, still had the burning desire to improve. Davis Jr. also questioned whether he was the right person to take his son to the next level, or whether Davis III should start relying on someone else to improve his game, a thought that frightened young Love. As he wrote in his book, "The words were coming from Dad's mouth, but they did not sound like him. I could not imagine my world without my father as my golf teacher."

When the airliner landed in San Francisco, Davis sprinted to a pay phone where he called his mother's home. When his brother Mark answered, the first words out of Davis's mouth were "What did you find out?"

"They found the plane," Mark Love said. "There were no survivors."

It took Davis Love III many years to effectively deal with his father's death. For the first couple of seasons he went through the motions of answering questions at every tour stop about the crash. He knew fans and reporters meant well, but that didn't make it any easier to discuss. On more than a few occasions he was short and quick-tempered with autograph seekers and rookie reporters, something so completely out of character for the always-accommodating Love that it worried those who knew him best. Bob Rotella, a sports psychologist who worked with a number of tour players, including Love, finally told him he needed to look at what he was doing to himself. "You're trying to be the head of your family and your mother's family. You're trying to be a lawyer and an accountant for your father's estate. You're trying to play the tour. You're trying to be your own swing coach. You're trying to put your father's death behind you. You're trying to prove to everybody that you can do everything! The thing is, you can't."

Time, love, and the closeness of his family allowed Love to work through the tragedy of his father's death. In 1997 he won the PGA Championship at Winged Foot in New York, discarding the moniker "Best Player Never to Win a Major" and moving into the elite class of major championship winners. Because he led the championship throughout most of the weekend, Love endured a new barrage of questions about his father: What would it mean to the memory of your father for you to win this championship? What sort of advice would your father give you right now? All the questions he had fielded for two years came back one more time, but Love didn't mind. He still lived with the pain of losing his father and he could never forget the tragedy, but he had grown and grieved and gotten on with his life the way he knew his dad would have wanted.

Those looking for mystic metaphors weren't disappointed in the final round. When Love's final putt fell on the 18th at Winged Foot a rainbow appeared overhead, providing one of the most lasting visual images in professional golf. He took off his visor and waved it across the sky, then embraced his brother, mother, and wife, tears flowing from every eye in the family and in the gallery. It was golf drama at its highest.

For over a decade after his father's death Love had gotten on airplanes with an understandable sense of apprehension. "Sure, you think about it every time you get on an airplane," he said. "But it's part of our lives, and things happen. We put a lot of faith in machines, and sometimes they break. You can't live your life scared."

After his son, Davis IV, was born, Love bought fractional ownership in a Hawker 1000, and he was traveling on that jet to Nashville to visit Legends Ridge, a golf course he was designing, when Stewart's plane crashed. Like Stewart, Love was venturing into the architectural field with a handful of design projects, the Nashville project being the fourth course in his portfolio.

When the Hawker landed at Nashville International, Love turned on his cell phone. It chirped immediately. Just as had been the case in Hawaii when he learned his father's plane had crashed, Love received the horrible news from his mother. "Mom was obviously concerned that we had arrived safely," Love said. The news stunned him, and for a moment he didn't know what to do or what to say. Payne and Love shared the fraternal bond of having played on the 1999 Ryder Cup team together, but they also shared the bond of having won their first majors at the PGA Championship: Stewart's coming in 1989 and Love's in 1997. "I had a copy of the Wanamaker Trophy made," Love said. Like the Claret Jug and the U.S. Open trophy, the Wanamaker Trophy was kept by the champion for the year of his reign and returned before the next year's competition, and like the others, the PGA of America inscribed the winners' names on the base of the Wanamaker Trophy. Just as it was on the original, Stewart's name was etched on Love's replica along with all the other PGA Championship winners. "It's going to be a lot more special to me now," he said.

A few days after Love won the PGA Championship, Greg Norman came up to him and said, "Welcome to the club," meaning the Fraternal Order of Major Championship Winners, an elite group among the most elite golfers in the world. "There is a bond among major championship winners," Love said. "Partly because you have all accomplished a similar goal, and stepped up the ladder, but part of it is because you end up being together for more things like past champions dinners or special events. Much like our bond on the Ryder Cup team, I think major winners somehow get thrown together a little bit more."

Now a member of that fraternity was gone, and Love felt the decade-old wounds open up again. "A gentleman in Nashville gave me a devotional book with a nice inscription in it," Love said. "Then he told me, 'You need to go home and tell your kids that this doesn't happen every day.' From a person I don't know, that was probably one of the greatest pieces of advice I have ever had. I went home and talked to my kids about it."

Because of the history of his father's accident, Love knew the press would want a statement from him, so he contacted Lee Patterson, the tour's on-site media official in Houston, and the two of them worked out a short, three-paragraph statement that ended with "May God bless Aaron, Chelsea, and Tracey and bring them peace."

Love wouldn't have gone to Houston if he hadn't called his friend Justin Leonard, who had already arrived at the Champions Club. "It feels better once you get here," Leonard told him. "Everybody is kind of together."

Love still wasn't sure, thinking that it didn't seem right to play golf. It didn't seem right to do anything other than try to help the Stewarts in any way possible. But he had been on the receiving end of too much help back in 1988, and he knew how draining and stressful that could be. When his father had died all of Sea Island sent food and good wishes to the Loves. Davis had appreciated the gestures, but there was only so much a family could eat, and there were only so many people you could see. The Stewarts had plenty of support from friends and family and several Orlando restaurants had even sent over their chefs to prepare meals for them. As much as his heart told him he should be in Orlando, Davis's head knew he would only be in the way. "I said to myself, 'I'm not doing anybody any good sitting at home watching the Braves game,'" Love said.

After hanging up with Leonard, Love called Ben Crenshaw, the captain of the 1999 Ryder Cup team. During their discussion, Love discovered Crenshaw's plans to drive to Houston from his home in Austin. "I want to come to be with some of the guys, talk to them about this, and I am going to come and walk a practice round," Crenshaw said.

That settled it for Love. "I'll see you tomorrow," he told Crenshaw.

Tiger Woods was already on the ground in Houston on Monday night. He left his Orlando home not long after watching the final moments of the crash on television and rode to the airport where he boarded his private jet. Like Love, Woods thought about the flight a little more, but as he said when he arrived at the Champions Club, "You have accidents. It's part of the risk that we all live. But you're not going to ride a bike to work. That's not realistic."

Woods played in the Tuesday pro-am, which commissioner Finchem made optional after Payne's death. Since Tuesday and Wednesday pro-ams are cash cows for the tour, players are normally required to play in one of them in order to be eligible for the tournament. This keeps the corporate sponsors happy, since they are the ones shelling out the $15,000 per group so that ridiculously bad golfers can play 18 holes and have their pictures taken with their favorite touring pros. But this week was different and everyone knew it. Under the circumstances even the most jaded corporate executive understood why it was not the time to push pros into playing. If they wanted to participate, fine. If they didn't, it was no problem. Woods, to the surprise of many who hadn't followed his maturation over the previous two years, was one who decided to play.

"From a selfish standpoint it was good for me to get out here and play with these guys. It allowed me to get away a little bit and enjoy their company," Tiger said. "They wanted to play in a pro-am and in order to do that you have to have a pro, and when you have an obligation to play, you play. I was fortunate enough to play with four great guys today and we had a great time, but this was a different feeling."

This from a man who shocked spectators and fans with his temperamental eruptions in 1997! Phrases like "in order to play in a pro-am you have to have a pro" couldn't be coming from the same young man who was chastised for turning down a request to attend a game at Shea Stadium honoring the 50th anniversary of Jackie Robinson's landmark debut in the major leagues. It couldn't be that such simple, reflective eloquence as "It allowed me to get away a little bit and enjoy these guys' company" could come from someone who had to have a pool reporter shadow him in 1997 because of the high likelihood he would tell members of the media to go fuck themselves. Yet there he was, patiently and poetically answering even the most inane questions on a day when most professionals would rather have taken a beating than talk to reporters.

"The tournament should go on, but obviously it's not going to be an easy week for any of us," said Woods. "When I was driving in with Butch Harmon, my coach, and when I got onto the golf course, it was so silent. It was just eerie, and nobody was really asking for autographs or clamoring for pictures. I think that's indicative of everyone's reaction. It was such a shock to everyone. I was telling Butch today, 'I almost feel like he is going to show up. I just saw him the other day.' It's hard to believe he is not going to be here.

"From what I've been told and from what I've seen on TV, Payne was sometimes a difficult person to be around. I never found that to be the case. When I came out, especially in the last year and a half when I really got to know him, he had gone through a change. He became more dedicated to his religion and it changed his life. That is the Payne I knew. I knew Payne as a carefree guy who was nice to everybody, open-hearted, and who loved to share and talk. That is the Payne I will always have inside of me. That's the Payne I know."

For many hearing this, it was Tiger who had undergone the change. In three and a half years Tiger had grown up, and now he was delivering a eulogy that could have come from a philosopher or spiritual counselor, but it came from neither: he was simply Tiger, golf's most noted one-name athlete, and a player television producers had once watched closely in order to cut away if a club was about to be slammed into the ground, or profanity was seconds from spewing forth.

This was clearly a different Tiger, older and much wiser than the youngster who turned pro amid media hoopla unlike anything seen since Muhammad Ali was in his heyday. He was far more mature, a man who, while still enjoying fast food and a good dirty joke, had come to grips with his fame and celebrity, who had sought and listened to the advice of mentors like Michael Jordan and Arnold Palmer, and who had realized that his blinding wealth and star power had a price. Tiger couldn't make the mistakes of youth afforded most men in their early twenties. An impetuous error in judgment became an epic event when it was Tiger Woods doing the erring, and in the first year or so of his professional golf life, there were plenty of errors to be exploited. It was a wonder Tiger played as well as he did in the early going. Even though his golf skills were magnificent, Tiger handled the pressures of competitive golf better than many of the pressures of stardom. He wasn't comfortable being recognized by screaming teenyboppers at McDonald's, and he certainly wasn't prepared for the demands of thousands of media requests ranging from Oprah Winfrey to *Business Week* magazine. There were three biographies written about him before his 21st birthday, and by the time he won the Masters in April 1997, just eight months after turning pro, he was the most recognized athlete on the planet.

He also became the target of cynics who openly opined that Tiger might become the next Jennifer Capriati, the teenage tennis star who went through a public meltdown when she finally rebelled in her late teens and early twenties. Superficially, Tiger fit the mold: talented athlete at a young age; hordes of marketing potential; even bigger hordes of people willing to "help" him exploit that potential; and at the center of it all, a father who shared the credit and the spotlight, and who made statements about his son being chosen by God for some higher purpose. Without knowing much about Tiger's resolve or his ability to mature, it was easy to predict a bad ending to this promising career, and many did just that.

But the cynics were wrong on several fronts. Despite countless reasons to believe otherwise, Earl Woods never pushed Tiger the way Stefano Capriati pushed his daughter, and the way thousands of parents who wish to vicariously relive their dreams push children into unhealthy regimens. Earl didn't push because he didn't have to. Tiger wanted to be the best golfer in the world, and, from an early age, he was willing to do whatever it took to reach that goal. Sure, Earl paraded his 2-year-old son in front of a nationwide audience on the "Mike Douglas Show" in the '70s, and he put him on display with other child prodigies anywhere and everywhere he could, but Earl never had to Krazy-Glue a club into Tiger's hands; Tiger was never without a golf club in his hands because that was the way Tiger wanted it.

As he made his comments in Houston—reverent, thoughtful, empathetic, and in no way self-centered—it was hard to reconcile the mature superstar athlete who went out of his way to make a group of amateurs feel good about playing on one of the worst days in golf history, with the child who, only four years earlier, had lived with his parents in a low-rise two-bedroom middle-class house in Anaheim close enough to the Lockheed Martin plant for Earl to get a job, and close enough to the Navy golf course for Tiger to play and practice every day of his childhood. He even looked different now, having grown from a skinny kid with both the innocence and the awkwardness of a teenager into a physical specimen, a lean, fit, muscular, and driven prototype for the "golfer/athlete" of the 21st century.

Tiger also came to Houston in the middle of a history-making streak he hoped would quiet his critics once and for all, and raise the bar so high only he stood a chance to clear it. He had just come off a victory at Disney, his second win in a row and his sixth PGA Tour win of the year, and his game was better than it had ever been, even though it had always been good. "I was in awe," Ernie Els, the fifth-ranked player in the world, said of the way Tiger was playing. "Nobody can touch this guy at the moment. He has gone to another level that I don't think the rest of us can really find right now."

That was the plan. Despite the snickers of a few who thought Woods was full of it when he insisted he was getting better every day during the 18-month period where he had only two wins and dropped to second in the world rankings, he had, indeed, improved his swing, matured in his demeanor, controlled his emotions, fulfilled his obligations, fired his agent and his first caddie, improved his attitude, and elevated himself back to the number-one spot with a statement second-half of 1999. But more than his golf (which was stunning), Tiger's feelings for the game and those around it had taken on a new quality—a Michael Jordan–Arnold Palmer—influenced respect to accompany his natural persistence.

At the 1997 U.S. Open, after his Masters victory and more pretournament coverage than any golfer had ever received, Tiger shot a 74 in the opening round and declined (rather forcefully) an invitation to speak to the media. The next day, when Tiger agreed to answer questions, he used more than 300 words to explain why he hadn't come into the media center the day before. Bev Norwood, a vice president with IMG, Tiger's management company, pointed this out to Tiger, saying, "You spent more time and used more words explaining why you didn't come in on Thursday, than you would have if you had just come into the press room on Thursday and answered a few questions about your round."

Tiger listened and learned. From August 1997 through the end of 1998 he was the only player to give a pretournament press conference at every event where he was in the field, something a younger, less experienced Tiger would never have done. His junior clinics and his Tiger Woods Foundation functions were always well attended, with Tiger's skills as host and teacher rivaling veterans 10 and 20 years his senior. He was also having genuine, unmitigated fun. "When I was in junior golf, I thought I could never love the game as much as I did then," Tiger said after winning in Disney. "Until I got out here and started winning more! I love it more than ever! I love to play. I love to practice, and I love to compete. I can honestly say I love it more now than ever."

Even though he knew golf would be far down the priority list for most of the players in Houston, Tiger came to the Tour Championship with a job to finish. "Occasionally I get a few flashes in my head of Payne and some of the memories I have with him," he said. "I'm sure it's going to happen to every one of us. You just have to understand that you have a job to do, and my job this week is to go out and try to win this golf tournament. It's not going to be easy, but it is just a matter of dealing with it, understanding it, and coming to peace with the fact that Payne is in a better place now.

"I learned from many of the deaths in my family to accept that they are in a better place. There is no struggling where they are now. They are happy; they are peaceful; they are looking over us; they are taking care of us. It is nice to know that. Maybe Payne will be, in essence, a guardian angel to all of us."

He gave a somber nod, and offered a hint of strong but silent sadness in his eyes as he prepared to embark on the remainder of his season: a Jules Verne marathon that would take him around the world in 30 days. As he walked out to the quiet parking lot, a boy, probably 12 years old, shyly approached. "Please, Tiger . . ." he started but didn't finish.

"Sure," Tiger said, taking the boy's hat and a Sharpie and scribbling his signature on the bill, not all the way across so as to leave no room for others, but appropriately sized and spaced. He then patted the boy on the shoulder. "You have a good day now." And he was off, leaving those who watched to say to themselves, "This couldn't possibly be the same Tiger Woods."

For the first time in their careers Tiger and David Duval, two players who had been part of a much-ballyhooed and often contrived rivalry for

two years, were finally paired in an official event at the Tour Championship, and nobody cared. The pairings were dictated by players' position on the money list, and since Tiger and Duval were one and two,
respectively, they drew side-by-side parking spaces in the player lot and
a first-round (in this case, 27-hole) pairing. The only way that might
have been a story is if anyone had asked Tiger and Duval what Payne
Stewart would have thought about them being paired, but the golf tournament was the least important activity of the week.

Crenshaw had, indeed, driven up from Austin, and he did speak to
the members of the 1999 Ryder Cup team, including Sutton, Love,
Leonard, Furyk, Duval, Woods, Lehman, and Jeff Maggert. Crenshaw
also spent an hour on the driving range recounting his Ryder Cup experiences with 2001 captain Curtis Strange and Champions Club founder
and former PGA Champion Jackie Burke, who captained the 1973
Ryder Cup team. For a few moments they forgot the gravity of the
week, and the three captains laughed at Burke's dry Texas humor.
"How many times did they call you asking what clothes to wear the next
day?" Burke asked Crenshaw.

"Every night," Crenshaw said. "I posted the next day's uniform in
huge letters on a board in the players' lounge, and they still called and
asked me what we were wearing."

"I got that beat," Burke retorted. "I put notes in everybody's room
the night before, and every night about midnight my phone would ring.
I'd say, 'Can't you read?' Hell, you're the best golfers in the world, but
you can't dress yourselves."

Strange chimed in that he was absolutely serious when he had said
his uniforms would be white and khaki in 2001. All three men had
another hearty laugh. It was the only refreshing levity of the week.

The following morning, with a three-quarter moon still hanging in
the early-morning sky and a blanket of fog draped over the landscape
like the fine mist of a Scottish moor, 35 players and their wives marched
single-file onto the first tee and sat in five rows of neatly aligned white
folding chairs while 300 silent spectators waited solemnly in the adjacent
grandstands. Once everyone was seated, the lonesome sounds of a single
bagpiper broke the eerie silence. Steve Agen, a bagpiper from the
Hamilton Pipe Band, played "Coming Home," a slow Scottish hymn
that seemed wholly appropriate. It took almost a full minute for Agen's

shadowy figure to appear in the mist, slowly marching out of the cypress and pines toward the gathering. By the time he arrived at the edge of the first tee there were few dry eyes in the assemblage.

It was a brief service, if service was even the right word to describe the gathering. Tim Finchem made a few introductory remarks in which he called Payne "a great champion, a tenacious competitor, and a real showman." Then Finchem turned the podium over to Tom Lehman, who had been up all night worrying about what he would say and how he was going to get through this without breaking down in uncontrollable sobs. "I didn't want to completely collapse and not be able to blubber a word," Lehman said, and he wasn't alone. Curtis Strange turned his eyes downward and took his wife, Sarah's, hand as Agen marched slowly toward them, while Amy Mickelson, wife of Phil and recognized as the most genuinely cheerful and consistently friendly of the tour wives, put her head on her husband's shoulder and gasped between silent but overwhelming moments of emotion. Even the normally jaded golf media succumbed to the anguish of the symbolism.

When he finally reached the lectern, Lehman said, "Payne was my friend and when he died, a big part of me died, too." He paused, then said, "Payne was a very emotional guy. He loved to laugh, and he wasn't afraid to cry. So I'm not going to be ashamed of my tears this morning and neither should you."

These were not revisionist views. Payne Stewart was, indeed, an emotional man who wore everything from his insecurities to his ego on his sleeve. His laugh, a high tenor with a slight edge to it, was louder than any other in the locker room, and his fire was only one bogey or one untoward interruption away from rearing its head. He was the loudest parent at Aaron's basketball and football games, often yelling at the officials to the point of being threatened with ejection if he didn't tone it down—just the kind of threats Payne's father, Bill, had received when Payne was a youngster. Payne was a little louder than Bill Stewart had been, but only a little. When Payne was in the region finals of his eighth-grade basketball league, Bill became so loud and obnoxious in his referee-ragging that the team received a technical foul.

"Who's the technical on?" Payne's irate coach demanded.

"That guy in the stands in the orange sweater," the official said, much to Payne's chagrin.

Almost 30 years later it was Payne who had become the man in the orange sweater. When his Isleworth neighbor and friend Ken Griffey, Jr., invited Payne, Mark O'Meara, and John Cook to Tampa to watch the Seattle Mariners play the Tampa Bay Devil Rays, Stewart was effervescent in his chiding of Griffey and the rest of the opposing team. After Griffey was caught in a rundown to end an inning, Payne led Cook and O'Meara out to the centerfield seats where Payne went to the railing and heckled his friend. "Junior!" he shouted. "Hey, Juuunioooor. Does this remind you of anything?" Payne then ran back and forth along the front-row aisle mimicking the rundown Griffey had just experienced. After several minutes of this obnoxious ribbing, the second-base umpire turned and pointed an accusatory finger at Payne. Of all the fans in the stands that night, it was Payne Stewart, the reigning U.S. Open champion, who came closest to being ejected.

He often had a political tin ear, and a knack for saying the wrong thing. Just four days before he died, Payne was interviewed during a rain delay at Disney and asked about the comments British commentator Peter Alliss had made concerning the American Ryder Cup team. Alliss told the *Daily Telegraph,* "Americans are totally different to us. They might as well be Chinese. In their eyes, pretty much everything in Europe is rubbish. Everything, everything, everything is crap! That begins to wear on you after a while." To which Payne dutifully responded by squinting into an ESPN camera, sticking out his top teeth, and saying in a mock Asian accent, "I juss want Peta' Arriss to know dat all of us American golfers on the Ryder Cup team, we are Chinese, too. Tank you very much." Within minutes of that segment's airing, Stewart was back on camera apologizing to anyone and everyone he might have offended, except for Peter Alliss, whom Payne said he "meant to offend." It was just the kind of naively inappropriate thing Payne did regularly, and the kind of thing only he could get away with.

Part of it was his overgrown kid personality, and part of it was his faith. His Christianity was well chronicled and genuine in every respect, but while he was strong in his religious convictions, his ecumenical skills still needed a little work. In his Bible-study class, Payne referred to the New Testament books of Thessalonians as "Theologians," and he once told his pastor that he had just read the Book of John and "you know what?" he said, "it wasn't bad." Payne was a well-meaning, good-hearted Baptist who donated a half-million dollars to his kids' Christian academy. He was also someone who called the Apostle Paul "a guy," as in, "Now, Paul was a guy who . . ." But he never claimed to be anything other than what he was. That, even with his foibles, was what endeared him to so many people.

Bill Stewart died of cancer in 1985, and it took Payne many years and many tears to get through the loss. He stood in the living room of his rented house in Pinehurst and openly wept as he watched an NBC segment on his father that ran before the final round of the 1999 U.S. Open, and his tears flowed again in Boston when he invoked the memory of his father during the Saturday-night team meeting. Almost every time the subject of Bill Stewart came up, Payne's voice would quiver ever so slightly as if the pain of his father's death were almost too much to bear. As he said later, "[Dad] prepared me for everything. Everything, that is, except his own death. That, he neglected."

None of Payne's peers, it seemed, were prepared for his death, either. There was a palpable silence on that solemn Houston morning, broken only by a few sniffles and one deep sigh from Tom Lehman as he opened a small black book entitled *Funeral Services* by James L. Christensen. Another breath and Lehman began reading, "In such a time there is but One who can bring light out of darkness, who can heal the heart that is broken by grief, who can bring peace of soul and strength of spirit. That one is the God whom Paul called 'the God of all comfort.' He did not fail Job. He did not fail Paul. He did not fail Christ. He will not fail you."

After a moment of silence, Agen's haunting bagpipes swelled the air with the recognizable notes of "Amazing Grace." Then, just as he had come, Agen marched back into the fog, disappearing to a reprise of "Coming Home."

As they were walking across the putting green after the service, Justin Leonard turned to Davis Love and asked, "When are you going to Orlando?" A note had been posted in the locker room informing all the players about the convoy of jets leaving on Friday morning, but some players were making their own arrangements.

"I might just go in a little while," Love said, implying he had seen enough. Playing a golf tournament was the last thing he, or any of the other top 29 money winners, wanted to do at that moment.

Fortunately Love had a few hours to collect himself after the memorial service. Bob Rotella, who had been in Houston all week counseling players, told Love he needed to focus on his routine. "Every time you think of something that is not golf, let it remind you to get into your normal routine," Rotella said. "That is the only way you're going to get through." This wasn't an ordinary session for a sports psychologist, but Rotella wasn't ordinary. When he was in high school Rotella had lost seven friends in Vietnam, an experience he recounted to many of the players during the week.

Love got through, shooting 64–35 to lead after the opening 27 holes, but he couldn't have cared less. "Every time you had some fun you chastised yourself for being excited," he said. At one point during Love's second nine, a small single-engine plane flew over pulling a banner that read, "We will remember you Payne." "When that little plane flew over, I couldn't putt," Love said. "I had a four-footer straight in for birdie, and it took me ten minutes to putt it. You shouldn't be out here playing golf with tears in your eyes."

Tiger shot 100 for 27 holes and was one shot back after trying to play a shot through a rock on the 15th hole. After driving his ball against a small stone in the rough, Woods examined his options and decided the best play was to hit the rock (which was about twice the size of his golf ball) and hope to advance the ball back to the fairway. "If I moved the rock the ball would have moved," Tiger said. "I would have incurred a penalty. If I took two club lengths [for an unplayable lie] I would still be in the rough with a tree in my line, and I probably wouldn't have saved par." So Tiger attempted to hit the rock first, and hoped the force of his swing would somehow move the ball back into play. It worked from the standpoint that Tiger advanced the ball back into play. The only problem was the pain. Rocks are harder than golf balls and they don't give quite as easily, as Tiger would attest to after his shoulder, wrist, arm, and neck stung for the remaining three and a half holes.

"I had a hole in my club," Tiger said. "It squashed the clubface so the grooves were completely flat. It was an interesting shot."

With no play on Friday Tiger was sure he would be fine for the remaining rounds. "No worries," he said. "I'll be all right." The rock couldn't stop him, and neither, it seemed, could anything else.

It was with no small sense of irony that players and their wives boarded a fleet of private jets on Friday morning for a three-hour flight from Houston to Orlando. Commissioner Finchem made the tour's Astra available, and The Southern Company, the title sponsor of the Tour Championship, provided two Citation Vs. The two men at the top of the tournament leaderboard flew together, as Robin Love left word for Davis to "just fly back with Tiger," while Phil Mickelson, one of several players who had their pilot's licenses, flew himself, along with his wife Amy and his daughter Amanda, in his Hawker 700. Hal Sutton flew in his Diamond 1A, a smaller jet Sutton had purchased outright after examining all the fractional ownership options and deciding the peace of mind of knowing the pilots and the maintenance history of his own jet were more important than the economics of time-share, while Jeff Maggert passed on the private transports altogether and took a commercial flight out of George Bush International on Thursday night.

No matter how they arrived, the procession into the First Baptist Church of Orlando was moving and enormously sad. Photos, trophies, and other memorabilia of Payne's life littered the sanctuary, a pastel megaplex seating 6,000 people. As he was walking down the aisle and past a table full of Stewart family photos, PGA Tour rules official Slugger White didn't know if he could remain composed long enough to get to his seat. He held himself together reasonably well until he saw a small plaque beneath Payne and Tracey's wedding photo that read, "We Love You, Dad. We Will Miss You." White's knees buckled and he slumped forward, gasping for air between sobs. Right before he hit the ground, a strong hand clasped White's shoulder and steadied him. "It's all right," the man, a minister from the church whom White had never met, said in a calming voice. "Come on, it'll be all right."

In fact, it was better than all right: it was the most moving funeral service any of the thousands in attendance or the millions watching on television had ever seen. In a stately black dress with long sleeves and a high neckline, Tracey Stewart stood like a pillar of faith before the assembled congregation, giving a moving and remarkably composed eulogy. She smiled when recalling how she and Payne first met. It was at a cocktail party before the 1980 Malaysian Open. "He was the most beautiful man I had ever set eyes upon," she had said then. It took a little cajoling from his friends, but Payne finally asked Tracey out to dinner and within a year the two were married.

She had never been one to let her husband rest on his laurels. It was her drive as much as his that lifted Payne out of complacency and back into the winner's circle at an age when many players were setting their careers on cruise control until their 50th birthdays and their debut on the Senior tour. Tracey had been strong when he was alive, and now she was stunning those who saw her with her strength, poise, and grace in the face of his tragic death.

Payne's close friend, Paul Azinger, shoved his pants legs inside argyle socks and donned a tam-o'-shanter while giving a eulogy that moved the audience from tears to laughter and back to tears again. Azinger recalled the outrageous Payne, retelling the story of how he bought a new fishing boat and (being a less than avid sailor) cranked the engine in his garage just to hear its throaty purr. There was only one problem: outboard motors require water. Within minutes Payne's little foray had become an inferno as the engine ignited and spewed flames onto the ceiling of his garage. With the outboard engine still running and burning simultaneously, Payne pushed the boat out of the garage before his house caught fire. He then compounded his mistake by sheepishly recounting the tale to Azinger, who promptly told everyone he knew. A week later Azinger cut out a photo of an outboard engine from a boating magazine, and taped it to Payne's locker along with the words "JUST ADD WATER." "I loved Payne Stewart," Azinger said, "and I will miss him."

"He ought to be a preacher," Hal Sutton said of Azinger's performance. "I'd sure go to his church."

Chuck Cook, Payne's long-time teacher, also did an admirable job remembering his friend. Cook spoke of a time when he and Payne were visiting Pebble Beach in anticipation of the 1993 U.S. Open. Payne had won the Open the year before, and, as tradition dictated, he was returning the trophy. But without his knickers and cap Payne went unrecognized, even to a group of golfers in the bar at Pebble Beach. "No, he's not," one man insisted when told that the stranger standing next to him was Payne Stewart. Rather than produce his driver's license or sign his name, Payne chose to prove his identity in a more demonstrable fashion. "If I bring the U.S. Open trophy in here, will you fill it with whatever we want to drink?" Payne asked. The man agreed. When Payne returned with the trophy he ordered a bottle of Cristal and sent the bill to the gentleman in the corner with the embarrassed look on his face. Cook vowed to return to Pebble Beach in 2000, where he said he would sit on a wall separating the golf course from the sea and "talk to my friend about life."

As the service continued ushers moved down the aisles with baskets of cloth strips. The strips, everyone soon realized, were bracelets with

W.W.J.D., a common Christian acronym for "What Would Jesus Do?", woven into the fabric. Payne had worn such a bracelet during his 1999 U.S. Open win, and now his pastor was asking the players and assembled friends to wear the same bracelets and send the same message. Most complied immediately, with a majority of players wearing the bracelets the rest of the week and some wearing them the rest of the year. Ben Crenshaw even posed (with his wife, Julie) for a *Sports Illustrated* swimsuit layout while wearing the W.W.J.D. bracelet, and some said they planned to wear the cloth strips forever as a permanent tribute to Payne.

Before reboarding their jets and returning to Houston, Mississippi, or their homes, the assembled tour players lined the aisles of the church and hugged Tracey, Chelsea, Aaron, and Payne's mother, Bee Stewart. There were golf tournaments to finish, but no one wanted to think about that at the moment. If his wife hadn't insisted he fly straight back to Houston, Davis Love would have withdrawn and spent the weekend on Sea Island with his kids, even though he was leading the Tour Championship at the time. Most felt the same way. Golf was the least important thing, yet it was crucial. "We need to be on TV and keep his memory that way," Love said.

Saturday's 27-hole round was more of the same. The skies wept like everyone else, and players slogged their way through a steady drizzle interrupted by an occasional downpour. When the day finally ended Tiger held the lead, having completed three disjointed rounds in 13-under-par. Love fell six shots back and into a tie for fifth with Sutton. Still, nobody cared. Even Tiger couldn't get as fired up as he might otherwise have been. "If I do win, it will be a nice thing, obviously, but I don't think I will feel quite as high, just because of what has happened this week," he said. "Today was tough, but nothing compares to yesterday."

He had held his emotions in check reasonably well until the memorial service, but when Tracey Stewart took his hand in the reception line, he "lost it." Tiger said, "I started bawling. Just to hear her voice and to hear her understanding of the whole magnitude of the situation put everybody's mind at ease. Seeing Tracey up there talking and speaking from the heart, that was incredible. If she can have that kind of strength then we should be able to do it easily."

Tiger did it on Saturday, opening up a three-shot lead, which meant the biggest story of the final round would have been if he had failed to win. Tiger was 10 for 11 when he led with 18 holes to play, and he arrived in Houston with six wins in nine events including the prestigious Memorial Tournament, the Western Open, the PGA Championship, the NEC Invitational (the second World Golf Championship event of the year), and Disney. His other finishes in that stretch had been a third at the U.S. Open, seventh at Carnoustie in the British, and 37th at the Sprint International, a modified-Stableford tournament held in Colorado the week after Tiger's PGA Championship win. The streak had people comparing Tiger with Ben Hogan, Byron Nelson, Palmer, and Nicklaus. It was clearly one of the most dominant stretches of golf in over two decades.

But the focus and attention remained where it should have remained: on remembering and properly honoring Payne. President George Bush and Mrs. Bush came out for the weekend, and the president spent a little time talking with Love about Payne. The Bushes had last seen Love and Payne and the rest of the players at the Ryder Cup Matches in Brookline, where they were weeklong staples in the gallery and off-course cheerleaders for Team USA. President Bush remembered having "a delightful inside-the-ropes chat" with Payne during Saturday's matches, and he shared those memories with some of the players. Players and fans appreciated their presence. George and Barbara Bush were not only the former President and First Lady, they were the reigning First Parents of Texas, with their son George W. Bush in the middle of his second term as governor of the Lone Star State. That made the elder Bushes more popular in Texas than they had been while serving in the White House. Everywhere the Bushes walked around the Champions Club there was respectful applause, followed by the president's always good-natured wave.

Even an ex-president was second fiddle, though. Stuart Appleby summed it up best that Saturday afternoon when he said, "The tournament is like, 'Big deal. Who cares?' We're playing for Payne."

That became overtly apparent on Sunday, when 24 of the 29 players in the field showed up on the range wearing knickers. The idea was originally Hal Sutton's, who said it would be "a neat tribute" if everyone wore Payne's trademark clothing for the final round, but it was Tom Lehman who called the makers of the Payne Stewart collection and requested two boxes of cream plus-fours. When the box arrived on

Saturday afternoon, the world's best players scrambled to find pants that fit. Some did, and others didn't. Vijay Singh was distraught Sunday morning when he arrived on the range wearing his regular long pants. "I don't want anyone to think I'm being disrespectful," Singh lamented to Lee Patterson. "They didn't fit." Patterson came up with an easy solution. Singh donned a pair of argyle socks and tucked his pants into the socks, just as Azinger had done during the memorial service. Everyone was happy.

Tiger chose not to wear the outfit, saying, "You don't have to wear knickers to honor someone. I'm comfortable handling things internally. I don't need to show the pain I feel inside, or how much I honor Payne Stewart. That's my way of handling things." He did wear a black ribbon on his cap, but he also chose not to wear the W.W.J.D. bracelet for the same reasons, and because he was a Buddhist. Tiger had been a regular attendee at temple with his mother in California, and during his first season on tour Tiger told reporters he "didn't practice [Buddhism] every day," but he did wear a chain with a Buddhist icon around his neck as a symbol of his devotion to both his mother and his faith.

Love wore the knickers, the bracelet, and the ribbon, despite some initial reservations. It was his brother and caddie, Mark, who convinced Love that the knickers were a good idea. "He said, 'They're not for you. They're for everybody who will see you,'" Love said. "So I snuck through the pile early and made sure I got a pair that fit."

The eeriest contestant was Appleby, who took the process a step farther and actually wore Payne's clothes. On Thursday night after he had arrived back in Orlando, Appleby went to the Stewarts' residence, where he asked Tracey what she thought of the idea. Tracey said it was fine, so, in Appleby's words, "three or four of us went up there and rummaged through his closet. There's about four million square feet of space in there. Every player in this field could wear a Payne Stewart outfit all four days and not have a duplicate." Ian Baker-Finch helped Appleby pick out a red, white, and navy-blue tartan pair of knickers, a navy shirt, matching socks, and a hat. Appleby even wore the deceased's shoes, which he said "fit perfectly. The cap's a little tight, though. Payne was losing some hair, you know." Throughout the day, players and spectators were stunned by the remarkable resemblance Appleby bore to Payne. When asked if wearing knickers might become a habit, Appleby replied, "If I thought I was going to win majors, I'd wear spandex."

Tiger shot 69 in the final round and won going away. He dedicated the win to Payne, looked skyward, signed enough autographs to make his fans happy, and said the right things afterward. "We've all had to come to grips with the barometer of emotions, and it's been a very draining week. Seeing Tracey up on that podium on Friday made it a lot easier. Without Tracey's strength there is no way I could have been as resilient in the way I played this weekend."

As the sun set that Sunday afternoon and players scurried to the airport to catch the tour's charter to Spain, a steady procession of fans continued through the parking lot, stopping briefly to pay their final respects. Some took pictures, some left flowers, some knelt and wept openly while others stood silently nearby. Until the moment, well after sundown, when a Harris County deputy closed off access, the lone five-and-a-half-foot-wide parking spot became part chapel, part shrine. It was the one spot where fans completely ignored passing players. No autographs or pictures or congratulatory handshakes or hugs. It may have only been a parking lot, but for those who found their way to it, the fourth lined space nearest the locker room door was much more important than any five-second conversation with the likes of Duval, Woods, Love, or Lehman. This was a special place.

Sarah Cleil was the last visitor. She prayed on her knees at the asphalt memorial, tears flowing freely as her husband removed his cap and waited behind her with his head bowed. Sarah stayed only a couple of minutes. Like most who visited she left nothing but her prayers and took nothing but her memories.

Others shared their feelings by leaving flowers and other items that might have meant little to Payne, but meant a lot to those trying to honor his memory. Cindy Marshall Henderson left a 20-year-old Southern Methodist University T-shirt with a handwritten sign that read "Class of '77. We will miss you." Someone else draped a towel from the 1999 U.S. Open over the three-foot-high temporary railing separating the parking lot, while others tied a half-dozen W.W.J.D. bracelets like ribbons beside Payne's nameplate.

A photo had been taped just below the PGA Tour logo on the nameplate. It was Payne between two teenagers, brothers from the similarity of features, one in his early teens, the other old enough to have attempted a mustache and goatee. The boys were beaming with pride, as their idol put his arms around them in an obvious if not amateurish pose for whoever held the camera six or seven feet away. It looked as though this was the highlight of their young impressionable lives. The picture, in a clear plastic frame with the words "Houston Open 1999" scribbled along the top, fluttered in the breeze beside a bouquet of orchids and a printed card of the 23rd Psalm.

Some of the visitors wrote notes. A woman who signed her name Anita W. penned a moving tribute to a man she may or may not have ever met. "Gathered at your feet are many gifts from God," she wrote. "Knowledge of yourself, love of family and the ability to be loved by them and by dear friends, and also a great love and talent for the sport of golf. You have earned your fitting place in the history of that game. Congratulations on a remarkable year. Now go to your God in peace knowing that He and your dear friends will be with your family. They will not be alone in this time of sorrow. And may they later know the serenity and peace you now feel."

Arthur Davis, a large black man with a noticeable limp and an infectious smile who was a maintenance worker at the Ramada Inn in Jasper, Texas, read those words during his Sunday-dusk visit to the shrine. "That's just right," he said with a satisfied nod. Davis had brought an arrangement of azaleas, which he carefully removed from a plastic grocery bag and laid on the ground beneath Anita W.'s handwritten card. "I've been watching him since he first started coming here," he said with a subdued grin. "I've only missed four Houston Opens in 36 years, and I watched Payne every time he played." Then, as his face tightened and his voice began to crack, Davis said, "I lost my daughter when she was one year older than Payne. 'Course, she knew it was coming with the cancer."

After a moment when the only sounds from the parking lot were a courtesy car trunk being closed and the deep breaths he took as he considered the location of his gift, Arthur Davis finally gathered himself enough to say, "I brought azaleas. I always thought red was his favorite color."

A week later, Davis Love III sat in the players' lounge, half a world away from Houston. The screen from a 60-inch television glowed from against the north wall of the room, and there was chatter as players filed past a buffet table filled with Spanish hams and flavorful cheeses. The leaderboard flashed across the screen for a second and Love could do nothing but shake his head and smile. Tiger Woods was 10-under-par on a golf course where only three players were under par for the week. Ten-under-par! Tiger was four shots ahead of Miguel Angel Jiménez, a native from nearby Málaga who had won twice in Spain on the European tour already, but the nearest player behind Jiménez was Dudley Hart at one-under, nine shots off the lead! With the exception of two players, Tiger had lapped the field by double-digits, just as he had done in his historic Masters win in 1997. Now, as then, he was playing against the top players in the world—62 of them to be exact, straight off the world rankings—but Tiger was proving why he was head and shoulders above everybody else in the game. Ten-under-par, on a day when the wind was whipping off the Mediterranean and swirling around the Costa del Sol with a fury unlike anything Love had seen in either of his trips to Valderrama. It was incredible.

Love hadn't planned on making the trip to Spain. His hip and back had been bothering him (a condition worsened by extended air travel), and Payne's death had been emotionally and physically draining for him. He had said he was "fifty-fifty" early in the week of the Tour Championship, then on Sunday, after finishing second to Tiger, Love said, "I was convinced I was going to Spain until I saw Aaron Stewart catch a touchdown pass (in his Pop Warner football game on Saturday) on SportsCenter. I'm looking for any excuse not to go and that's a pretty good one." Throw in the fact that Lexie was showing her Paso Fina in a national horse show at the Georgia International Fairgrounds in Perry that week, and Love became sure he was staying home. But Robin Love convinced her husband to make the trip. Despite a third-place position on the money list and 11 top-10 finishes, Love had failed to win in 1999, which meant he wouldn't be eligible for the 2000 Mercedes Championships at Kapalua on Maui unless he won the season-ending WGC American Express Championship at Valderrama. As much as Lexie wanted her dad to see her horse show, she wanted to go to Maui even more. A win was the only way to get there. Plus, Love was a company man, a player representative on the PGA Tour Policy Board as well as the Player Director on the board of the PGA of America, so it would be untoward for him to miss one of the inaugural World Golf Championship events. The tour had expended a lot of goodwill getting the WGC off the ground, and it was up to players like Love to ensure its success. So after traveling across the state to Columbus, Georgia, on Monday to get a checkup from his back specialist, Tom Boers, Love and brother Mark caught the 5:00 P.M. Delta flight on Tuesday from Atlanta to Madrid, connecting on to Malaga where a courtesy car whisked them away for the 90-minute ride to Valderrama. At least he thought he would have more time to view the countryside on this trip. His only other visit to Spain had been during the 1997 Ryder Cup, when Love barely found time to sleep. This week should be different.

Now, as he rolled a Romeo y Julieta Habana Churchill cigar between his fingers, Love considered the implications of what he was seeing on the television screen. Tiger was about to become the first player since Ben Hogan in 1953 to win four tour events in a row. Palmer hadn't done it; Nicklaus hadn't done it; Watson, Player, Miller, Norman, and Price hadn't done it; but Tiger was about to not only win his fourth in a row but also whip the undisputed best players in the world in the process, becoming the first player since Johnny Miller in 1974 to win eight PGA Tour events in a season. The numbers were even more impressive than that. If you counted his win in Germany on the European tour (which Tiger did), he was about to win his ninth event of the year and his eighth in 11 starts. The American Express was Tiger's 22nd tournament of the year and he had been out of the top 10 only five times. This wasn't a Player-of-the-Year performance; it was a Player-of-the-Last-Quarter-Century coronation ceremony! And he wasn't beating a bunch of club pros in the Citrus Open or the Cajun Classic: Tiger's streak included a major championship, the Tour Championship, and, if the current situation held, two of the tour's prestigious WGC events where he had resoundingly trounced the very best in the game.

Love hadn't completed the math, but he knew Tiger's 1999 earnings would exceed his and Duval's combined winnings. It would be an obscene amount of money, somewhere north of $6.5 million on the U.S. tour and over $7 million worldwide if he won at Valderrama. That was more official money than Jack Nicklaus had earned in his entire career! Money, Love knew, could no longer be a barometer. "I was hoping to catch Greg Norman (as the all-time leading money winner) before Tiger passed me," Love said to Jeff Sluman and Stuart Appleby, who sat next to him with plates of food from the buffet. "I don't know if that will happen."

Tiger had certainly raised the bar on all fronts. Endorsement dollars were more than anyone could have imagined because of his presence, and golf, while not yet on par with the NBA, NFL, or Major League Baseball, had grown in popularity since Tiger's emergence on the scene, with player compensation moving upward accordingly. In his first season, Tiger had raised the standard by uttering his simple, yet profound, philosophy on golf. "Second place sucks," he had said. It was the perfect mantra, Lombardiesque in its classic simplicity, but groundbreaking in its audacity and certitude. Golf wasn't like football, where the championship team might have two or three losses in a 19-game season, or even like baseball, where a hit every three out of ten at-bats was pretty good. Professional golf was a long-term venture with incremental gains. Two wins in a 25-tournament season was stellar, and sometimes (as was the case with Mark O'Meara in 1998) good enough to earn Player of the Year honors. Two wins a year for three or four years in a row put you in the upper echelon. But Tiger had changed all that. In three and a half years he had 21 worldwide wins, eight seconds, 10 thirds, and 59 top-ten finishes in 87 starts with only one missed cut during that period. Curtis Strange, the interviewer sitting next to Woods when he made his "second place sucks" proclamation, had smiled and told the youngster, "You'll learn." But it was everyone else who had learned. The game had changed. The tide had risen because of Tiger. Professionals were working out to increase muscle mass and decrease body fat like never before. Practice sessions were longer, more intense, and more focused than they had been before and the drive to win on tour, while always big, was more important among players than ever. Second place *did* suck, after all, but it had taken a 20-year-old to remind them of it.

"Isn't that illegal?" Appleby asked, pointing to Love's Cuban cigar.

"Not if I smoke it here," Love said with a smile as he continued to roll the cedar wrapper between his fingers. A friend had picked up a box of cigars on Gibraltar, about a 20-minute drive from Valderrama and rumored to be the most economical place in Europe to buy Cuban smokes. They were having a pretty big ape shoot in Gibraltar from what he had heard. Barbary apes, a long-protected species, were coming down off the big rock and attacking people for food. With no natural predators and tourists more than willing to feed and photograph them, the apes had taken a more aggressive stance, so authorities were organizing a primate hunt for the coming weeks. Love hadn't paid much attention to all that. There were plenty of things to keep his mind occupied on the Spanish mainland.

When he looked up from his cigar, Love saw that Tiger had made a bogey at the 16th. So he was nine-under instead of 10. He still seemed to have a lock. Then, after hitting two perfect shots on the par-five 17th, Love watched as Tiger hit a beautiful knockdown nine-iron just beyond the pin. Tiger had turned away after hitting his shot, thinking it was perfect. Then as the crowd noise began to elevate, he looked up and saw his ball rolling down the slope of the green, picking up speed, and heading for the front edge. To call the 17th hole "goofy" was an insult to other goofy but charming holes like the 17th at TPC of Scottsdale. The 17th at Valderrama was, as Colin Montgomerie put it, "the worst hole we play all year." It was an unfair test that rewarded poorly played shots and penalized good ones, as was the case at that very moment. The cheering increased as Tiger's ball trickled off the front edge of the 17th green and it became an all-out roar when the ball slid down an embankment and into a pond, the ripples spreading outward as the fanfare from the grandstands intensified.

The shot had been perfect, but it had ended up in the water, a testament to the awful design of the 17th. Fan reaction, however, had been rancorous, rude, and completely anathema to the spirit of the game. This wasn't the Ryder Cup! Still, they were cheering a perfectly played shot that had ended up in the water! "Unbelievable," Love said. But then a lot of things in golf were unbelievable these days, and many of the epic changes could be traced back to this very hole, on this golf course, with this same player, Tiger Woods, in almost the same circumstances. In 1997 it had been a Ryder Cup, and the crowd had been just as vocal, and just as wrong. But such things were expected in the patriotic biannual contest. This was a stroke-play tournament comprising players from all over the world. To cheer a man's misfortune in an event like this . . .

My, how the game had changed!

*Four*

# THE DEAL—
# SEPTEMBER 1997

BY 1997 THE RYDER CUP had ceased being a good deal for the players, especially the American players. No one ever referred to the Ryder Cup as a "deal" in either the business or the academic sense of the word. "Deal" insinuated a transaction, a give-and-take in a dispassionate commercial venture, the connotations of which were far too smarmy for the puritanical biannual matches, even though by 1997 the Ryder Cup had become the most commercialized and lucrative golf event in the world. Deals were what agents worked out with commercial endorsers, or what club manufacturers worked out with players to entice them to play their clubs. To somehow look at the Ryder Cup as a "deal," good or bad, bastardized the saintly essence of the competition. Players used words like "privilege" and "honor" when discussing the matches, usually using each word two or three times, as in, "I can't tell you what an honor and privilege it is to represent my country in the Ryder Cup, and I'm honored to have the privilege to compete in such an honorable and privileged event." Nevertheless by the time Team USA landed in Spain for the 32nd rendition of the matches, the Ryder Cup presented the best golfers in the world with a deal that, while being honorable and privileged, was financially bad, competitively bad, and in many ways bad for a player's image.

First there were the financial considerations, or lack thereof. Even though they received a $5,000 stipend, which never came close to covering expenses, the Ryder Cup was the equivalent of a professional freebie, a competition among people who made their livings playing golf in which no money was awarded to the competitors. Journalist and author Michael Bamberger called it "the ultimate amateur event played by professionals," which was as apt a description as any. But for all the lofty posturing of the Ryder Cup as a benevolent "good of the game" creation (the PGA of America called it "one of the last great sporting events based upon prestige rather than prize money"), the entire concept of the matches came about as a commercial venture. James Harnett, a circulation director of *Golf Illustrated,* proposed the matches in 1920 in hopes of increasing paid readership, paid circulation, and paid advertising for his magazine. He accomplished none of the above and the matches floundered. Benevolence didn't enter the picture until 1927, when seed merchant Samuel Ryder commissioned a two-and-a-half-foot-tall gold trophy, then covered the financial shortfalls of the matches so the best players in Britain and the United States could "get to know one another" every two years during a friendly game. Even Ryder understood the value of remuneration, saying in the early days, "I will give £5 to each of the winning players and give a party afterwards with champagne and chicken sandwiches." It wasn't much, but quite a few golf pros in the late 1920s played for a lot less.

For half a century nobody cared about the money because there wasn't any money to care about. The Ryder Cup bled red ink for years, staying afloat only because of subsidies from the dues-paying members of the PGA of America. There were no huge television contracts, no licensing and merchandising fees, no big galleries, and no corporate hospitality tents. Things were so bad that when the PGA Tour split from the PGA of America in 1968, the tour chose to take the World Series of Golf (a cash cow) as part of its separation package, leaving the floundering Ryder Cup in the hands of the sweater-selling club pros. Players certainly didn't mind the lack of compensation. The Ryder Cup was, after all, an event to promote goodwill and harmony among nations, and the PGA was losing money like everybody else. It would have been unseemly for players to expect compensation. Even when they realized they were losing money on things like extended family travel and lodging, Ryder Cup participants weren't upset. It wasn't much money, and besides, it was an honor and privilege to play. What most Ryder Cup rookies didn't realize was, not only did they lose a little money during the week of the matches, they had another round of losses waiting for them when tax time rolled around. All the uniforms and gifts, from the jackets, slacks, and sweaters worn in the opening ceremonies to the bottles of wine and custom-made golf bags, were taxable income in the eyes of the IRS. Not only did Ryder Cup players have to wear uniforms (something golfers never did), they had to pay taxes on those uniforms at the end of the year. It was, quite simply, a bad deal. Still, nobody complained. It was only every other year, and the Ryder Cup provided a chance for the best golfers from the United States and Britain to play for God and country and all the other noble platitudes thrown out by the PGA like "good of the game," and "promotion of goodwill," and "camaraderie through competition." If there was an alliteration to be found concerning the virtuousness of the Ryder Cup, the PGA of America used it.

For years no one questioned the fact that the Ryder Cup was a financial dog. It was always held in September after the PGA Championship, when most Americans were engrossed in football and most Europeans were preparing for the Rugby World Cup. Plus, the matches were usually routs. From 1927 through 1977 the U.S. teams won the cup 16 times, lost it three times, and tied once when the Americans already possessed the cup, which meant they got to keep it. "It was usually just a question of whether we would win on Saturday or Sunday," Hale Irwin, who competed in five Ryder Cups, said of the early years. "They had good individual players but, depth-wise, it was clear we were going to win. We still had to do it and we still had to give the opponents the respect they deserved, but all in all our teams were too talented."

Which was another reason the Ryder Cup was a bad deal for the U.S. players: they were always expected to win. The Americans were predominant favorites every year. If the Europeans won, it was an upset victory, a David and Goliath story with the triumphant underdogs toppling their bloated and overconfident opponents through strength of will and character. On the occasions when the Americans lost the Ryder Cup, their collapse was big news. When the U.S. team won, nobody cared because they were supposed to win. According to Irwin, "Nobody paid much attention until we started losing the thing."

And lose they did. In the decade from 1985 through 1995, Team USA posted two wins, three losses, and one tie in Ryder Cup competition. Every year they were heavily favored, and with every loss they were resoundingly vilified. "Soft" was the most common characterization used to criticize the Americans. "Spoiled" was another favorite. Somehow the American players didn't have the heart, or the fortitude, or the resilience, to win the Ryder Cup anymore, critics claimed. Forget the sixty years of dominance: U.S. golfers didn't know how to play as a team, couldn't compete in match play, and, perhaps the most stinging criticism of all, they choked. Every time a U.S. squad was "upset" in the Ryder Cup, no matter how strong the competition, loud voices decried the defeat as a choke, a gag, or a perennial taking of the gas. Those who leveled such charges conveniently forgot that, starting in 1979, the complexion of the Ryder Cup changed. That year, and for every Ryder Cup thereafter, the competition moved from a head-to-head match-up between the United States and Great Britain and Northern Ireland to a showdown between the United States and all of Europe.

"In 1977, we were playing at Royal Lytham," Jack Nicklaus recalled. "I sat down one night with Lord John Derby, the head of the PGA of Great Britain, and said, 'John, you know that for everyone on the American team it's a great honor to make the team and it's a great honor to play in these matches, but frankly, when the matches start there isn't much competition. We win every year, and I don't think that's right.' I said, 'You've got a European tour that you're a part of, and I think if you included the European players and made it Europe versus the United States, I think you'd have some really great matches that would add to the Ryder Cup.' John agreed with me and he said he'd take care of it from his end, which he did. I suppose the most difficult aspect was getting the British PGA to include Europe. When [John] got it through, the Americans went along with it."

That opened the door for players like Seve Ballesteros, José María Cañizares, José María Olazábal (all from Spain), Bernhard Langer (Germany), and a contingent of players from Sweden. Nicklaus had been right: change was swift and dramatic. The first signs came in 1983 at the PGA National Golf Club in Florida, when the United States eked out a one-point win. The Americans actually trailed after the first day, and were tied with the Euros after the second. It wasn't until the final match on Sunday, when Tom Watson defeated Bernard Gallacher 2 and 1, that the United States locked up the win in the PGA of America's backyard. Compared with 1981 in Surrey, England, when the United States trounced Europe 18½ points to 9½, and 1979 when the Americans won by six points (17 to 11), 1983 was a wakeup call. This new crop of Europeans actually believed they could win the Ryder Cup, and they had proved themselves capable of playing against America's best.

In 1985, the unthinkable finally happened. At the Belfry, an English golf course that looked like it belonged in central Florida, Scotland's Sam Torrance made an 18-foot birdie putt on the 18th hole to defeat Andy North and secure a victory for Europe, the first time the cup hadn't been retained by the Americans in 28 years. Not only did the Euros beat the Americans, they thumped them, winning 13 out of 20 points in the final two days. The final tally was Europe, 16½ and the United States, 11½. It was, as Ryder Cup rookie Hal Sutton would say, "a good ole-fashion whippin.'"

Two years later, things got worse for Team USA. At Muirfield Village in Dublin, Ohio, Jack Nicklaus's landmark course, and with Nicklaus himself serving as captain, the greatest players in America, which included Curtis Strange, Hal Sutton, Lanny Wadkins, Larry Nelson, Tom Kite, Ben Crenshaw, and a promising Ryder Cup rookie named Payne Stewart, were once again embarrassed by such European stalwarts as Ken Brown, Howard Clark, and José Rivero. In the final tally, Europe stunned the United States with a 15–13 victory, the first time the United States had ever lost the Ryder Cup when the matches were played in America.

"Some of our younger players appeared to enter the matches saying, 'We're better than you and we don't have to work as hard,'" Irwin theorized. "That clearly manifested itself in losses. I think it became two things: overconfidence and underrespect by our players, and the other teams got better players."

Two of those "better players" were Spaniards Ballesteros and Olazábal, who teamed up for the first time at Muirfield Village to win three points as partners. In 1989 they paired up again to win 3½ points, which was the same point total they accumulated in 1991. By the time they picked up two more points in the 1993 matches, Ballesteros and Olazábal were Europe's most dominant twosome, a dynamic duo with more cumulative points than any single pairing in history. Suddenly, thanks to the Spaniards and the consistently stellar play from Germany's Langer and England's Nick Faldo, the United States was no longer the pretournament favorite, which earned the Americans criticism, not only from their fans but also from their peers.

"The country club atmosphere over here, where our guys are taken care of, doesn't translate well to the trenches of a Ryder Cup format," Irwin said. "Call it depth of character or whatever you want, but they had it and our guys didn't." Irwin was profoundly qualified to offer such opinions, having won three U.S. Opens and 20 PGA Tour events before adjourning to the Senior PGA Tour, where he won 26 times in five seasons. He had also played on five Ryder Cup teams, competing in both the Great Britain–Northern Ireland biannual route days, and in the highly competitive European years. It was Irwin who picked up the critical half-point in the final singles match to give the United States a 14½ to 13½ victory on Kiawah Island in 1991, a Ryder Cup that became known as the "War by the Shore"; and it was Irwin who was never far from the top of anyone's list for a captain's pick or, perhaps, to serve as captain. He understood, maybe better than anyone else, the differences between a Ryder Cup and a regular week on tour.

"It doesn't come from great golf," Irwin said. "We've seen that. It comes from great courage and great character, and that's where our guys have missed out throughout the years. Our players go week to week either hopping on their own airplanes or traveling alone, eating alone, and staying alone, while over there [Europe] you still drive to some events and maybe room with someone else. Those guys might rent a car together or hop on a train to get from one event to the next. All the Swedish guys travel together, and you have those groups that literally live together throughout the year. They are more at ease with one another, so when they come together as a team it's no big deal. Everything outside the game is different for the Europeans. The golf skills are pretty much the same, but it's how those outside things affect you inside that determines whether or not you are good at team competition.

"When you look at any of our players who make these teams, their personalities as competitors inevitably change a little bit. Rather than seeing the guy next to you as someone you are competing against every week, these are now men you are playing with. Tweak that as you may, it still changes the way in which you look at someone. In Ryder Cup play, you get to know the player, but you also get to know the individual because of the environment. You're sharing every meal with him, you get to interface with the wife in a way that you never would in the normal course of a tour event. You're thrown together with people you might not ordinarily choose to be with, and during the week you learn that, hey, these are nice people. You get to know them differently. You become a team."

In other sports that "jelling" occurred during spring training or summer camp, but because golf was uniquely individual, the Ryder Cup Matches (and in recent years the Presidents Cup played in even years when the Ryder Cup isn't contested) were the only times players abandoned their individuality to play together as a unit. For 51 weeks they were individuals, millionaire entrepreneurs playing a solitary sport. The 52nd week they were partners, teammates, playing for pride and country and praying they wouldn't be the ones to let the team down. Irwin understood that dichotomy, and he understood what it took to overcome it. That understanding, coupled with his ability to hit laser-beam iron shots, was why, at age 52, Hale Irwin found himself in serious contention to be one of Captain Tom Kite's two picks for the 1997 Ryder Cup team.

Tom Kite looked like a patrician: his fair skin scrubbed and slightly pink from a week in the New York sun, and his large-framed glasses perched precariously on his nose. "Athlete" was not the first word that came to mind when people saw Kite, and in that respect he was somewhat lucky. He could go about his off-course business in relative anonymity, eating out with an open notebook by his side, drawing no more attention to himself than if he had been an economist struggling to calculate the latest interest rate models, but the models Kite was examining were far more important than that. This was after all the Ryder Cup, and every player had a win-loss record and a mountain of stats that needed examining. Kite was an analyst, a right-brain, logic-driven, calculating thinker who knew all the permutations and statistics that should have helped him decide which two players to choose as captain's picks. There was no more important decision than the one Kite was about to make. As he had said about the Cup, "Thirty years ago, you invited the British over, beat up on them, had a couple of cocktail parties, and sent them home. That's not true anymore." Now he was less than 14 hours from announcing the final two members of his 1997 team, and as he studied the numbers, Kite felt the pressure of the closing moments. He knew how long the players hit their tee shots, how often they hit the fairway, how many greens they missed, and how many putts they made. All the scores were charted to show trends, and performance in the majors was taken into account. But in the end, nothing on paper would help Kite with his decision. When it came right down to it, he had to go with his gut, something that was easier said than done. Even his gut was sending mixed signals.

One thing was certain: if Davis Love somehow fell out of the top ten in Ryder Cup points during the PGA Championship at Winged Foot, he would be one of Kite's picks. No question. Love was in. He had made the key putt to win the 1993 Ryder Cup at the Belfry, and he had ground out three hard-earned points in five matches for Lanny Wadkins in

1995. Love had been on a winning team and a losing team and he was a leader and competitor, the kind of man Kite wouldn't mind his own sons looking up to. Love had character and the "it" Hale Irwin said was necessary to win the Ryder Cup. He also knew what to expect from a European crowd, and even though no one had ever played a Ryder Cup match in Spain (1997 was the first year the matches ventured onto the Continent), Kite felt comfortable with Love's ability to handle anything thrown his way.

By the weekend of the 1997 PGA Championship Kite's choices became tougher. Unless he fell down and hurt himself, Love was going to at least finish in the top 10 even if he didn't win, so he was on the team. That opened Kite's options and made his decision more difficult. He could go with experience, leadership, age, and good iron play. That meant Irwin. But picking a player from the Senior tour would be the most controversial thing Kite had done in the almost two years since he had taken the job of captain. Still, experience was something he needed. There were four Ryder Cup rookies on his team. Fortunately, one of them was named Tiger, and the other three were named Justin Leonard, Jim Furyk, and Scott Hoch, who, at 41, would be the oldest man on the team. Experience was important, but as Paul Azinger had said, "How much experience does a Tiger Woods, a Justin Leonard, or a Jim Furyk need? These guys don't need babysitters."

The one thing Kite didn't need was more advice. "To me, all the talk about experience is absurd," David Duval, who was number 15 on the Ryder Cup points list, offered. "It's like trying to get a job. They won't hire you without experience, but how do you get experience if they won't hire you?" Kite paid attention to Duval, not so much for his analogies on job experience as for his ability to make a lot of birdies. His 4–0 performance in the 1996 Presidents Cup hadn't gone unnoticed, and Kite was looking for someone who had proved himself in match play. But Duval hadn't won on tour, even though he had played himself into contention many times, and while Kite knew the youngster was right about the experience stuff being overblown, he also knew that having a win or two under your belt was a big factor. Kite had the statistics to prove it. Since 1979, Ryder Cup rookies had 59 wins, 63 losses, and 8 ties, and in 1995, even though the United States had lost, the rookies were 11–6. But all those rookies had been tour winners. The stats showed that a player who made the Ryder Cup team with no wins was twice as likely to post a losing record as someone who had won on tour. Still, with all the statistics pointing against him, Duval had promise.

"I think you need somebody who has been there," Payne Stewart offered. Stewart had been there four times, accumulating an 8–7–1 record, obviously the kind of experience he thought Kite needed. "You know what a Ryder Cup is like? It's chaos. No matter how good a young guy is you can't imagine how wild it is. They've never had people pulling against them before, people everywhere, people hanging in the trees."

Stewart's point was well made, but even if Kite chose to go with experience it wouldn't be from Stewart. There were plenty of players with Ryder Cup experience who were higher on the points list and who were playing better than Payne Stewart at the time. Fred Couples was one of those. Lee Janzen was another. As Janzen walked off the 18th green at Winged Foot after shooting 67 to take the second round in the PGA Championship, Kite said to him, "Hey, you know any Spanish?" He wasn't a lock, but the way he was playing Janzen stood a good chance. Jeff Maggert was perched precariously in the 11th spot on the points list and was in a six-way tie for fifth going into the weekend at Winged Foot. A good weekend put Maggert over the top. A poor showing dropped him off the chart, but a mediocre showing might leave him in 11th spot, which would put Kite in another awkward position. Should he choose Maggert? Love thought so, pulling Kite aside and saying, "Go with Maggs and Freddie . . . unless I screw up, then pick me."

Kite was restless, sleeping in intermittent spurts throughout the week. He would wake up at all hours and sit upright in his bed at the Rye Town Hilton with a new angle, a new variable, or a new idea in mind. "I'm sure I woke my wife [Christie] up every night yelling the names of guys in my sleep," he said. In addition to all the headaches and confusion that went with making his captain's picks, Kite had a golf tournament to play. He was one shot off the lead in the PGA Championship after the second round and was tied for third with Janzen going into Sunday's final. "I was making my selections on Monday, and I was also trying to win the golf tournament. I had a good chance, and at the same time I was playing with and watching my team. It was definitely a challenge to have the mental discipline to separate the two."

Kite kept saying he was "waiting for somebody to show me something, not with words, but with shots," and during Sunday's final round

Janzen did just that. Paired with Kite, Janzen shot a solid final round of 69, birdieing the last hole to finish alone in fourth—one better than Kite, who jokingly told Janzen, "You made the team until you cost me money with that last putt." Maggert played himself onto the team with a 65 on Sunday, the lowest score of the day, while Love won the championship (his first major) by five shots.

That Sunday night Tom and Christie Kite nestled into a corner booth at the hotel restaurant along with Tom's assistant captain, Dennis Satyshur, a long-time friend of the Kites and the head golf professional at Caves Valley in Maryland. In his notebook filled with statistics and lists, assets and liabilities, scribbled names and scratches, Kite had a printout of the Ryder Cup points standings with all the names listed from 11 through 20, including himself. He quickly narrowed the field to four players: Irwin, Duval, Couples, and Janzen.

Couples was his first choice, and an obvious one. He was the 10th-ranked player in the world, and he had four Ryder Cups under his belt even though he wouldn't turn 38 until four weeks after the Valderrama matches. The only question marks were his health (Couples consistently fought back problems) and the distractions in his personal life. Couples's father, Tom, was losing a battle with leukemia, and as if that weren't enough to distract the laconic former Masters champion, his girlfriend, Thais Bren, had also been diagnosed with cancer. Most people would have had trouble remembering their own names under those circumstances, but Couples, while distracted, seemed to use golf as an escape. He played better when his personal life was in turmoil. Kite had seen this before when Couples's divorce had been splashed across the front of the tabloids.

Fred's first wife, Deborah, had been a tennis pro until her inability to keep her opinions to herself alienated too many club members, which led to a career change. She met Fred when he wasn't making the soundest decisions in his life (like neglecting to call his parents, his coach, or his roommates when he dropped out of college and turned pro on a whim), and the two were soon married. Almost immediately, Deborah Couples became her husband's most vocal and often most obnoxious fan, shouting obscenities when his ball took bad bounces and squealing with unbridled delight when his putts found the hole. But as Couples's career took off, Deborah's penchant for spending money and frittering away her days in the company of the super-rich became evident. She was a deb circuit wannabe who never understood why the powder blue sundresses and white cowboy hats didn't quite cut it with the Palm Beach polo crowd, and when her frustrations finally ended in a divorce, the tabloids covered the proceedings with a fervor normally reserved for people named Pulitzer or Kennedy. Through it all, Fred played well. While the *New York Times* was reporting on Deborah's petition for $160,000 a month in alimony to support her polo pony habit, Couples was finishing third at Riviera. When the proceedings dragged on several months longer than expected and Couples had to ask several tour friends to be deposed on his behalf, he won the Buick Open. After the episodes with Deborah were finally and mercifully over (although she resurfaced later when she advertised a "Yard Sale" in the *Palm Beach Post* featuring "Fred Couples Ryder Cup Memorabilia"), Fred's game slumped until his next personal relationship, with a lady named Tawnya Dodd, became shaky. Then Couples played well again. The more turmoil he went through in his personal life, the more his golf game seemed to thrive. When things were going fine at home, his game suffered. Couples hadn't had a great PGA Championship at Winged Foot (a tie for 29th), but he made it a point to approach Kite and say, "With all that's been going on, it was easy for me to say I was ready for the PGA, but I really wasn't." He vowed to practice every day and go to Valderrama early if chosen, telling Kite, "I'll be ready. You can count on that." The captain didn't need to hear anything else. Fred Couples was in.

The next pick was tougher. Duval's game had shown signs of brilliance, but with no wins and no Ryder Cup experience it was hard to justify him over veterans like Irwin and Janzen. Duval (age 25) more closely approximated the ages of the other Ryder Cup rookies Kite would be carrying to Spain, but that wasn't necessarily a good thing. A few gray hairs in the locker room could be important if things got tight. Plus Duval was a mercurial sort, "different," as some of his fellow pros called him. He wore a goatee and chinos and in wraparound sunglasses he looked more like a roadie for the Dave Matthews Band (one of his favorite musical groups) than a professional golfer. On the golf course Duval couldn't seem to keep the tail of his shirts tucked in, nor did he appear to care. Unlike most of his fellow tour players, he didn't particularly like watching *SportsCenter,* but he did read 31 books in his rookie year, including *Zen and the Art of Motorcycle Maintenance* and Tom Robbins's *Jitterbug Perfume.*

A little rebellious bohemianism could be a good thing, and Duval definitely fit the bill as the Gen X poster boy of golf, but there was something else about him—an edge and an element of arrogance that made those around him uncomfortable. While younger players like Justin Leonard and Phil Mickelson would do everything in their power to beat you on the golf course, once the final putt fell they were the most congenial and accommodating people you could imagine, perfect ambassadors. While he was polite, Duval was dismissive of those he didn't care to engage and blunt with those he did. According to his best friend, Kevin Cook, "He doesn't care about being liked." That attitude had alienated Duval from his college teammates at Georgia Tech and most of his peers on the Nike tour (where he spent his first two professional seasons), and it caused him to draw the ire of many journalists once he made it onto the PGA Tour. Reporters were frustrated by the fact that Duval's favorite answers seemed to be "no" and "I don't know," even though by all accounts he was an extremely bright young man. He collected fine wines, but Duval's only visible contribution to golf's social graces appeared to be his ability to drink a diet Coke with a pinch of snuff between his lip and gum, a skill that would no doubt be lost on the game's European pundits.

None of those factors were as important to Kite as Duval's record. He hadn't done anything inspiring on the golf course since finishing second in May at the BellSouth Classic in Atlanta. Had Duval posted a top five at the PGA Championship, his chances would have certainly improved, but a 71–73 weekend dropped him into a tie for 13th and he had fallen behind Kite on the yearly money list. Without a great deal of debate from the other members of his dinner party, Kite scratched Duval's name from his list.

That left Irwin and Janzen. Either one would make news. At 52, Irwin would be the oldest pick since the rules were changed in 1989 allowing the captain two wild card choices, and Janzen, at age 32, would be the youngest. Either way, a benchmark would be established. Irwin had surprised a lot of people by tying Couples, Mickelson, Tiger, Azinger, Lee Westwood, and Payne Stewart at Winged Foot, but where the tie for 29th was considered a disappointment for Couples, Tiger, and Mickelson, Irwin's finish was looked upon as good "for a man his age," a phrase that sent Irwin into an apoplectic fit. He was a good Ryder Cup choice, but a risky choice, especially since he hadn't played a regular PGA Tour schedule. Irwin was the best on the senior tour by a mile, but they played only 54 holes a week out there, and that was riding in carts! If Kite chose Irwin and he played great, it would be seen as the most brilliant move in Ryder Cup history. But if Irwin had a losing record, or even lost a critical point or two, both Kite and Irwin would be roasted. It would make Lanny Wadkins's controversial decision to select Curtis Strange look conservative, and Kite was in no mood to take any unnecessary risks.

Janzen, on the other hand, had shown him a lot on Sunday. Both men knew the round was an audition, and Janzen had performed beautifully. If there was any greater pressure than the Ryder Cup it was trying to qualify for the Ryder Cup, especially with the captain walking beside you inside the ropes, and Janzen had proved himself with Kite watching every shot. He also hadn't lost any brownie points when he said, "Tom, you should pick yourself," as they walked off the final green. There had been talk of Kite, who was 23rd on the money list after his fifth-place finish at Winged Foot, choosing himself, a concept that drew a fair amount of criticism even though Kite was clearly playing well. "You can't do both," Tom Watson had said. In his heart Kite knew Watson was probably right, but it was a heady thought for a while. In the final analysis, though, Kite knew that choosing himself would not only distract from his duties as captain but also create unnecessary controversy—in addition to being, as one well-dressed Manhattaner in the Winged Foot gallery put it, "just tacky." After talking over his options with Christie and Satyshur, Kite put a check mark by Janzen's name, and by the time the server brought coffee to their table, the 1997 U.S. Ryder Cup team was set.

Kite called Couples first, and, after the proper thanks had been tendered, Couples said, "You know all this talk about distractions? Something like this sort of helps. I get on the golf course and forget all about them." But Kite already knew that.

Then he called Janzen, who was like a kid waiting up for Santa Claus. "Lee?" Kite said.

"Yeah."

"It's Tom. You're in."

"I'm in?"

"You're in."

"I'm in!" Janzen dropped the phone and cheered like a football fan at the Super Bowl. "I'm in! I'm in!"

The excitement didn't wane on Monday when Kite officially announced his choices. Tom Lehman could hardly contain his glee. "This team looks like the future of golf," he said, coming just a breath shy of calling them the 12 best golfers in the world, a line Ben Hogan had used to introduce his 1967 team.

Love chimed in as well, saying, "Look at this team!" as if he were opening a present and seeing its contents for the first time. "I mean, you put Woods and Mickelson on a team and I'd feel like I'm two down when I walk to the first tee."

Kite appreciated the enthusiasm, but he sounded an early note of caution when he said, "It does look awesome, but you know how it will be."

No one really knew how it would be because the Ryder Cup Matches had never been outside the United States or Britain before. Now, the Ryder Cup was being contested in Spain, and even the Europeans weren't quite sure what to expect. Choosing Spain had been a big "thank you" from the Ryder Cup committee to Seve Ballesteros, who was almost universally recognized as the man who had done more for European golf than anyone else since Harry Vardon. "He gave us everything we've got," Mark Wilson, a PGA European Tour official said of Seve. "There is no exaggerating what Seve did for the Ryder Cup. The man is magic. Absolute magic!" And in recognition of that magic and all it meant to the European tour, the 1997 Ryder Cup would be held in Spain, even though more than a few European traditionalists considered the move a mistake. The golf courses in the region were more than adequate, and the weather would be much better in Spain than on the coast of the Irish Sea, but trepidation was still palpable.

The venue wasn't the concern. Spain was fine. It was the Spanish that worried many in Europe's golf community. "The Spanish couldn't run a raffle," said Tony Jacklin, a veteran player in seven Ryder Cups and a captain in four more. As sharp as that comment seemed, it was the unspoken but prevailing opinion throughout much of Europe. Everyone who followed European golf held his breath and waited for the first of what they anticipated would be a series of Spanish snafus.

They weren't disappointed. Not long after the committee indicated its leanings toward Valderrama as the site for the 1997 Ryder Cup, Seve strolled into the press center at the Montecastello Golf Club in Jerez after shooting a 66 in the Spanish Open. He was expected to drone on about his good play, perhaps throwing in a few comments on the golf course (a Nicklaus design) and a plug or two for his own course, Novo Sancti Petri in Cadiz. Instead his face tightened in a feigned attempt to look distraught. Then Ballesteros calmly accused the Ryder Cup Committee of corruption, calling the Spanish Golf Federation "a cancer" and claiming that Valderrama owner Jaime Ortiz-Patino had offered a million-dollar bribe to Ballesteros if he would back Valderrama's bid to host the Ryder Cup. With a sad and worried frown that was belied by a slightly sinister twinkle in his eyes, Ballesteros said, "I don't like to be bought. I have my principles." He went on to question why, after a technical commission had advised the Ryder Cup Committee that Valderrama didn't have the necessary infrastructure to host the world's largest international golf event, former captain Bernard Gallacher informed Ortiz-Patino that Valderrama was still high on the list. "One has to ask if those gentlemen on the Ryder Cup committee have received similar offers to the one I received," he said.

David Hurish, a member of the Ryder Cup Committee, responded to the accusations by saying, "If Seve said that to my face I'd punch him on the nose. I can't believe it! If he's suggesting that members of the committee have been offered inducements I'd take it all the way to the courts. It would be like winning the pools."

Ballesteros didn't stop with the Ryder Cup Committee. He also blasted the Spanish Golf Federation, saying, "The Federation has always been a cancer. Their job has been to maintain the social circle. It seems incredible to me that these people who have done nothing for golf are arm-wrestling with me when it is I who have brought the Ryder Cup here. When we got the Cup in Spain nobody called me, nobody congratulated me, and nobody asked me for my opinion. It is quite possible that if I hadn't played in the 1983 match, the Ryder Cup would not be what it is now. It is possible that the event would have disappeared altogether. It is bad that I have to say so, but I have to because no one else does."

It was classic Seve. When he hadn't been showered with enough praise to satisfy his eggshell ego, he lashed out, claiming it was he, not

Nicklaus or Watson or Sandy Lyle or Nick Faldo, but Seve, who single-handedly rescued a half-century-old event no one else realized needed rescuing. Forget that it was Nicklaus, not Ballesteros, who spearheaded the effort to include all Europeans in the matches. Dismiss the fact that it was Watson who restored decorum to the matches after the contentious "War by the Shore" in South Carolina. In Seve's mind, none of it mattered. He, not them, had elevated the level of play, bringing competitiveness back to the Ryder Cup and therefore, in his mind, rescuing the event from certain extinction. Seve deserved praise, and he deserved to be listened to, and if you didn't oblige him, you were an enemy. "I have become stronger mentally," Seve said. "And have confirmed what I already knew, that I have a few friends, many acquaintances, and very many enemies . . . many more than I thought I had."

"He has a personality that is highly confrontational," Curtis Strange said of Ballesteros. "The public may not see it very often, but the players do. It seems like everything he's done in this game, as well liked as he is, he's been unhappy. I could never understand that. He's a very unhappy man. He's got to realize the whole world isn't out to get Seve Ballesteros. He had his chance to be loved in America and he blew it."

During the early and mid-1980s Ballesteros was arguably the best player in the world, and certainly the most influential. He traveled five continents, winning tournaments and building his legend with a swash-buckling style, imaginative game, and charismatic personality. It didn't hurt that he was Spain's most handsome export, complete with a fan club and groupies, not bad for a kid who grew up in a modest home in the small fishing village of Padrena between the Bay of Biscay and the Cantabrian Mountains. Even after he married one of the wealthiest women in Spain, Ballesteros continued to be a worldwide heartthrob. "When I was twenty-one I had just gotten out of the Rhodesian Air Force," Nick Price, who was two months older than Ballesteros, remembered. "Seve was already winning major championships. Just as everybody who's now twenty-one wants to be Tiger Woods, we were twenty-one and comparing ourselves to Seve. And he was light-years ahead of us."

While the 21-year-old Seve was winning majors, he was also developing a reputation as a manic competitor who alienated his peers and did whatever it took to win, including gamesmanship and an often liberal interpretation of the rules. Former PGA Tour pro Tommy Valentine once recalled that "Seve would hit tee shots all over the place, but when he got in the rough there suddenly became all these loose impediments around his ball. By the time he finished putting his hands around [the ball] you could have hit a three-wood from the lie he had. When you'd say something to him he'd pull that *'No habla Ingles'* line. He was unbelievable."

Seve's expansive interpretation of the rules led to a heated confrontation with Paul Azinger in the 1989 Ryder Cup, when Azinger took issue with Seve's desire to take a ball out of play. Seve responded with a little gamesmanship of his own, questioning a drop Azinger took from a hazard on the 18th hole, even though Seve had actually suggested the spot to Azinger and referee Andy McFee. That incident spilled over even further when Azinger accused the Spaniard of conveniently coughing during his opponents' shots, warning players on the 1991 team at Kiawah and the 1993 team at the Belfry not to "let him get away with it."

Mac O'Grady, Seve's one-time instructor and good friend, claimed that at the 1994 U.S. Open, Ballesteros flew into a tirade when O'Grady tossed two bottles of water to Payne Stewart and his caddie. "He was incensed," O'Grady said. "He was like some crazed general in the middle of a great holy war. He said I was helping the enemy. He yelled at me on the course and he yelled at me after we got in the courtesy car. This is a megalomaniac who suffers from major insecurities."

Even with his reputation well known throughout the golf world, people were still shocked by Seve's bribery accusations. Everyone knew he wanted the course he designed, Novo Sancti Petri, to be the Ryder Cup venue in 1997, but no one thought he would go *this* far. Valderrama owner Jamie Ortiz-Patino, a slight man in his 60s with a tremor in his hands, was one of the wealthiest men in Europe, having sold the family's Bolivian tin-mining interests to the government for a figure rumored in the high–nine figures. In addition to being a financial heavy-hitter who regularly opened his checkbook to the PGA European Tour, Patino was a wonderfully charismatic figure, a Pablo Picasso look-alike who called President George Bush and King Juan Carlos II good friends. To accuse a man like Patino of bribery was beyond scandalous, even by Seve's standards.

Patino responded by confirming he had, indeed, offered Seve a percentage of Valderrama greens fees that would equal approximately a million dollars, ostensibly for the redesign work Seve had done on the course's par-five 17th. Once an unreachable dogleg right par-five with a meandering creek down the left side of a crowned fairway, Ballesteros had shortened the hole to 511 yards, and, in an attempt to make it look like the par-five 13th at Augusta National, designed a sloping green with large flash bunkers behind and a newly created pond in front. While reachable in two, the new 17th was a marked departure from the rest of the course, which meandered through a cork-oak forest, and the green was, by all measures, a joke. Perfectly hit shots would roll into the water, and downhill putts to front pin placements had a better chance of trickling into the pond than going in the hole. Ballesteros called his new hole "spectacular," but almost none of his peers on the European tour agreed. Still, Patino, who in addition to owning the course was also the de facto superintendent, seemed pleased with the changes—pleased enough, in fact, to offer Ballesteros a generous compensation package for all his help. Like all savvy businessmen in the region, "Jimmy" Patino, as his American friends called him, put a small caveat in his offer to Seve. He was prepared to compensate Ballesteros for his design services and "for your agreement to support our candidacy for the Ryder Cup and in particular if you are prepared to publicly communicate your support to the press." As much as that looked like a bribe, Patino insisted that, "knowing politics in Spain, it could become very nasty, which it did in the end. I felt I could avoid all this nonsense. I knew we had the best course and if we had Seve on my side, there would be no opposition. There's nothing wrong with making someone a business proposal."

The bribery scandal died down soon enough. Then, just as it appeared the first Spanish Ryder Cup would commence without further incident, Ballesteros did it again, this time manipulating the process to get an extra captain's pick and pitching a fellow countryman aside in the process. It was a sorry scene all around, and, for many, the first time their Ryder Cup hero, Seve Ballesteros, had shown his dark side to the public.

The groundwork for the incident started in early 1995, when José María Olazábal started experiencing problems with his foot. He had difficulty walking. The pain was excruciating—not the kind of discomfort caused by a corn or an ingrown toenail, but the kind that left Olazábal bedridden. For 18 months he struggled with his foot, at times in so much pain he could only lie in bed at his parents' home in Fuenterrabía, crawling to the bathroom and watching golf on television. The entire ordeal was devastating. He did everything he could, saw everyone he knew to see, but nothing seemed to work. Olazábal's problem had been misdiagnosed as arthritis. Finally, in October of 1996, German doctor Hans-Wilhelm Muller-Wohlfarhrt told Olazábal his problems stemmed from a pinched nerve in his lower back. Corrective measures were taken and Olazábal clawed his way back into the competitive mainstream with the same fervor Ben Hogan had shown after a near-fatal car crash in 1949. By the time the 1997 Ryder Cup qualifying came to an end, Olazábal was back on tour with a win under his belt and an 11th-place spot in the European standings. He was a perfect pick for Seve's team. But that presented a problem: Ballesteros wanted to save his two captain's picks for Nick Faldo (the all-time leading point winner in Ryder Cup history) and Sweden's Jesper Parnevik (a full-time member of the U.S. tour who hadn't played in enough European tour events to qualify for the team on points).

Enter Miguel Angel Martin, a journeyman 35-year-old Spaniard with only two career wins in Europe who had played himself into the 10th spot and earned the final automatic berth on the Ryder Cup team. Martin, also a Spaniard, had played the best golf of his life. Other than Colin Montgomerie, he was the only European player to retain a spot in the top 10 for the entire 12 months of qualifying. Then, on July 10th in Glasgow, Scotland, as he was trying to protect his position in the standings, Martin injured his wrist at the Loch Lomond Invitational when he tried to thrash a shot out of the high rough. There was concern from Martin, not about his health but about the prospect of missing the British Open at Royal Troon and jeopardizing his spot on the team. Against the advice of doctors, Martin took a cortisone shot at a Scottish hospital and played in the Open Championship. As a result he aggravated the injury and was forced to undergo surgery on August 5.

Ballesteros had his chance. All it would take was a wink, a couple of nods, and a little rule bending—nothing unusual for Seve. Four weeks after Martin's surgery Ballesteros held a news conference to announce that he was booting Martin from the team due to injury. The next player in the points standing would replace him. That player just happened to be José María Olazábal. Voila! A bend here, a boot there, and Seve got his three picks and his old buddy on the 1997 team. All he had to do was destroy the lifelong dream of a fellow Spaniard, a man who had taken a needle in the wrist to play in the Ryder Cup.

They didn't even give Martin a chance. In a letter to European PGA Tour commissioner Ken Schofield, Martin wrote, "I will only play in the Ryder Cup if I am in the best physical and psychological condition. Have no doubt that if I am not fit for the demands of the Ryder Cup week I will withdraw. There is no need for the committee to take any action at this time. All that I want is the best for the captain and the team."

Martin's commitment to do the right thing was ignored because doing the right thing had nothing to do with this. The decision wasn't about Martin. It was about fielding the team Seve wanted, the team he felt had the best chance against the Americans, and the team that would generate some excitement about European golf. If Martin and the general principles of fair play and sportsmanship had to be sacrificed for that purpose, so be it. Seve was already taking four rookies (Ignacio Garrido, Darren Clarke, Lee Westwood, and Thomas Björn). Parnevik would be the fifth first-timer. The last thing Seve wanted or needed was Martin, another Ryder Cup rookie. The fact that he qualified was irrelevant. Olazábal was the better man for the job.

The cries of foul were loud and angry. Garrido, another Spaniard, risked his relationship with Captain Ballesteros by standing up for Martin, and for what was right. "Seve has tried to have four or five picks all year long," Garrido said. "We must respect the ranking system, but that is not what we are doing. This is the most unfair decision in golf." To which Seve responded, "Ignacio is Martin's best friend, and I think he is a little too young [Garrido was 25] to be making such a strong statement." But Seve had no response when his own brother, Manuel Ballesteros, the president of the Spanish PGA, wrote a letter to Schofield condemning the action and calling for Martin's reinstatement. Tommy Tolles, an American player who failed to qualify for the U.S. team and was not on Kite's short list of candidates, said, "Martin has a right to play. He's earned it. I hold Seve responsible. He was caught with three players and only two picks and he looked for an excuse. When Martin hurt his wrist, he found it." And Carl Suneson of Spain chimed in by saying, "A major wrong has been done here."

Martin hired lawyers and attempted to file an injunction against the Ryder Cup committee and the European PGA Tour, which prompted

Seve to call Martin "a little man." Seve, the Dark Prince, revealed himself at the press conference where the Martin scandal was made public, ranting and spewing the kind of venom that had always been a part of his personality, but that had remained hidden from public view. "I thought Miguel was more intelligent than this," Seve said. "He must have a square head. He has had very bad advice, and he is making things worse and worse. You think Martin can stop the Ryder Cup? You are crazy! Lawyers can only do so much. Martin is only thinking of himself. He is like a kamikaze pilot flying toward a ship. You think he wasn't welcome before, what about now?"

Schofield sat in uncomfortable silence as Seve continued his diatribe. When he finally spoke, while avoiding eye contact with the reporters who were peppering him with questions, Schofield confirmed his support of Seve's position. "We've been informed that it is very unlikely an injunction would be successful," Schofield said. "But the reality is that when lawyers are involved, different processes ensue."

Martin made it clear whom he blamed for this sorry debacle. "The captain is responsible for this," he said. "The other players are with me. The only people against me are the Ryder Cup committee and Seve Ballesteros. If Olazábal had been number seventeen [on the Ryder Cup points list] this would not have happened. This is an economic problem, not a personal one. It's not the same having Miguel Angel Martin playing Tiger Woods as having Nick Faldo play Tiger Woods. For publicity, Woods–Faldo is much more attractive. They are squeezing me to get better known players on the team."

The Martin affair typified the final reason the Ryder Cup had become a bad deal. As much as it was touted as a "sportsmanship" and "goodwill" competition, after 31 contests the matches had become a political tool for the organizing bodies that ran them (the PGA of America and the European PGA and European PGA Tour). Players who actually competed and fans who supported the Ryder Cup were secondary, and, in the case of Martin, expendable. By 1997 the event was a cash cow, and a biannual show where the European golf establishment and the PGA of America could engage in a breast-beating week of self-ingratiating pageantry. Martin was simply the most visible casualty of this systemic change. He didn't make for good television, and he didn't paint the European PGA Tour in its best light; therefore, a little rule bending to send him on his way was perfectly acceptable.

The Ryder Cup was also more important to the European organizers than it was to the U.S. players. The fact that both of Seve's picks (Faldo and Parnevik) lived in Florida and were full members of the U.S. PGA Tour wasn't lost on Schofield and the members of the European Ryder Cup committee. The U.S. tour was far more lucrative than its European counterpart. Plus U.S. players didn't change countries and currencies every week, nor did they have to deal with spotty weather and dodgy golf courses. Endorsement riches were far greater in the United States, and with Tiger-mania on the rise things were only getting better. Faldo had defected to America years before. Parnevik soon followed, and Schofield knew there were more European players shopping for real estate in Orlando. The European PGA Tour needed a dramatic show to reassert itself as an equal to the U.S. PGA Tour. As *Golf World* columnist John Huggan put it, "The likelihood is that in a couple of years the majority of the better European players will be more familiar to viewers on NBC than the BBC, so perhaps understandably, tour officials are in a bit of a panic."

There was one gem left in the European treasure chest—the Ryder Cup—and if Europe could successfully retain the cup at Valderrama, the European PGA could shirk the claims that it ran a secondary tour. To the organizers of the Ryder Cup, holding on to legitimacy was imperative. Right and wrong be damned! At Valderrama, winning was all that mattered.

*Five*

# A SPANISH RAFFLE

CADDIES WERE FLOWN COACH from New York to Malaga, which in the entire scheme of things wasn't a big deal. They normally traveled the cheapest way they could. Like their bosses, caddies were independent contractors, and most paid for their own travel expenses, which meant discount coach fares and sharing cars with three or four buddies during tournament weeks. Standard compensation normally included a base salary of around $700 a week and a percentage of their players' winnings beginning at 5 percent, jumping to 7 percent for a top-10 finish, and capping at 10 percent for a victory. Some players paid more, some less, but the range was pretty consistent, as were the agreements on travel. Caddies picked up their own expenses except when traveling overseas, then the boss picked up the tab. It was a perfectly acceptable arrangement for most caddies, and coach travel was the norm, even for the highest paid loopers. But the Ryder Cup was different. During normal weeks on tour, decisions on how to travel, where to stay, and what time to arrive at the golf course were made by the caddie and his boss. On Sunday afternoon in Phoenix a player might tell his caddie, "Be on the range at Pebble Beach at 7:30 Tuesday morning," and the caddie would say, "See you then." The PGA Tour didn't dictate when and how a caddie traveled to an event. They loved the lifestyle and the entrepreneurial aspects of what they did. That was why this particular travel decision rankled them. Everybody knew the PGA of America was making millions on the Ryder Cup—enough in fact to fly the players, their wives, and top PGA of America officials on a chartered Concorde. Even second- and third-tier PGA of America officers, staffers, and some volunteers were flown first class. Only the caddies were relegated to the back of the bus (or in this instance, the plane), and neither they nor their bosses had any say in the matter. It wasn't a big deal. Most caddies thought it was barely worth mentioning, but all were perplexed by it, and it became one more festering sore for those who actually participated in the Ryder Cup Matches caused by those who made all the decisions.

Most caddies would have paddled to Spain in a canoe to work the Ryder Cup, so no one would ever complain about the transportation arrangements. To have made it this far, a caddie had to have known his job and his place. The role of a caddie was to help his man shoot the lowest scores possible, period. They weren't supposed to sign autographs, appear in commercials, or give press conferences. Caddies were not the show, even though some, like Tiger's man, Mike "Fluff" Cowan, had gained celebrity status and had even been featured in a *People* magazine profile. That sort of thing made most caddies, including the ones who flew coach from New York to Madrid and Madrid to Malaga, uncomfortable. All they wanted to do was help the American team win back the Ryder Cup. But first they had to figure out how to get to the golf course.

After flying coach to Malaga a handful of caddies were supposed to be met at the airport by a PGA of America volunteer. Malaga International wasn't far from the ocean, and the morning sun was bright as the tourist city came to life. It was early, and the caddies figured they would have no trouble getting some work done before their players arrived. They already had their yardage books—hand-drawn pamphlets filled with scribbled numbers, arrows, and codes like ST-5-DAT, which means "standard five-iron, downwind a tad"—but the really good caddies, and none who worked for Ryder Cup players were bad, always got to the course early to confirm yardages and to get a feel for what they could expect during the week. After an hour in the airport, however, they started wondering if they would make it at all. Finally a woman from the PGA arrived, but when the caddies requested they be taken straight to the golf course, the woman told them that was impossible, not because of some rule prohibiting an early visit but because she had to make another airport run to pick up more PGA of America staffers, flying first class into Malaga, no doubt. The caddies were dropped off at their condos (which, at the time, had no electricity, no hot water, and more than a few ants) where they remained stuck the rest of the day. None of them bitched. It wasn't their place, and again it was not a huge deal. It was simply another minor illustration of the skewed priorities and questionable decision making that had become standard fare at the Ryder Cup.

"It's very easy to make decisions without taking responsibility for them," Larry Nelson, a two-time PGA Championship winner and veteran of three Ryder Cup teams, said. Few were more uniquely qualified to criticize the PGA of America than Nelson. Before he joined the PGA Tour, he was a club pro and PGA of America member in Marietta, Georgia, a man who drove a caged range picker and folded sweaters between lessons and practice sessions. He also was the man everyone assumed would be the 1997 Ryder Cup captain, primarily because of his club pro background, his PGA Championship wins in 1981 and 1987, and the fact that Nelson had a 3–1 head-to-head record against Seve Ballesteros in Ryder Cup play. To the shock of many observers, not only was Nelson never called about being captain but he never received a courtesy call from the PGA of America explaining their decision to go with Tom Kite.

"I've always thought the PGA of America hides behind its emblem," Nelson said. "It's funny that individuals within the PGA make decisions, but nobody seems to know who makes them. We know someone does, but nobody knows who it is. It is the most closed 'open' organization I've ever seen."

The "hiding behind the emblem" criticism was one that caused officers at the PGA of America to bristle. From 1968, when Jack Nicklaus and Arnold Palmer led the separatist movement that became the PGA Tour, to the present, the PGA of America had maintained a testy relationship with the players. While the PGA Tour ran the week-to-week events from the Sony Open to the Tour Championship, the PGA of America ran the PGA Championship and the Ryder Cup, and spent the rest of its time ostensibly perpetuating the interests of its club-pro membership and growing the "grass roots" of the game. Even though they shared the same acronym, the PGA of America and the PGA Tour couldn't have been more different. The tour ran golf tournaments, owned TPC clubs, gave gobs of money to charity in a very public forum, and had a visible presence on television every week. The PGA of America was made up of 30,000 club pros, and while the organization piggy-backed off the tour's exposure and recognition with such catchy slogans as "We make the game fun," when it came to the interests of the players and the general public's perception of professional golf, it was the PGA Tour, not the PGA of America, that took the lead. Even their offices spoke volumes. The PGA of America headquarters was in a beautiful white glass-front building at PGA National in Palm Beach Gardens. With a marble-floored atrium foyer, sweeping staircase, and layers upon layers of bureaucratic staffers shuffling through the political maze of the organization, the PGA of America could have easily been mistaken for the Department of Agriculture or the E.E.O.C. if those government agencies had moved their headquarters to south Florida. The PGA Tour offices, on the other hand, looked like a connected series of low-rise cedar bungalows discreetly hidden behind a canopy of oaks a quarter mile from the TPC at Sawgrass. The tour's corporate presence was discreet and understated. Unless commissioner Tim Finchem walked by, a visitor would never know he was standing in the command center for the richest professional golf tour in the world. Most of the time, the PGA and PGA Tour coexisted peacefully. But, starting at the Valderrama Ryder Cup, their interests appeared destined for a collision course.

"The PGA of America is a bit like a firing squad," Nelson continued. "Somebody in the line always has a gun that's not loaded and everybody assumes they have that gun. But you know that twelve guys are shooting real bullets. At the PGA, you know that when the meeting doors open and they come out having made a decision, somebody had to actually make the decision. It didn't just grow out of the meeting, but you can't put a name on who did it. Nobody is responsible."

The week before players, wives, caddies, and throngs of reporters were to fly to Spain, Earl Woods tried to find the person who had made what he considered a particularly bone-headed decision, but, as Nelson predicted, Earl had no luck. His question was simple: Earl wanted to know who decided that it was fine and dandy for Tiger to bring a wife or a girlfriend to Valderrama as part of the Ryder Cup entourage, but, since he had neither a wife nor a girlfriend, Tiger could not bring Earl instead. PGA of America policy (a decision with no name attached) was that wives and girlfriends could attend team functions and follow the matches from inside the gallery ropes. Parents of an unattached player, however, were not allowed to substitute. "It makes no sense and it's not justified," Earl said. "Tiger is twenty-one and does not have a girlfriend, but they don't think enough of the parents to invite them instead." He had a legitimate point and one that PGA of America officials probably would have responded to if Earl hadn't continued by saying, "I can unequivocally state that I'm more responsible for Tiger being where he is today, and have made a bigger contribution to the team, than all the wives and girlfriends combined." With that little addendum, Earl shifted the focus from what was a valid issue, the PGA's policy, to his own outrageousness. He went on to say he would "boycott" the Valderrama matches, asking rhetorically, "Why should I go all that way to be treated like dirt?" When news of Earl's boycott filtered through the golf community, Lee Trevino quipped, "I didn't realize he had qualified for the team."

None of the mechanics of the decision-making processes mattered to the "heavily favored" U.S. players who were all honored and privileged to be competing in such an honorable and privileged event. Even after arriving at the course and finding their locker facilities to be alarmingly small, with six small lockers stacked atop six even smaller ones next to a line of even more lockers set aside for PGA of America officials, the players never complained or made any suggestion that things were anything but perfect. Not a big deal. A petty annoyance. Nothing to fuss over. The fact that PGA officers, some of whom the players had never met, would be putting on deodorant and changing shirts next to them in the players' locker room during the biggest golf week of their lives was a minor inconvenience, barely worthy of mention, just like the caddies' travel arrangements and the lack of consideration to those players without wives. Even when the team was kept out late and put on display almost an hour longer than Tom Kite had been told they would at the Gala Dinner, the players never uttered a peep. This was the Ryder Cup, and everything about it was "neat," as Kite said. Forget that players were hustled between functions to the point of exhaustion. That was what the event was all about. As Jim Furyk put it, "We didn't get a feel for anything. We were there to play the Ryder Cup, and from the moment we arrived we had something to do for about fifteen hours of every day." It was a hectic power-packed schedule that cut into everything. "I never got eight hours of sleep at one time," Furyk said. "Not even close."

The only player who made any negative noises was 40-year-old Mark O'Meara, who was in his fourth Ryder Cup and who had seen enough over the years to know that it wasn't the be-all and end-all a lot of people made it out to be. Sure, the competition was tough and the golf was exciting, but as O'Meara put it, "All you can do is give it your all. If you don't come out on top, you're not a bad person. Unfortunately, players on both sides have been lambasted in the press for losing matches. I don't think that's fair. You win or lose as a team. I mean, players aren't getting paid, and a lot of people are paying a lot of money to watch." O'Meara went on to suggest that players should, in fact, be paid, and that as professionals it was their duty to be compensated. "This isn't about greed," he said. "It's just the right thing to do."

To purists there was no greater heresy than what O'Meara was suggesting. Payment to Ryder Cup participants would make the Ryder Cup no different from the silly-season matches where the only real competition was who could come up with the best on-course one-liner for the television mikes. For an American player of O'Meara's stature to suggest the injection of money into the Ryder Cup equation was an adulterous evil, a sentiment even his peers condemned. "I think it would destroy the integrity of the competition," Paul Azinger, one of the fiercest American defenders of the Ryder Cup, said of the notion of paying competitors. "Getting paid to play for your country doesn't sound all that right to me. Having played in three Ryder Cups, knowing the amount of pride and pressure you feel, there's no need for money to be doled out." Azinger also tried to discount O'Meara's comments by saying, "He's not the kind of guy who's motivated to get on the Ryder Cup team. He doesn't enjoy going to the dinners and all that. He would probably want to be on the team more if they didn't have the dinners."

Kite had even approached O'Meara about his ambivalence, pulling him aside and saying, "Look, I know you haven't been the biggest fan of the Ryder Cup." O'Meara assured Kite that once he got to Valderrama he would do "whatever it takes for our team to win." No one questioned that, nor did any of his teammates question his honesty and sincerity in voicing his opinions. O'Meara was a 40-year-old, slightly balding, slightly gray, slightly pudgy father of two who coached Little League baseball and took his kids fishing when he wasn't on the golf course. A pizza and a good night's sleep was his idea of a perfect night, and the hoopla of the Ryder Cup dinners, parties, ceremonies, and glad-handing pomp and circumstance was simply bad for his system. He also believed professionals should not give away their services unless it was for the charitable cause of their own choosing. Lawyers worked pro bono on *their* terms, usually when their clients were indigent and the causes were just. The same was true of doctors, accountants, and every other professional service group he could name. The PGA of America was neither indigent nor, in O'Meara's view, wholly noble. For him to stay up late, put on a tie, and glad-hand a bunch of executives from Volvo and Johnnie Walker so the PGA of America and its European counterpart could make a financial killing while wrapping themselves in the flag didn't make a lot of sense.

Not that O'Meara was antisocial: exactly the opposite was true. There wasn't a more congenial man in professional golf. O'Meara was a corporate sponsor's dream. He never let an interview go by without thanking all the right executives and dropping all the right names, wearing his logoed clothing at just the right angles for maximum television exposure. When the cameras were on he was ready with the perfect sound bite, earnest and genuine in his delivery and wearing just the right feel-good smile. He was the kind of person who, once he learned someone's name, would use it two or three times in every subsequent sentence, almost forcing his verbal syntax to ensure the name was repeated. During one post-round interview, O'Meara used *San Diego Union-Tribune* writer T. R. Reinman's name six times in a single answer, prompting *Golf World*'s John Strege to rib Reinman by saying, "So, T. R., does this mean we have to use your name in our quotes?" But that was Mark O'Meara. At banquets he was always perfectly dressed, with his suit pressed in all the right spots and his tie knotted just so. When he shook a stranger's hand he would clasp it in both of his, gently drawing his newfound friend closer as he expressed what a pleasure it was to meet you. O'Meara was a lot of things, but antisocial was not one of them.

He was a late starter as golfers go, having taken up the game at age 13 after his father, a furniture salesman from North Carolina, moved the family to Orange County, California, and into a house just above the Mission Viejo Country Club, a Robert Trent Jones, Sr., design dubbed "Mission Impossible" for its difficulty. The family didn't join the club right away, but Mark received playing and practice privileges in return for picking up all range balls in the late afternoons. Many evenings, as the young O'Meara would steer the bouncing picker around the range, squinting as the sun set in order to see the balls, he would dream of someday becoming the best golfer in the world. Soon he was the best junior golfer in Orange County, and later the best golfer at Long Beach State, the California college where O'Meara studied marketing.

His real test came in 1979, when he made it to the finals of the U.S. Amateur. He was playing John Cook, an Ohio State player who was nine months younger than O'Meara, but who was also the defending

U.S. Amateur champion. Cook was heavily favored, and it was a surprise to many when O'Meara trounced him 8 and 7 in the finals. Two decades later, O'Meara and Cook were close friends and neighbors at Isleworth, but 19 seasons after their U.S. Amateur battle, O'Meara regularly recalled that U.S. Amateur win, especially when asked about being labeled "Best Player Never to Win a Major." "Hey, Bud, I've won a major," he would say. "I won the U.S. Amateur. If Jack Nicklaus can count the U.S. Amateur as a major, why can't Mark O'Meara?" Nicklaus did, indeed, count his two U.S. Amateurs among his 20 major championship titles, but when you own 20 majors like Nicklaus a little more leeway is afforded than when your only "major" is the U.S. Amateur, as was the case with O'Meara in 1997.

Still, being labeled one of the best players without a professional major title wasn't a bad thing. It certainly beat being the worst player to have lucked his way into a major. Even though he hadn't won one of golf's four biggies when he arrived at Valderrama, O'Meara had 14 tour victories, more than any other player on the Ryder Cup team. Two of those wins had come back-to-back earlier in 1997, at the AT&T Pebble Beach Pro-Am and the Buick Invitational at Torrey Pines. By all rights, O'Meara should have been the go-to guy, the gray-haired leader Captain Kite so desperately needed. Instead, O'Meara said things like, "Let me ask you a question. There's a champion's dinner after the matches. If you've lost, would you want to go to a victory dinner?" While the question was rhetorical, O'Meara's feelings were not. "I wish I could tell you exactly what I think of the Ryder Cup, but I won't. When my career is over, I can say I was on four Ryder Cup teams [although making the 1999 team pushed that number to five]. That's an honor, I guess."

Once on the ground in Spain, however, O'Meara put forth his most honored and privileged decorum, saying things like, "The spirit of our team is very high. This is my fourth time and of all the teams that I've played on I'd say that talent-wise this team is very, very strong, and very compatible. It's very close. Even though Scott Hoch and I might be the oldest players on the team, we've still been very much in touch with the younger players and I think we're all pretty good friends."

For Hoch, the oldest member of the team by two years, there was little that could have spoiled this first Ryder Cup experience, or so he thought when he arrived. It was all new and different, and so exciting! By his own admission Hoch's career hadn't panned out exactly as he had wanted. There had been missed opportunities in major championships and fewer wins than he thought he should have had by his 42nd birthday, but he was finally on a Ryder Cup team, and that made this a moment to remember.

The first thing Scott and Sally Hoch noticed was the town, or in the case of Sotogrande, the lack of a town. Valderrama's official address was the village of Sotogrande, but "village" turned out to be a purely academic term. Sotogrande was a large, rather modern real estate development with a harbor, several high-rise high-dollar condominiums, a small commercial area, some very nice homes, and two golf courses. It was a town only in the sense that mail was delivered there; much like the Woodlands in suburban Houston was technically a town, even though, as a practical matter, it was a golf course subdivision with a post office. The two golf courses in the village of Sotogrande, Club de Golf Sotogrande and Valderrama, were the best in the Andalusia region by a fair margin, and of those two, Valderrama was the most meticulously maintained. Jimmy Patino had spent well over $50 million seeing to that. But the Hochs had no basis of comparison for either the "village" or the golf course, since neither of them had ever been to Spain. Nor did they have any frame of reference for the Ryder Cup. And that made them a little nervous.

"I had talked to a lot of people and read every story I could find on the Ryder Cup," Hoch said. "In some of those stories people couldn't eat, couldn't sleep, it was the sickest they had ever felt, and I just couldn't imagine golf being that way. What I remember most from watching past Ryder Cups were some of the awful shots hit by some of our best players. I remember thinking to myself, 'Gosh, how can there be that much pressure?'"

Hoch was about to find out, and he was understandably nervous. He also knew some of his teammates were less than thrilled about being in Spain. "There are guys who make the team who don't really want to be on the team, but it would be political suicide in a golf sense not to play," Hoch said. Coach Kite didn't have to worry about Scott Hoch in that regard. "One time before I got out of this game I wanted to make it," he said. "I was right on the verge of qualifying several times before, but I was never chosen [as a captain's pick]."

His blunt honesty had never endeared him to many of his fellow professionals, and he knew that if he was ever going to play on a Ryder

Cup team, he would have to qualify. "Perhaps the most frustration I have ever experienced as a professional was at the [1989] PGA Championship at Kemper Lakes," Hoch said. "I had to finish fifth to make the team, which meant I had to make a thirty-footer on the last hole to qualify. I missed the putt, and ended up three-putting just because I was so deflated from having missed my best opportunity." After Scott missed the putt, Sally went to the parking lot where she crawled into the courtesy car and cried. Scott, visibly upset by the whole ordeal, punched a hole in his locker.

"I was so happy when I made it [in 1997]," Hoch said. "And I was happy with the fact that we were playing away. I like it when the crowd is pulling against you, because a lot of times over here when I'm in contention, most people are rooting for the other guys and not me, especially if it's a Tiger or a Duval or another name player in contention. I also really like match play, and I wanted to prove to the other captains who I thought should have chosen me in past years that I could, in fact, perform. Then there was the fact that Tom Kite was captain. He is one of the top three or four guys I admire in terms of the combination of family, golf, and how he treats people. I thought he was as good a captain as there could be."

Hoch wasn't put off by the whirlwind of dinners, ceremonies, and receptions; in fact he thought they were pretty impressive. President Clinton met the team in New York the night before they boarded the Concorde, and his remarks, while brief, meant a lot to the team, even though most professional golfers were staunch Republicans. "He was the president, and we respected that regardless of party," Hoch said. Once in Spain, the Hochs attended functions with George and Barbara Bush (a President and First Lady they could all relate to) as well as King Juan Carlos II, Jimmy Patino, Prince Andrew, and countless other dignitaries, intoxicating stuff for a down-to-earth couple from Raleigh, North Carolina. Neither Sally nor Scott felt the least bit put-upon, even though they knew these functions were a dog-and-pony show with pros from both sides being the dogs and the ponies. It was the Ryder Cup. And from all they had read and heard there was nothing else like it in the world.

Meanwhile Seve the crusader was preparing for battle. His first order of business was setting up the golf course to give his team the best possible advantage. Nature and the course's original architect took care of some of that. Valderrama was nestled on a rolling stretch of land between the Andalusia Mountains and the Mediterranean Sea, within site of Gibraltar and the Moroccan coast. The course had been carved out of a cork-oak forest, with many of the low-limbed arbors hanging out into the fairways and over the greens. During the course's construction, Robert Trent Jones, Sr., had battled to cut down more of the trees, particularly in landing areas and around the greens, but the original developer would have none of it. "I'll trade you a tree on the next hole" was Jones's standard line as he tried to negotiate another cutting, but more often than not, he lost the battle, the trees stayed, and as they grew and matured over the years, Valderrama became a much tighter golf course than anyone had ever imagined.

"The golf course is what it is," Kite said. "We have to accept it and play with it. It's certainly unique. It's a tight, very tricky golf course and it's one of those that will suit a certain type of player and not necessarily another one. It's easy to understand why some of the Europeans who have played it for a number of years think it's wonderful and other people don't like it very much."

The fourth hole, a par-five, was particularly goofy. The elevated green was guarded on the right by a man-made pond and stacked stone waterfall that looked like an amusement park ride. A deep bunker guarded the left side with an overhanging cork oak between the sand and the green. "You're basically hoping the ball goes through the tree on your bunker shot," O'Meara said. The fifth and ninth holes were much the same, with trees encroaching into the line of play, jutting out into the players' lines and generally causing havoc with well-played shots. The only hole where trees weren't a factor was Seve's redesigned 17th with its impossibly contoured 19-yard-deep green, shaved slope, and controversial pond. As if that hole weren't interesting enough, Seve had the greens staff at Valderrama grow a strip of rough across the fairway at the dogleg, making it impossible for the long-hitting Americans to use blast drivers around the corner. That was the captain's strategy throughout. Seve knew the Americans had the advantage of length with players like Tiger, Mickelson, and Love regularly reaching par-fives in two and hitting short irons into par-fours. To take away that advantage, Seve narrowed the already penal fairways, making it virtually impossible for the Americans to hit driver anywhere.

NBC commentator Johnny Miller, who was immensely popular with the fans but loathed by a number of players who thought his commentary crossed the line, said, "If I were to pick one golf course in the whole world that would be bad for Tiger Woods, this is it. It has the narrowest fairways I've ever seen and the smallest greens I've ever seen. There are trees overhanging the fairways. This is a precision golf course, a Ben Hogan golf course, not a Tiger Woods golf course."

"It's not really up to me to approve or disapprove of the golf course set-up," Kite said. "The determination of those in control of how the course will be set up has already been made."

Once the course was adequately set up to his advantage, Seve, growing more manic by the minute, attended to other details, most of which he closely guarded. "How will you greet your team, Seve?" "It's a secret, but I have everything ready." "What about the American team?" "I will only talk about my team." But he barely did that. This was Seve's war, and he would not discuss any of his plans. When he handed out the team uniforms, which included new dress shoes, he warned all his players to scuff the bottoms of the shoes before wearing them. The grand ballroom floor, where the Gala Dinner was being held, was wooden and would likely be slick—a detail only Seve would have considered. He was, as it turned out, right. During the dinner, Jimmy Patino's wife slipped on the slick floor and broke her wrist. While a number of the European players had chuckled at Seve's suggestion, after Mrs. Patino's accident they were all glad he'd made it.

Captain Ballesteros also rearranged the rules a bit to gain what he hoped would be an advantage. In all previous years, the morning matches (four in total) were foursomes or alternate shot. One player would tee off, and his partner would hit the next shot, and the players would alternate shots throughout the rest of the round. The afternoon matches (again a total of four) were four-balls, which most Americans referred to as "best ball." Every player would play his own ball and each team would take the best score on each hole. The same format applied on Saturday, with the final day, Sunday, featuring 12 singles matches. That was how the Ryder Cup had been contested for decades and it was how everyone assumed it would be contested again in 1997. But Seve had other ideas. He thought the Europeans had the edge in the four-ball format, so he changed the order. Rather than playing alternate shot on Friday and Saturday mornings, it would be four-ball, with foursomes coming in the afternoon. Tom Kite offered a half-hearted protest when he first heard about the change, but he quickly let it drop. This was just Seve being Seve. Everybody knew it, and everybody expected it.

Finally there was the lingering matter of Miguel Angel Martin. On Wednesday before the second full day of practice, Seve finally got that "little man" out of the way when Ken Schofield issued a statement on behalf of Martin and the Ryder Cup Committee. "The Ryder Cup Committee and Miguel Angel Martin are pleased to announce that they have met and discussed the publicized disagreement regarding Miguel's exclusion from playing in the 1997 Ryder Cup," Schofield said. "The issue centered on who should decide the right to play and at what time this decision should be made. Both parties believe that the members of the team must be fit and in good competitive condition, and both parties recognize that Miguel Angel earned the right, subject to fitness and competitiveness, to participate in the 1997 Ryder Cup as he finished tenth in the points table. However, Miguel Angel, despite making great progress with his recovery, would by now have unilaterally decided to withdraw from playing. Therefore, the Committee and Miguel Angel do not feel there is any remaining issue between them."

Martin was given the Ryder Cup uniforms and allowed to pose in the team picture (although Seve had the photographer take two shots—one with Martin and one without). Martin was then hustled into the media center for a brief press conference, where he said, "I'm not going to say much, because I don't think I have much to say. What's past is past." He then thanked all those who supported him, including Seve's brother, Manuel, the other European players, and the media whom, Martin said, "treated me very decently at such a difficult time." He closed by saying, "I have come to Valderrama because I was invited to come by the Committee, but I'm leaving today. I don't feel much like staying here for the Ryder Cup."

With that, the sorry affair of Miguel Angel Martin was put to rest, and Seve went back to his crusade.

At 5:00 A.M. on Friday, a little less than four hours before the first shot of the 32nd Ryder Cup Matches was to be struck, Sally Hoch sat straight up in her bed in the Club San Roque hotel, awakened by what she initially thought was artillery fire. "There was this series of huge booms," she said. "It sounded like we were under attack." In a sense they were, but not by an invading military. Valderrama and surrounding areas were under assault by a series of severe thunderstorms rolling in from the African coast. For three hours the rains fell, often in sheets so thick visibility was cut to 10 feet. Play was suspended, and for over an hour thousands of spectators who drove out the narrow, winding road to the golf course were forced to sit in their cars until the storms cleared and the golf course was properly drained. Back at the Club San Roque, players from both sides anxiously awaited word on when the matches would begin.

The official delay was one hour and 40 minutes. Then, at 10:42 local time, Davis Love, dressed in a bright red shirt, khaki slacks, and a blue sleeveless rain vest, struck the first shot of the Ryder Cup, a one-iron that split the middle of the fairway. His partner, Phil Mickelson, hit a three-wood in the middle. Love and Mickelson were playing Olazábal and Costantino Rocca, the Italian Love had beaten in singles in 1993 to clinch the Ryder Cup for the United States at the Belfry, and the man most known for the 65-foot putt he made from the Valley of Death on the 18th at St. Andrews to tie John Daly in the 1995 British Open. Daly went on to win the playoff to become the "champion golfer" of that year, but it was the slightly overweight Rocca who captured everyone's imagination that day. Now he was paired with Olazábal against two of the Americans' top guns.

Love birdied the first hole to take the first lead, but Rocca drew all square with a birdie at the seventh. The match seesawed back and forth, each team getting into their respective rhythms and overcoming the nerves that always accompany a Ryder Cup appearance.

On the par-five 11th, the first disturbance occurred. Mickelson had laid up in the fairway, leaving himself a 45-yard pitch shot to the up-sloping green. As he was going through his routine, a fan began dialing his cell phone, watching Mickelson's every move. As Phil waggled the club and glanced at the hole a second time, part of his standard ritual, the man in the gallery pressed the SEND key, and at the top of Mickelson's backswing another cell phone chirped. Mickelson noticed and hit his chip shot well short.

Phil made birdie and won the hole to put the Americans 2-up, but the incident was still disturbing. Even in the old days the Ryder Cup fans were always more demonstrative than other golf galleries. That was understandable enough: it was a nationalistic event and people always became more engaged when pulling for their country. Plus, the Ryder Cup attracted fans who might never have seen a golf tournament in their lives; much like the Olympics attracted novices to gymnastics and Greco-Roman wrestling matches. But there was a big difference between cheering for your team, even cheering bad shots hit by the opposing team, which had become a frequent occurrence at the Ryder Cup, and fans injecting themselves into the competition and disrupting play. That was something relatively new. At the Belfry in 1993, fans had attempted to trip players by poking umbrellas beneath the gallery ropes, and in 1995 at Oak Hill, Americans had brutally heckled the Europeans, especially Colin Montgomerie. Now fans were becoming more sophisticated in their ploys, mapping strategies for ringing cell phones at inopportune times, and that was a fundamental change, even for the Ryder Cup. Cheering a missed putt was one thing; this was something altogether different.

Those sorts of incidents were minimal on Friday, in part because the week was young, and in part because Seve's strategy in switching the order of play had worked brilliantly. Mickelson and Love lost to Olazábal and Rocca in the morning when both Americans missed birdie putts inside 10 feet on the final hole, and Mickelson's college teammate from Arizona State, Per-Ulrik Johannson, along with Florida resident Jesper Parnevik, beat Tom Lehman and Jim Furyk 1-up. The Americans won the other two morning matches with Tiger and Mark O'Meara beating Montgomerie and Bernhard Langer 3 and 2, and Fred Couples and Brad Faxon coming away with a 1-up win over Nick Faldo and Lee Westwood (or "Young" Lee Westwood, as he was called so often throughout the week that one began to wonder if that was actually his name). What should have been a strong morning for the Americans had ended in a split, and with each win and each match that went down to the wire, the European team gained new confidence.

Scott Hoch had plenty of time to think about his Ryder Cup debut. Kite benched him in the morning, but paired Hoch with his friend Lee Janzen in the afternoon, a match that didn't get under way until well after 3:00. "If anything threw us off golf-wise it was having to start so late," Hoch said. If he was nervous about his rookie appearance Hoch didn't show it. From Janzen's tee shot, Hoch hit a hard-spinning nine-iron shot on the first hole that stopped 6 feet away. When Janzen made the putt, the team was quickly 1-up on Olazábal and Rocca. But Hoch was disturbed. "I didn't think our team had the fire it should have had," he said. "The weather screwed everything up, and there really wasn't time for us to bond as a team. Plus, I didn't think we were as humble as the other team. To me, some of the guys appeared to be out there just filling a spot."

Even though the match was tight, Hoch kept feeling that there should be more to this experience. On the eighth hole, he finally turned to Janzen and said, "Is this all there is?" For a moment Janzen didn't know what to say, so Hoch continued. "I don't feel the least bit fired up. In fact, I don't feel anything! This feels like a practice round and I don't want it to feel that way."

Fired up or not, Hoch and Janzen won their match against Olazábal and Rocca 1-up, but they knew they wouldn't end the day with any sense of closure. There was no way all four afternoon matches would finish before dark. In fact, when the sun set on Friday two matches remained on the golf course. Langer and Montgomerie had come back from their morning loss to beat Tiger and O'Meara 5 and 3, but Faldo and Westwood were 1-up on Maggert and Lehman through 15 holes, and Lehman and Mickelson were 1-up on Garrido and Parnevik with five holes to play.

Even though the afternoon matches weren't decided, the matches were tied after the first day with the United States earning three points and leading in one match, and the Europeans also winning three points and leading in the other. It was the kind of day that led Tom Kite to say, "Gosh, isn't the Ryder Cup neat?"

It might have been neat for Kite, but some members of his team weren't quite as enthused. "With all the rain delays you never got a sense of how you stood," Furyk said. "We went to sleep Friday night with matches still out on the golf course. That's frustrating. Whether you're favored or not favored, to leave without the lead is a frustrating feeling. This was my first Ryder Cup, so I didn't know what to expect. You can talk to as many people as you want, but until you are there you can never really get a feeling for what to expect."

No one expected the heavily favored Americans to be in such a dog-fight after the first day, except for Johnny Miller, who had been sounding the warning signals for several weeks prior to the opening day. "If the U.S. jumps out to a two-point lead early, it will be a rout for our guys,"

Jean Van de Velde came to Carnoustie as an unknown and left as the poster child for spectacular collapses. Months later, as people got to know him, he became one of the most liked and respected players in Europe—a true gentleman who takes neither himself nor his profession too seriously.

The plane crash that killed U.S. Open Champion Payne Stewart along with Bruce Borland, Robert Fraley, Van Ardan, and pilots Michael Kling and Stephanie Bellagarigue sent shock waves through the close-knit golf community.

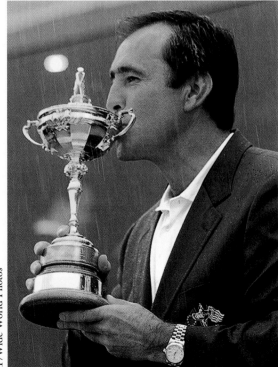

Passionate, charismatic, driven, and maniacal are all words that accurately describe legendary Spanish golfer Seve Ballesteros. During his reign as Ryder Cup captain he was called everything from the Mad Genius to Captain Outrageous. In the end, however, he did the only thing that mattered: He won.

Monty reacts to crowd jeers at the 1999 Ryder Cup in Brookline.
Behavior like this has built animosity between Europe's number-one player,
a genuinely nice guy off the golf course, and golf fans in America.

True Grit. Hal Sutton provided inspirational leadership in the locker room and on the golf course during the Brookline matches. He will make a great captain someday.

The Comeback Kid. After suffering from a foot ailment that threatened to end his career, José María Olazábal came roaring back in 1999 to win his second Masters title.

Sergio Garcia captured the hearts of golfers everywhere during the
PGA Championship at Medinah. This six-iron shot from behind a tree
solidified his reputation as one of the most exciting and imaginative
players in the game.

A familiar pose for Tiger Woods, who capped off the 1999 season with four consecutive wins, starting at Disney World in Orlando and ending with the WGC American Express Championships at Valderrama on the Spanish coast.

By winning the 2000 U.S. Open in record-setting fashion, Tiger removed all doubt about his ability and star quality.

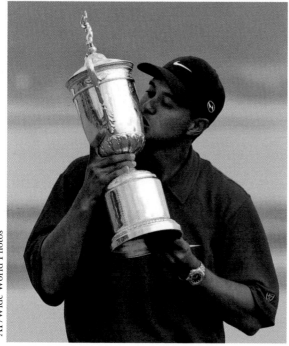

Conservative projections place Tiger's career earning potential at between $2 and $6 billion dollars, more than any athlete in history.

William Payne Stewart, September 1999.

Miller said two weeks before the matches. "But if Europe can end the day with a small lead or even come away tied with the Americans, look out. They'll get the idea they can actually win, will pull together emotionally, and send the match to the wire." Miller's early prognostications had come true, as had his theories on the golf course and the crowds. "If you thought the British Ryder Cup galleries (or American galleries, for that matter) were loud and partisan to a fault, wait until you see the crowds in Spain. These are people who love seeing bulls get killed, so you can only imagine how they will respond to good shots by Europeans and bad shots by Americans." By Friday afternoon everyone knew how they would respond. But Miller's most dire prediction for the Americans had to do with the golf course. "The Europeans are very familiar with Valderrama," he said. "It's a short golf course by professional standards and tricky, too. The Americans' biggest advantage, power, has been taken away. The controversial par-five 17th is made for drama and can be a great equalizer. Goofy holes favor the underdog." As the players tried to eat dinner quickly to get a good night's sleep on Friday, no one could have known how prophetic Miller's analysis would turn out to be.

In the wee hours of Saturday morning a blast of cool air moved down from the Northwest and collided with a wall of warm, dry air moving up from North Africa. The warm air moved up over the cool air like a balloon over the Spanish coast, and the results were catastrophic. Sally Hoch's artillery shells starting going off again about 5:30 A.M., only this line of thunderstorms made Friday's look like a mild drizzle. Water poured onto Valderrama, leaving greens, tees, bunkers, and swales flooded. By the time the rain stopped the situation looked bleak. The greens crew dug trenches and broke out squeegees, fans, vacuums, and every other device they could find to dry out the golf course. Thankfully the sun came out and the wind picked up, which helped dry things a little, and by 9:00 it looked as though 10:50 would be the starting time. That meant the remaining two matches from Friday would have to finish (in Mickelson, Lehman, Garrido, and Parnevik's case five full holes) before the first day's matches could be officially tallied. The second day's matches would be under way before anyone knew how the first day had ended, and with the late start, everyone knew Saturday would be more of the same. There wasn't enough daylight to finish 36 holes, so more matches would be left on the course again.

Garrido and Parnevik won the 14th with a birdie, and the two teams halved the 15th and 16th, leaving the final match of the first day (still on the golf course as the sun peaked in the sky on the second day) at all square with two holes to play. The pin on the 17th was cut back left, and both teams had good runs at birdie.

Tom Kite stood on the edge of the green, watching the play but staying out of the players' way. There wasn't much he could do at that point but watch, and look for the white paint dot that indicated where the afternoon pin placement would be. When he saw a white spot on the front of the green, he hesitated. That couldn't be it. The spot he saw was only two paces on the edge. Kite was a tour veteran. He knew that four paces was the minimum a hole would be cut to an edge, and that was marginal. Two paces was outside the acceptable norm by a good bit, not to mention the fact that this was two paces from a shaved bank that led straight to the water.

The crowd grew silent as the Europeans prepared to putt.

Kite looked again at the spot and decided that that couldn't be paint. It had to be bird dung. The folks at Valderrama were proud of the 104 species of birds that nested in and around the golf course, and the spot on the front of the 17th green must have been left by one of them. Nobody in his right mind would cut a hole that close.

The Europeans missed their birdie putt. The Americans made par as well, and the match continued to the 18th all-square. Kite took one more glance at the white spot on the 17th green and nodded as he walked away. That couldn't be it. It had to be bird dung.

It wasn't. Seve and the Committee cut the pin two paces from the front edge, thus ensuring that the controversial 17th, the hole Miller said was "goofy" and therefore favored the underdogs, would be the focal point of what were originally supposed to be the Saturday-morning, but were, as a practical matter, Saturday-afternoon matches. Love and Couples were the first victims. With their match against Montgomerie and Clarke all square through 16 holes, Love was forced to lay up on the 17th. He then hit his third shot long and left. Playing at the pin with only two yards between the hole and the water wasn't smart, especially with the pressure of a Ryder Cup Match on the line. Love had a 15-footer for birdie—not great, but not bad.

Clarke had hit his second shot in the water, which left it up to Montgomerie. With a wedge from inside 100 yards, Montgomerie hit his shot just beyond the hole and watched as it trickled back to within three feet, a "glorious shot," as the BBC called it. When Love missed and Montgomerie made, the 17th had claimed its first victim.

Every point was important to Love, but losing to Montgomerie was particularly souring. Before the matches, Montgomerie had been asked to compare the Europeans' chances against the Americans, and Monty, being the candid chap that he was, suggested that Brad Faxon would have other things on his mind since he and Mrs. Faxon were going through a divorce. Monty also opined that "Jim Furyk is a good advert for Callaway. He's a top-ten guy, but will that swing stand up under the ultimate pressure?" And Phil Mickelson: "Great touch, but you cannot rely on that every hole, which is what he tries to do. He's not accurate off the tee at all." None of the players escaped Monty's critique. Of Tom Lehman he said, "I've never found him to be a world beater." And when asked which American player he would most like to see with a four-foot putt to win the cup, Montgomerie said, "Hoch, because he has been in that situation before." He didn't actually say "choke" out loud, but the message was loud and clear.

Most of Montgomerie's comments were written off as blustering, something Monty had become famous for, but bringing up Faxon's divorce changed people's attitudes. No matter what other players had heard or read about him, most liked Montgomerie or at least tolerated him. He was always cordial, even funny at times. His wife, Eimear, whom he met as a child when they were neighbors in Troon, was a delightful woman, pretty and soft-spoken with a petite frame, milky complexion, a hint of freckles around her high cheekbones, and a wickedly dry wit she would employ with a charming Scottish accent. She had studied law at Edinburgh University, and although she never became a practicing barrister, Eimear's intellect was mighty. Most observers agreed that Monty had married up. The Montgomeries were the model tour couple until Colin opened his mouth: then, for some inexplicable reason, he became outrageous, the "Goon from Troon," as *Sports Illustrated* called him. In most settings there wasn't a more delightful person to be around than Colin Montgomerie. He never missed an opportunity to ask about a player's family. He remembered friends' birthdays and anniversaries, surprising them with gifts and cards. He moved his mother-in-law, Dorothy Wilson, into his London home to help Eimear with their two children, and he remained in London, even after it became evident his career would be better served in America on the PGA Tour, because of his family. When the British Lung Foundation needed his help, Colin was only too happy to oblige, and he became one of the organization's principal patrons. He also helped launch a campaign in Scotland called "Bypassing the Bypass," a heart-disease-awareness program for which he devoted a great deal of time. In all those respects he should have been a role model. But then, as if aliens had invaded his brain, he went off on tangents, ripping into anyone and everyone in his path. "He says some things that even I wouldn't say," Hoch, the U.S. standard-bearer for blunt opinions, said of Montgomerie. "I've played in tournaments with him on golf courses that weren't in very good shape, but we were both being paid to be there, and he would rip the condition of the golf course. He would rant and rave about how awful it was, saying that he should have been told how bad the conditions were so he could have saved himself a trip. I mean, sure, they weren't the best-maintained courses in the world, but even I wouldn't have said that."

A chubby lad, as Bill Ferguson, the pro at Ilkely Golf Club in Leeds and Monty's on-again, off-again instructor since childhood, called him, Colin Montgomerie was raised to be a proper gentleman by his father, James, who had served as a British army captain in the Suez before taking a job in northern England as the president of Fox Biscuits. James Montgomerie became club captain at Ilkely in 1979 and Royal Troon in 1986. The Montgomeries owned a cottage on the west coast of Scotland near Troon when Colin was a child, and it was there during the summers that young Monty learned the game. He wasn't much of a world-beater when he was young, in part because his golf was limited to the three summer months. The rest of the year Colin attended boarding school in Yorkshire where kilts were worn on Wednesdays no matter what the weather. His golf was good enough, though, that Dave Maddon from tiny Houston Baptist University in Texas thought Montgomerie would be a good addition to his team. After working through James Montgomerie, Maddon signed Colin to become a fighting Husky. Even after graduating Monty didn't believe his game was good enough to compete as a professional. In fact, he wanted to become a sports agent. "I met with Mark McCormack at Turnberry," Monty said. "[IMG] was looking for somebody to work under John Simpson [in IMG's London office]. We played golf as part of the interview, and I was six-under through ten holes that were played. Before the job was offered, they said, 'You shouldn't be working for us, we should be working for you.'" If he had been six-over-par on those 10 holes, Montgomerie might have been at Valderrama as Tiger Woods's agent, but McCormack and others at IMG convinced him he had what it took to compete at the highest levels.

A decade later he was the undisputed number-one player in Europe, and a man who had been called everything from "Mr. Doubtfire" to "The Fool Monty." Those who knew him couldn't speak highly enough of him, but even his best friends were perplexed by his Jekyll-and-Hyde personality. His caddie, Alastair McLean, said, "People see this grumpy, old-fart golfer, but working for him is probably the easiest job on tour." When McLean was out of commission with back surgery, Monty called him several times each week and sent expensive wine, food baskets, and handwritten notes to his house. Even his swing coach during the Valderrama Ryder Cup didn't quite get it. Denis Pugh, who had started working with Montgomerie in 1996, said, "Like everyone else in golf, I find him to be an absolute great guy away from the course and extremely moody around it. It may be extreme to call him the angel and the devil, but he really does take on a totally different character. Golf seems to change his entire mood. He's a genius, but he's definitely a flawed genius. You know that quote about how God doesn't give you everything? With Monty, it's the inability to control himself at given moments."

God-given disability or not, Monty's comments on Faxon crossed a line you just didn't cross, and no matter how vociferously he apologized afterward, it changed the way American professionals viewed him. None of the U.S. players mentioned Nick Faldo's tryst with an American college student during the 1995 Ryder Cup when it was apparent Nick and his then-wife Gill were steaming headlong for divorce court. It was out of bounds and everyone knew it. Even after Faxon tried to soothe matters by saying, "Monty was not being mean-spirited in what he said," the temperature when it came to Montgomerie was high. If it wasn't mean-spirited, it was stupid. Either way, everyone on the U.S. squad wanted desperately to beat Monty.

Love and Couples lost 1-up when Montgomerie parred the 18th, but it was the 17th, Seve's signature hole, that turned the match. Faxon and

Leonard were the next victims of the 17th. Thomas Björn, the only Dane ever to play in the Ryder Cup, hit his second shot into the middle of the green and two-putted for birdie to close out the match 2 and 1.

By the time Phil Mickelson reached the 17th it had become the pivotal hole of the Ryder Cup, and his had become one of the most pivotal matches of the day. Phil drove his ball 272 yards, but caught a bad hop off one of the many mounds in the fairway and the ball nestled into a deep cut of rough. The lie was testy, but not terrible. Phil knew he could get a long iron on the ball if he needed to, and this was the kind of make-or-break situation where he needed to execute a shot. After taking a look at his ball, Mickelson checked the yardage. He had 237 to the front of the green and 239 to the pin. Phil took a second look. Was that right? Could it be that the pin was 2 yards on the front of this green? Mickelson couldn't help smiling. Seve was a cocksure gamer. Putting the pin there was a helluva risk, but one that had obviously paid off for him. Phil chose a two-iron and started his routine. It was time to execute a shot.

The ball landed in the only spot it could have, a square no bigger than the top of a small desk. It jumped forward 15 feet behind the hole, then slowly rolled back to within 6 feet. It was a shot Tom Lehman would later call "the greatest single golf shot I've ever seen." When the ball stopped rolling, Tom Kite came running across the fairway, his hands in the air for an obligatory high-five. "You've got big brass ones!" he shouted to Mickelson. It was one of the best compliments Phil had gotten all week.

Even Mickelson's miraculous two-iron wasn't enough. Ignacio Garrido hit his second shot over the 17th green into the back bunker, a huge mistake. Par would be a good score from there if Garrido was lucky. But Garrido had some brass ones of his own, and when his bunker shot rolled to within 10 feet, the crowd behind the 17th green erupted. When Garrido made his birdie putt the crowd went wild, and when Mickelson missed his eagle putt to keep the match all square, pandemonium broke out on the hillside. Another of Miller's predictions was coming true: the bullfighting golf fans could smell blood, and they wouldn't rest until the Americans had been gored.

The ultimate insult, however, came when the third group reached the 17th. Young Lee Westwood had just birdied his fifth hole of the round to give him and his partner, Nick Faldo, a 1-up lead with two holes to play over O'Meara and Tiger. Westwood, a baby-faced 24-year-old with a slightly bigger midsection than his age might warrant, had been the surprise of the matches. He had taken all three of his matches to the wire, winning one, losing one, and, unless O'Meara and Woods could mount a miraculous charge, winning his third. When his three-iron shot stopped 3 feet from the hole at the 17th, the closest second shot of the day to that pin, Westwood elevated himself from rookie kid on the coattails of Nick Faldo to Ryder Cup warrior. Tiger was the last to play, hitting his iron shot long onto the back portion of the green, but on nonetheless. Two putts for birdie and he could, perhaps, extend the match.

Then Tiger hit the shot that typified the 1997 Ryder Cup for the Americans. The ball had barely left the blade of his putter when Tiger and O'Meara simultaneously said, "Slow down." As the ball crested the ridge and began its descent, still 20 feet from the hole, a BBC announcer said, "My goodness, that's in the water." He was right. Tiger Woods, the world's number-one golfer, the man who had demolished the field and the record book at Augusta National in April and the man whom every knowledgeable pundit described as the best match play competitor in the world, watched in stunned disbelief as his ball trickled off the green, down the embankment, and into the water.

O'Meara tried to keep his expression as even as possible. The last thing he needed was for Faldo and Westwood to see how shocked he was. Tiger had just putted his ball in the water. In the water! It was all O'Meara could do to gather himself to play his delicate pitch shot. To his credit O'Meara came within an inch of holing his chip for eagle to halve the hole. But when Westwood made his putt, the match was over.

Many who were watching thought the Ryder Cup was over as well. Back home in Milton, Florida, Isao Aoki was in the process of shooting a 60, the lowest round in the history of the PGA Senior Tour at the Emerald Coast Classic, and nobody cared. The locker room at the Moors Country Club was filled with senior players watching the Ryder Cup Matches unfold on NBC, and when Tiger's ball plopped into the water on the 17th, there was a collective gasp from the over-50 crowd followed by a slightly audible "Holy shit." Lee Trevino said, "That putt was going so fast it would have dented your car." Trevino and the rest of the seniors thought Tiger's putt was a death knell for Team U.S.A.

Despite those dire prognostications, Scott Hoch continued on his quest to prove he belonged, not only on this team but also on all the other teams that had passed him over. During Hoch and Maggert's afternoon alternate shot match against the energized team of Faldo and Young Lee Westwood, Hoch stared down Faldo and took the momentum on the seventh hole. Westwood and Maggert had both hit approach shots to within 8 feet. "You're away, putt," Faldo had said to Hoch.

Hoch looked at his putt and decided he wasn't away. "You putt. You're away," he said.

Faldo gave his patented dispassionate stare and said, "No, you're away."

Hoch looked at both putts from behind the hole and respectfully disagreed with Faldo. "It's your putt," he said.

A referee was called in to arbitrate the matter, and after exhaustive measurement, it was determined that Faldo was, indeed, away. He proceeded to miss his birdie putt. Hoch made his putt and the United States went on to pick up its only full point of the day. It was a big win for Hoch and Maggert and a good win for the United States, but most thought it was too little too late.

After another exhaustive day, Kite didn't know where to turn. "I knew I was going to have to say some hard things to them to kick them a little bit," Kite said. "We needed to get them out of the down emotions and get them motivated to play on Sunday. It's hard to kick somebody when he's down; I thought we needed something to lift them up and get them going. I knew President Bush was there, so I went to the press room and had Julius Mason [the PGA of America media director, and one of the truly good guys in the organization] find out where the president was and where he was going to be."

The president and Mrs. Bush were having dinner at the club when Kite found them. "We were walking into a black-tie dinner and Tom asked me to come speak to the team," President Bush said. "I told him I would have to check with Mr. Patino. Jimmy said 'OK' but he urged me to get back as soon as possible because of receiving-line problems and dinner speeches. I drove over [to Club San Roque] with Tom, whom I had known over the years and with whom I had played in a Texas celebrity event several years before. I don't recall exactly what I said. It was a very informal setting. The players were sitting around chatting. I wouldn't call it a 'speech.' Just remarks of encouragement, nothing that will live in history to rival the Gettysburg Address. I've never been accused of being a great speaker, and I don't know if I connected with the team or not. I do know I was very pleased Tom invited me, and the players were very receptive."

It was the first time anyone could remember that a former president gave a locker room pep talk to a group of professional athletes, and while President Bush might not have considered himself a great speaker, it was a moving experience for many of the players in attendance.

"I was impressed and inspired by him," Furyk said of the president's remarks. "He seemed very proud of us, and he instilled something in us. It made us feel pretty good."

"He certainly inspired me," Hoch said.

But the president's inspiration wasn't enough. As many predicted, the Europeans won the Ryder Cup on Sunday, but not before the United States came within a point of pulling off, as Tom Lehman put it, "one of the greatest comebacks of all time in any sport."

"At one point we were leading in nine singles matches and were tied on one or two more," Furyk said. "Still, there weren't that many blow-outs, so you couldn't get a real sense of what was going on out there."

In fact there was only one blowout on Sunday. Fred Couples made seven birdies in the first 11 holes and tied the Ryder Cup record for blowouts by drumming Ian Woosnam 8 and 7.

Furyk showed his mettle on Sunday as well. After holing a chip shot on the 14th to halve Nick Faldo, who had hit an approach shot to within 2 feet, Furyk hit his approach on 15 in a greenside bunker. After Faldo hit his shot to 4 feet, Furyk climbed into the bunker, stalked the shot like a hunter, then, just before he hit it, Furyk turned to his caddie and said, "How about two in a row?" When the bunker shot went in, Furyk knew he had his man. He beat Faldo 3 and 2.

And so it went. Mickelson defeated Clarke, Maggert beat Young Lee Westwood (whose real name was Lee John Westwood), Janzen made two critical putts in the closing moments to defeat Olazábal 1-up, and Lehman trounced Garrido 7 and 6. But America's three major championship winners—Woods, the 1997 Masters winner; Love, the PGA Champion; and Leonard, the British Open "champion golfer of the year"—could not muster a single point on Sunday. Love lost to Johansson 3 and 2, Leonard halved his match with Björn, and, in the biggest surprise of the Ryder Cup, Costantino Rocca, who was nicknamed

"Rocca the Choka" by the British press after losing to Love at the Belfry in 1993, handily defeated Tiger Woods 4 and 2.

The U.S. run looked promising for a while, but the matches were too close for too long for the Americans to pull it off. Once the Euros got to the 17th they knew they had it. Even the omnipresent Seve, who established a Ryder Cup record for most miles logged on a golf cart by a captain, couldn't foul up his team's inevitable victory, although he did everything in his power to get on as many nerves as possible. "Sometimes he gets a little bit too intense," Monty said of Seve's weeklong histrionics. "We're doing all right until he arrives, then the whole thing buckles and shuffles around. Sometimes he's better off just staying in his buggy and watching."

By Saturday afternoon, Jesper Parnevik had seen enough of his captain. When Seve approached Parnevik with his arms waving in his intense "Captain Frantic" way, the Swede looked directly at Seve and said, "Just get the fuck away from me." It was the silent opinion of everyone on the European team by the end of the week. "He would have loved to be even more involved than he was," Parnevik said of Seve. "Everywhere you looked, there was Seve, basically being Seve. I don't know what he did, but whatever it was, it worked."

Indeed it did. When Bernhard Langer closed out Brad Faxon on the 17th, the Ryder Cup was over. The most heavily favored team in two decades had gone down in flames to five Ryder Cup rookies who had followed Seve to the altar and been baptized by his Ryder Cup magic. It was the most important victory in European golf history.

Some Americans were more disappointed than others, for a variety of reasons. "I didn't think I played as well as I have on other teams," Davis Love said.

Faxon was simply stunned. "It's mind-boggling," he said. "If you look at the records on paper, our guys have done better in the majors and have won more tournaments. We've got higher rankings. We've got a captain we love and respect. We all got the pairings we wanted, and we *still* lost. There's no rhyme or reason to it."

Hoch was perhaps the most profoundly disappointed. He had waited 20 years to make a Ryder Cup team, and, while he finished with the best individual record of any of the American players, the experience was, in his eyes, completely forgettable. "After experiencing the whole thing, I couldn't imagine anything any more overrated than the Ryder Cup," he said. "After we lost, Sally and the Lehmans and I were standing outside the team room and a lot of our guys were inside having a good ole time. I mean, we had just lost the Ryder Cup! I remember saying to Tom, 'We just lost. I'm not in the mood to celebrate.' The Ryder Cup was most disappointing to me personally, because what I was expecting and what I experienced weren't even close. Tom Kite did everything he could do, but there just wasn't a bond there."

For Kite it had been the culmination of two years of hard work and sacrifice, of crunching numbers and examining stats, taking time away from his kids, and gathering advice and wisdom from others. He had visited with past captains, taken them and their wives out to dinner, probed them about things they did right, things they did wrong, what worked, what didn't. Tom Watson told him things that Lanny Wadkins contradicted, and vice versa. Finally, Kite realized he had to run the team his way, and that's what he had done. The result was a one-point loss, and another major "upset" victory of the Europeans.

For months afterward Kite was ripped in the media and in letters from golf fans for everything from his failure to play Justin Leonard in the opening matches on Friday to his decision to let Michael Jordan (who was in Spain for four hours while his family vacationed in Monaco) ride in his golf cart. Kite was out-captained by Ballesteros, some said. He was too soft, others chided. He let Seve get away with too much.

Almost two years after that Sunday afternoon in Spain, Tom Kite still got tears in his eyes remembering the details of the entire experience. It was overwhelming for a man to pour himself into an endeavor, come away just short of his goal, and spend months dodging spears from those who would second-guess his every move. "I look back and I have no regrets," Kite said, his back a little straighter as he made the proclamation. "I know I did everything I could do to get that team to play well. They just didn't do it. It wasn't from not being prepared. We were prepared. We just didn't get it done."

Tom Kite would never say it, nor would he ever acknowledge even thinking it, but after Valderrama, he knew—he was too smart, too analytical, and too reality based not to know—that the Ryder Cup had finally reached the point where, for American players and coaches, it was, quite simply, a bad deal.

*Six*

# DO NO HARM

OPELIKA, ALABAMA, A SMALL textile town on a rural stretch of I-85 between Atlanta and Montgomery, had been the source of a running joke among University of Alabama Crimson Tide fans for decades. The joke went like this: Cletus and U.L. are riding down the highway in their pickup when they pass a mileage sign that reads "Auburn 15." A few minutes later they see another mileage sign that reads "Opelika 30," at which time Cletus turns to U.L. and says, "Damn, Tiger's got beat again."

Redneck humor aside, Opelika had never been widely known outside the narrow reaches of southeastern Alabama until three weeks after the 1997 Ryder Cup, when the town hosted the Nike Tour Championship, the season-ending event that would determine who graduated from the elite mini-tour to the big leagues in 1998. It was the seventh year the PGA Tour had run a developmental tour where players had an entire season to earn their tour cards rather than hinging their futures on one week of qualifying school, and it was the fifth year Nike had been the title sponsor. In that time, Tom Lehman, John Daly, David Duval, and Jeff Maggert had all pulled duty on the Nike tour, driving from Odessa to Boise and staying in Motel 6s rather than flying from Phoenix to Los Angeles and renting homes. Now, the tour had reached an agreement with the newly created Robert Trent Jones Golf Trail, a series of public golf courses throughout Alabama, to host the Nike Tour Championship in various towns like Opelika and Dothan for the next four years. As he always did on such occasions, Tim Finchem flew to Opelika to announce the terms of the agreement, and to personally hand out PGA Tour cards to the top 15 money winners.

Lefthander Steve Flesch won the event, and Finchem gave cards and congratulations to such players as R. W. Eaks and Barry Cheesman. In his posttournament remarks the commissioner thanked all the sponsors, heaping praise on Nike for its continued support and showering accolades on Sunbelt Golf, the owners of the Robert Trent Jones Golf Trail.

But very few of the questions Commissioner Finchem fielded that day had anything to do with the Nike tour. Everyone wanted to know how on earth the United States had lost the Ryder Cup, again! In a small conference room in the Opelika clubhouse, Finchem was peppered with questions about the guts and veracity of the American players. Was Tom Kite the right man for the captaincy? Did the U.S. players have what it took to win in international team competitions? How could such a highly ranked, highly touted group of athletes—people with names like Tiger, Davis, Justin, and Freddie, who had been elevated to one-name status in the golf world—lose, yet again, to a bunch of guys with hyphens and umlauts in their names? What was it that turned the greatest golfers in the world into dysfunctional losers when the Ryder Cup was on the line? Was it money? Could the greedy bastards get motivated only when a winner's check was waiting? Did they simply not care? Or were the Europeans really better players than the Americans? Finchem was also questioned about the Ryder Cup venues. What did he think of The Country Club in Brookline? Why didn't they play the matches at TPC courses where our guys had an advantage? That's what Seve had done. Why didn't the United States employ the same strategy? And what about the captain? Who did Finchem think the United States needed? A field general like Hale Irwin? A coach and motivator like Tom Watson? What about Curtis Strange?

After diplomatically handling the barrage as best he could, Finchem finally said, "Look, these are all questions for the PGA of America. They run the Ryder Cup. Tour players obviously compete, but we don't make the rules and I don't have anything to do with the selection of venues, or captains, or anything else, and it would be inappropriate for me to comment on those things."

Inappropriate, maybe, but Finchem knew he was going to have to deal with questions that were outside his purview as commissioner. It was the price you paid when you were the most powerful man in the sport, and by the end of 1997 there was no doubt Finchem had assumed that role. In just over four years as PGA Tour commissioner, the 50-year-old had skillfully maneuvered his way through the complex web of power brokerage, influence, and panache that informally dictated who was and who was not "in" as a leader in the game. By the time 1998 was ushered in, he, Tim Finchem, a five-foot-seven-inch lawyer with a Virginia accent who pulled the bill of a bucket hat over his eyes when he was trying to break 80 on the golf course, had quietly and methodically elevated himself and his organization to the pinnacle of influence, eclipsing the PGA of America, the USGA, the R&A, and many other older, more established, and more traditional institutions in the process. The PGA Tour was the youngest of those organizations by a wide margin. Even the LPGA was older by 18 years, but age, and in some respects tradition, no longer mattered in the new arena of golf. Tiger Woods had proved that. If anything, being an old establishment golfer—wearing the blue blazer of the USGA or hiding behind the emblem of the PGA of America—was a liability in the game's new world order. The future was about innovation, expansion, and above all, image. Finchem understood that better than anyone. He had an uncanny ability to look at the broad and complex political horizon and chart a course to the top for both his organization and himself. By the end of 1997 he had become The Man, and while it appeared that Finchem's rise to the top of golf's food chain had been short and quick, it was, in fact, the culmination of forty years of life experiences that had finally grown to fruition.

It started in 1956, during the early stages of America's second golf boom, when Harold Finchem, USMC, took his 9-year-old son to the Camp Lejeune Golf Club in North Carolina. Tim wasn't allowed to play, or even hit balls, but he could watch his father and the other Marine Corps officers. For an impressionable kid, watching was good enough. By the time he was 10, Tim was allowed to hit a few shots here and there, but his golf consisted mostly of observing. This was the Eisenhower era, and golf among military personnel was serious business, not a place for prepubescent curiosities. Tim was fascinated, however. In addition to the officers in his dad's group, there was a young professional named Arnold Palmer creating quite a buzz, and in their single-story military home, young Tim Finchem would sit on the floor transfixed by the glowing black-and-white images from the family's RCA television of this swashbuckling golfer with big forearms and a charismatic smile. He had a connection with the game, one that would stick with him forever.

Two events in the summer of 1960 proved pivotal in the life of young Tim Finchem. First was his ability to play golf full time, all summer long. At age 13 it was the last summer he could romp and play and do kid things before the family expected him to get a job. He took full advantage of his nonworking status by playing as much golf as he could from the day school let out until the day it started back. "My mother would drop me off in the mornings and pick me up in the evenings, and I would play all day," he said. "I got to where I could play a little bit, but that was it. The next summer I went to work, and I've been working ever since." The second event occurred in mid-July. Margaret Finchem, an Irish Catholic and proper military wife, took more than a passing interest in national politics, and when John F. Kennedy, the first Irish Catholic ever to be nominated for president, stood at the podium in Los Angeles and accepted the Democratic nomination, Margaret and her son Tim listened to every word and watched the sign-waving delegates demonstrate their support. Tim was enthralled by it all: the booming voice of Adlai Stevenson as he gave the keynote speech and introduced the senator from Massachusetts; the falling balloons; the majesty of each state chairman standing and shouting, "Mr. Speaker, the great state of 'X' casts its support to the next president of the United States, John Fitzgerald Kennedy." It was all Tim Finchem had ever imagined it would be. During the entire week of the convention his mother picked Tim up from the golf course and they hurried home to watch the proceedings, listening intently as Walter Cronkite, Chet Huntley, and other experts explained the inner workings of the national political process. That was where Tim Finchem belonged, he told himself as he watched the grainy images on television. Politics was his destiny.

Golf went away for Finchem after his 14th birthday. When he wasn't studying, playing basketball, and making a name for himself as a skilled debater at Princess Anne High School in Virginia Beach, he was crawling around in attics and crawl spaces installing central heating and air-conditioning units. It was his brother-in-law's company, and with child labor laws somewhat relaxed in the 1960s, not only was it not inappropriate for a 14-year-old to climb into an asbestos-insulated 120-degree attic in the middle of the summer, it was expected. Work was something the Finchems prided themselves on, and like the rest of the family, Tim was expected to put in a decent day's labor. He played one year of high-school golf when he was 15, and he loved basketball, but with his growth stalled at five-seven, there weren't many colleges looking at him as a potential basketball star. His golf was nowhere near good enough to earn him a golf scholarship, so he turned his focus elsewhere. "A scholarship was the only way I was going to college, so I took up debate," he said.

He became a state champion debater, finding a satisfying niche in the mental discipline it took to craft a persuasive argument. Tim also thought his debating skills would serve him well in the political arena, where he was certain he would end up after college. During his sophomore year in high school, his neighbor came over and asked Tim to write a speech. "He was running for sophomore class president, so I wrote an election speech for him," Tim said. "The next year was the same thing. He came over, and I wrote his speech for him again. My senior year, we won the state championship in debate, and when he came over I said, 'I'm not going to write your speech. I'm going to write my own speech.'" Finchem was elected president of his senior class at Princess Anne, his first elected office. He loved it.

The University of Richmond offered him a debating scholarship, and, in addition to becoming an even more skilled deliberator, he was elected president of his fraternity and vice chairman of the Richmond student government. A path to the political mainstream seemed naturally paved for him. When he was accepted to the University of Virginia Law School, his future in the political system seemed even more certain.

He was elected vice chairman of the Virginia Democratic Party in 1972, the same year Nixon bugged the DNC and crushed George McGovern in the biggest landslide in presidential history. But Finchem's introduction to the big time, and his first exposure to the cruelties of the modern political process, came in 1976, when he became campaign chairman for Admiral Bud Zumwalt's U.S. Senate bid. Zumwalt, a conservative Democrat who was the youngest four-star admiral in history and the youngest man ever named as chief of naval operations, ran for the Virginia Senate seat against Harry Byrd, Jr., and was resoundingly defeated.

Undaunted by Zumwalt's defeat and energized by the political process, Finchem decided to give it a go himself. In 1977 he ran for chief prosecuting attorney in his hometown of Virginia Beach. It was a far cry from the U.S. Senate, but it was a start, an introduction to the process, and a chance to whet his appetite for elected office. But Finchem had a problem. While he imagined himself as a John Kennedy Democrat, and while he had been overwhelmingly persuasive when his constituency had been high school and college students, the real world of politics proved much different. In one word, Finchem was dull. His language skills weren't the problem; he was a masterful wordsmith. It was his delivery that put people to sleep. Tim Finchem was a lot of things; dynamic was not one of them. His body language was rigid, often stilted, as if too much movement were something to be avoided. Even his mouth didn't move much, the words coming out of this wooden character as though he had been wound up with a key. Despite the best platform, the best credentials, and a rock-solid background as a hard-working do-gooder, Tim lost the election. Twenty-three years later, he said of that time, "You know, it's interesting how some things in life turn you in one direction or another. If I had won that election, I'd be prosecuting cases in Virginia Beach. Recently I gave a speech back there and I told the people in Virginia Beach, 'I'm so happy today that you didn't vote for me back then.'"

The loss in 1977 moved Finchem back into private practice. He and two of his friends, Glenn Croshaw and William Williams, formed Croshaw, Finchem, and Williams, a Virginia Beach firm specializing in legislative issues, which was code for lobbying. Tim used his political connections, pulling strings and writing letters, like one in early 1978 he wrote to Tim Kraft, assistant to President Carter, on behalf of Cox Enterprises, a firm trying to gain EPA approval for a power plant in Portsmouth, Virginia. "It is my understanding that [Energy] Secretary [James R.] Schlesinger is a staunch supporter of this proposal," Finchem wrote. "Could you please have your office check into the status of the matter and determine if the President has had an opportunity to discuss it with Secretary Schlesinger? I cannot impress upon you too much the importance of this six-million-dollar plant to the economy of this area."

He was always polite but firm, subtle in his mastery of the language, but leaving no room for misinterpretation. Finchem was a quiet bulldog. He would bore you to death with his pontifications, but when he latched his teeth into your leg you knew he meant business.

In November 1978 Finchem left private practice and moved to Washington to become the deputy advisor to the president on economic affairs. In hindsight, it seemed ironic that the future commissioner of the PGA Tour—a man who would become the world czar of golf in the late 1990s—would work for the only president since Truman who didn't play golf, but at the time Finchem's foray into the Carter White House seemed like the next step in his political progression. He had a top-level security clearance, an office in the Old Executive Office Building, and was on a first-name basis with everybody in the West Wing, including President Carter. "I was not a part of the 'Georgia Mafia,' as they called Hamilton [Jordan] and Jimmy and those guys back then,"

Finchem said. "I came along a little later from a different direction. I still keep up with all those guys, though. They're good friends of mine."

On his fifth day in the White House, Tim was standing in the Roosevelt Room preparing to chair a meeting of the Intergovernmental Task Force on Inflation when it hit him. He had made it. The little boy who had watched John Kennedy accept the Democratic nomination for president was now in the White House chairing a meeting in the Roosevelt Room! When the meeting was over, Finchem returned to his office and made a phone call. "Mother," he said when his mom answered, "you're not going to believe what I did today."

It didn't take him long to realize why he had been chosen to chair that meeting. "When I got to the White House, Al Kahn [President Carter's chief economic advisor] and other senior White House staff saw some fresh meat," Finchem said. "Nobody wanted to mess with inflation. It wasn't fun, and it was a loser, as we later found out, so they dumped it on me."

He was one of the few noneconomists on the President's Council on Wage and Price Stability, a governmental task force chaired by Treasury Secretary Michael Blumenthal (father of infamous Clinton administration hit man Sidney Blumenthal), but most of Finchem's contacts were with Kahn, and his responsibilities were more pragmatic than ethereal. "The team needed somebody to pull together governmental action," Finchem said. "We organized a nationwide, public sector effort on wage and price stability, the theory being that if we could demonstrate discipline to the private sector it would have a rub-off effect." Then with the hint of a wry smile forming at the corners of his mouth, Finchem said, "It did a lot of good. We got inflation up to about 18 percent. When people ask why I left in 1980 and moved over the campaign, I say, 'There wasn't anything left to do. We had interest rates and inflation in double digits. We'd done our jobs, so it was time to move on.' We were sending the country right down the tubes."

Finchem was a quick study, and it didn't take long for him to maneuver through the political land mines of Washington politics. He also brought the same quiet aggressiveness that had served him well as a private "legislative" lawyer to the White House. When Al Kahn, a brilliant economist but political novice, became frustrated by a seemingly impenetrable wall around the president, Finchem drafted a memo outlining Kahn and the committee's concerns and told Kahn to pass it directly to Carter during one of their briefings. "I went around Phil Wise, the president's secretary, and you just didn't do that," Finchem said.

Wise was furious. "Mr. Kahn gave that memo directly to the president," Wise said to Finchem, his voice seething. "That's not going to happen again."

"Well, Phil, we don't need for it to happen again," Finchem said. "We only needed the president to see the memo once."

The next night at a State Dinner, President Carter pulled Finchem aside and said, "Tim, I would very much appreciate more direct communications like the memo of yours I got through Al Kahn."

Finchem smiled and said, "Yes, sir," but he didn't let it go at that. The next morning he sent a note to Phil Wise relaying the president's comments. "That really frosted him," Finchem said.

In 1980 Finchem moved over to the Carter-Mondale campaign, where he assumed the role of peacemaker, fund-raiser, and staff manager. When Bob Strauss, a heavy-hitting Washington contributor who would later be President Bush's ambassador to Russia, had a falling out with the Carter campaign, it was Finchem who was assigned to, in his words, "mend fences and put hands on troubled waters." He also took on some mundane tasks. In one of his memos from that time, Finchem requested that the president "pose for a photograph with The Commodores, a rock-and-roll group that has had nine gold albums and been key supporters of the campaign."

Tim wasn't the front man. He didn't show up on talk shows or give speeches at rallies, but he did organize and mobilize the national campaign staff, allocating funds and resources when and where they were needed. It was a job that earned him great respect among White House insiders, and the attention of the president. Hamilton Jordan, Carter's principal advisor and de facto chief of staff, announced he would be resigning after the election and returning to the private sector. Jordan also announced he had recommended Tim Finchem as White House staff director for the second term of the Carter presidency (if there was a second term).

There wasn't, and Finchem never got the chance to run the White House staff. Ronald Reagan won the 1980 election in a landslide, a political defeat that left Finchem scratching his head. "Carter was still leading in the polls two weeks out," he said. "But in peacetime, if the economy is bad, you're not going to get reelected, period. The Arabs drove the dynamics of that election. OPEC oil prices were through the roof and that drove up other consumer prices . . . there wasn't a lot we could do. Plus, [the Ayatollah] Khomeini had us by the proverbial balls."

Finchem was back to private law practice once again, using his political connections on behalf of a paying constituency. Not long after the election, an old friend named Tim Smith, a fellow Virginian who had served as President Carter's advance man, approached Finchem for advice. Smith had left the White House before the election to return to the law firm of Rogers and Wells, where he served as general counsel to the Carter-Mondale campaign. But since the election Smith had been spending more and more time with one of Rogers and Wells's most exciting clients: the PGA Tour.

"I'm really torn," Smith told Finchem. "The tour is becoming a bigger client. They've moved to Florida, and they want me to become general counsel." Smith was hoping Finchem would give him some thoughtful advice on how to consider the offer. PGA Tour commissioner Deane Beman was an exciting guy with grand visions for the tour, like owning and running golf courses, licensing the PGA Tour brand, and expanding the tour's influence beyond that of other professional sports organizations. Beman saw the PGA Tour as family entertainment, like movies or the circus, and his vision for growing professional golf was to position the tour as an entertainment alternative. It was exciting stuff, and something Smith was seriously considering.

Rather than giving him a dispassionate opinion, however, Finchem said, "Hell, I want that job. You don't even play golf!"

Eight years later, Finchem got that job. After Smith talked Finchem into working on the tour's TPC at Avenel project (where he met his wife), Finchem decided to accept Beman's offer to join the PGA Tour as a full-time employee. Ten months later, he became the deputy commissioner and chief operating officer.

When Beman retired in 1994, the tour's board of directors set out to find a suitable replacement. They didn't have to look far. Finchem had been the perfect second chair to the hard-charging, entrepreneurial Beman, a man who became so animated when sharing his ideas that he once scraped the side of his car down a concrete pillar while talking over a new strategy with Smith. "He never missed a beat," Smith said. "We got out of the car, and Deane didn't even realized he'd wrecked it." Like most who worked for the PGA Tour at the time, Smith was a huge admirer of Beman. "Deane would get into a zone and forget about everything else," Smith said. "He was one of the most focused men I've ever met." Beman's focus and drive built the tour from a 10-person, one-office operation into a sports monolith with over $500 million in assets. He also made a lot of enemies, including many of the players who benefited from his business strategies. Beman was a type-A hard-charger, a man who once fined Hubert Green for arguing with an official about a ruling on television, even though the network didn't carry the sound. "I was right about the ruling and you couldn't even hear what I said!" Green had insisted. "That doesn't matter," Beman said. "Your body language was hostile." Finchem, on the other hand, was a mild-mannered, politically savvy bridge-builder; softer, more politically astute, more conciliatory, and less threatening. He was the perfect candidate to replace Beman.

"The years Deane was running things, the tour was an entrepreneurial, fast-growth operation," Finchem said. "It was a one-man decision-making apparatus, which is fine in an entrepreneurial environment. Deane ruffled a lot of feathers, but you've got to remember, he built this operation from zip. When you're building a business you don't have time for small talk, and Deane didn't. He was just as focused in his attempts to build the tour as he was when he was trying to shoot 68 in the U.S. Open."

Beman had been a tour player, which was both good and bad when it came to assuming the role of commissioner. Many of the players looked at him as a peer, not as a CEO, and that caused conflicts especially when he tried to expand the scope of the tour from simply running golf tournaments into golf course development and marketing. "I don't think people understand the enormity of what Deane did," Finchem said. "He had to fight the system he was dealt, a system that was slow to change and slow to make decisions. He was a real idea man and innovator, and our skill sets worked well together."

Finchem was equally adept at fighting. His approach was simply more urbane. While still a bit stiff, Finchem could carry a controversial motion through a board meeting without offending a soul. He was far more debonair than Beman, and a master of political speech, using smooth, disarming language, replete with passive voice, to get his points across. But he also used the word "core" a lot, as in "core values," "core beliefs," "core principles," and "core focus." Finchem's vision was core, as was his belief that the PGA Tour could become even bigger and better than Beman had made it.

After Finchem assumed the reins, the substance of the PGA Tour remained intact but the presentation changed. "On the plus side, I'd say we're a little smoother now than we were when Deane was here," Finchem said. "This organization has assumed a high profile, and that dictates being cautious. On the minus side, we might water down the message a little bit in order to come off a little smoother."

As the 1998 season rolled around, the tour's message was anything but watered down, and Finchem's position as the most important man in golf was no longer in question. The defining moment had come during a one-week period in May of 1997, when Finchem and his lieutenants rented suites in the Waldorf Astoria for a series of meetings with television executives. "We had delivered packages to all the television networks and the other interested parties ten days in advance of the meetings," Finchem said. Those packages contained groupings of PGA Tour events, and the networks and cable outlets were invited to the Waldorf to bid on the right to televise PGA Tour golf.

While sending out packages to networks was standard procedure, Finchem threw a couple of ingenious twists into what had previously been a very cozy negotiating process. It was a standard rule of auctioneering that no matter what the item, whether it's a Monet or a Chevy Malibu, the more bidders you had in the process, the higher the bids were going to be. The creators of Ebay recognized that when they designed an online auctioning service for everything from retro clothing to viable human eggs, and literary agents had been driving up book advances for years using the same theory. Finchem understood the principle as well, so rather than inviting the Big Three networks to bid exclusively on tour television rights, he invited six bidders including cable outlets like the Golf Channel and Turner Broadcasting, as well as adding Fox to the network mix.

The feeding frenzy intensified when Finchem placed executives from each network in cozy rooms at the Waldorf, isolating them from the other bidders but making sure everyone was aware of everyone else's presence. Tim and his team then met with each group, using some of the oldest negotiating ploys in the book. The "I'll be right back" trick was the best one. After a network made an offer, the PGA Tour execs, all dressed in matching blazers, would march out of the room, leaving the television execs alone to ponder what must be happening with the other networks. NBC executives were left to fret over what CBS's people must be doing. CBS wondered what ABC was up to, and everybody worried about that rogue Fox network. It was enough to give even the most hardened New York television exec a severe case of angina.

Also helping the process was the fact that five weeks before the meetings, Tiger Woods had won the Masters and generated the highest numbers in the history of televised golf. The win had been the lead on every major newscast and Tiger's face had appeared on the cover of every major magazine in the country. If ever there was a time to gin up the bidders' emotions and push the "gotta have it" frenzy beyond the point of economic reason, the height of Tigermania was that time.

"Anytime you get into those kinds of discussions, the environment is very important," Finchem said. "There are always intangibles that affect that environment, and Tiger was a very positive intangible. Tiger coming through at Augusta with a 22 rating, something unheard of in golf, put a lot of topspin on the discussions."

The results of that topspin and Finchem's skillful negotiating tactics were a series of television agreements that would bring in over $400 million in revenues to the PGA Tour from 1999 through 2003, over twice the television revenues golf had ever generated. There would also be twice the amount of golf on television, with every round of every PGA Tour event covered on either a broadcast network or a cable outlet. After the contracts were signed, Finchem, a man who never stepped out on a limb in his public predictions, said, "It would be reasonable to expect purses for PGA Tour events to average in excess of $3 million."

As part of the new-and-improved PGA Tour, Finchem also announced the formation of the World Golf Championships, a series of three events in 1999 and four in 2000 that would pit the best players from the PGA Tour, the European tour, and the Australasian, African, and Japanese tours against each other in a series of worldwide, high-dollar events. This bore a remarkable resemblance to the World tour concept Greg Norman had tried to push through three years before, and Finchem acknowledged Greg's contribution to the process, even though Norman had no role in the new World Golf Championships. A "federation" made up of all the world tours ostensibly ran the WGC tournaments, but everyone knew it was Finchem who stood at the top of the world golf totem pole.

Under his tutelage golf had hit the big leagues! In the 1960s when Beman took over as commissioner from Joe Dey, PGA Tour golf was on a par with professional bowling in terms of its television audience, its prize money, and its influence over average Americans. Now it was approaching the majors. NFL football would always lead the ratings wars when it came to sports, and as long as Michael Jordan continued to play basketball, the NBA would remain a close second, but golf was moving up. Where baseball was losing audience and market share, professional golf was doubling its coverage and its dollars. According to Sean McManus, the president of CBS Sports, and one of the men who paid Finchem's handsome asking price, "The track record for golf has been very good. We're confident that the future is going to be even better."

Finchem shared that confidence. He also believed the tour could be doing more to promote the game, particularly to the youth in America, and more specifically the underprivileged minority youths who might never otherwise be exposed to golf. When he accepted the job as commissioner, Finchem openly lamented that "our tour doesn't resemble our nation. We need to work on that." Even with the arrival of Tiger Woods, the hottest minority golfer in history, there were still more minorities playing hockey in the NHL than playing golf on the PGA Tour. While Finchem couldn't sprinkle pixie dust over the projects and create a new crop of professional golfers, he could use the tour's influence and brand identity to build a coalition and expand the game into the inner cities.

On a breezy March afternoon, Finchem flew to Houston and ran his idea past former president George Bush. It would be called "The First Tee" program, Finchem told the president, the idea being to build 100 golf facilities around the country where inner-city kids could be introduced to golf and be mentored in the game by caring adults. Finchem asked the former president if he would serve as honorary chairman of The First Tee, and Bush, whose grandfather George Herbert Walker was a president of the USGA and the namesake of the Walker Cup, couldn't sign on fast enough. "I accepted Tim's offer because I believe the goal of making golf available to more kids, kids from all different backgrounds, is a great thing," President Bush said. "I am active, because I love the game."

With the president firmly on board, Finchem approached the USGA and the PGA of America with his plan. That was a little trickier. Both those organizations claimed ownership of the "grass roots" of the game, and while it would have been political suicide for any officials to speak ill of any plan to help inner-city minorities, there would no doubt be some turf guarding, especially from the PGA of America. It wasn't enough that the prima donnas who made a living with their clubs had broken away and stolen bragging rights to their acronym, that Beman character had been audacious enough to license the logo and open his own golf courses, putting the PGA of America in catch-up mode. Now the tour was trying to muscle into grass-roots-growth-of-the-game issues, right where the PGA of America claimed to live! But officers at the PGA of America could only smile and go along. This should have been their initiative, but it wasn't. Once again their "sister" organization, the PGA Tour, had beaten them to the punch, and all PGA of America officials could do was applaud Commissioner Finchem's outstanding efforts "for the good of the game."

Finally, Finchem needed the help of one of his players—not just any player, but the one everybody was talking about, the one who made this whole thing possible through his game and his ethnicity. Finchem needed Tiger. Nothing would cause this initiative to fall on its face faster than a lack of support by golf's most visible minority member. While he was sure Tiger would support The First Tee, Finchem shored up that support by inviting Earl Woods, who was serving as chairman of the Tiger Woods Foundation, on the whirlwind two-day tour to announce the program. "We must make it possible for all our kids to dream," Earl said.

As icing on the cake, Finchem convinced Augusta National Golf Club, the stoic home of the Masters, to join the party. Augusta National had recently come under fire for its lack of charitable contributions, even though it hosted the most watched golf event in the world. Some of the criticism was well founded, some wasn't. While the PGA Tour made visible contributions to local charities each week, Augusta National and the Masters didn't support any charities, local or otherwise. When they turned down a donation request from the Augusta chapter of the

NAACP, the club got hammered in the press. Their lack of munificence was silly and stupid, especially since most of the members of Augusta National were generous, philanthropic people. But Finchem helped Augusta soften its hard image when club chairman Jack Stephens announced a $5 million personal contribution to The First Tee. Augusta National general manager Jim Armstrong made the trip with Finchem, Earl, and President Bush to announce Stephens's contribution. It was a coalition unlike any assembled in golf, and Finchem deserved all the credit.

In early 1998, Finchem the politician tried to downplay his ascension to almost imperial power. "We are not the athletes," he reminded anyone and everyone within earshot in as emphatic a tone as he could muster without opening his lips any wider than normal. "We are not the players, and we don't take ourselves too seriously. We like to have fun with each other, but we take what we do very seriously. If you're not a team player, you shouldn't be at the tour."

Finchem was a team player, but he was also the head of the team and everyone knew it. He had been the driving force, the visionary, and the master politician who had pulled off this coup, and he would be the one to lead the professional game into the next century. All he had to do was spend 1998 building the infrastructure and waiting for the good times to roll. It should be a slow year, a year without many distractions or new items on the agenda. Finchem's primary goal in 1998 was to do no harm. The television, the money, the added exposure, the World Golf Championships, and tangible results from The First Tee initiative would all come around in 1999. Until then, he simply wanted to keep the convoy moving and, above all else, he wanted to avoid any and all hidden land mines.

Fourteen years removed from governmental politics (after working for the Mondale-Ferraro campaign in 1984), Finchem had obviously lost some of his touch when it came to recognizing a political firestorm on the horizon. The Tim Finchem who had somehow managed to keep Jimmy Carter ahead of Ronald Reagan in the polls through October of 1980 would surely have recognized the potential disaster the tour faced when it chose to deny a young Stanford graduate named Casey Martin the right to play on the Nike tour with a golf cart. It should have been a no-brainer, a political layup, as easy a decision as he could have possibly had under the circumstances. This 25-year-old kid from Eugene, Oregon, with a face that could have come right out of "Leave It to Beaver," and an "I Love God and America" wholesomeness that most sports would have killed for, had qualified for the Nike tour and become the buzz of the business, not so much for his golf but because the kid, Casey Martin, had a degenerative bone disease in his right leg called Klippel-Trenaunay-Weber syndrome. His right leg was withered and pale, shocking the first time you saw it because it seemed so out of place on this handsome, clean-cut Christian boy-athlete. When the realization that Martin's atrophy would only get worse sank in, most people initially felt sorry for him, but when they saw what he had accomplished and what he had overcome, people were universally inspired. This was a man who, at any moment, could take one wrong step, snap his tibia, and have his leg amputated; yet he had qualified to compete with some of the best golfers in the world, an achievement no less inspiring than Tom Dempsey's success as an NFL kicker despite being born with half a foot, or Jim Abbott's success as a Major League pitcher despite having only one hand. Casey Martin was a hero, a role model Finchem and the PGA Tour should have put on display as a shining example of all things good in golf.

There was only one problem: Section 6, Item G of the PGA Tour's bylaws stated, "Players in cosponsored and coordinated tournaments shall not use automotive transportation." Walking, according to Finchem and the tour, was an "integral part" of the professional competitive game, just as important to the integrity of the sport as holing all your putts or playing from the same tees as everyone else in the field. Never mind that the players on the Senior tour used carts. That was, in the remarkably lame words of the tour, a "different product." Tour players, both PGA and Nike tour, had to walk, period. Casey Martin could barely walk from his living room to his kitchen. Walking 18 holes of golf was out of the question.

Maybe the television deal, the World Golf Championships, The First Tee, and all the other positive things on his agenda had distracted him (although he vehemently denied it), but Finchem clearly took his eye off the political ball when it came to Casey Martin. Rather than defuse the situation by writing a one-time exception for Martin, then putting his arm around the kid and saying, "Look how great our game can be!" Finchem said no, Martin couldn't ride. It was against the rules and that was that.

Martin sued under the Americans with Disabilities Act and gained a temporary injunction. He could play with a cart until a federal magistrate in Oregon sorted out this unseemly mess. Until then, the PGA Tour would provide Martin a cart, and would in no way impede his ability to compete.

Suddenly, Martin became the center of attention, not just in the golf world but all across America. He appeared on CNN's *Crossfire,* and was the subject of debates on *Meet the Press, This Week with David Brinkley,* National Public Radio, *Oprah, Leeza, Geraldo, Jenny Jones,* and every other talk show north of Jerry Springer on the content scale. In every case, images of Martin hobbling from his golf cart to his ball, his clean-cut boyish face filled with determination, glowed on television screens, usually followed by the image of Tim Finchem, dressed in a coat and tie, hair perfectly combed, his manners just as stilted as they had been back in 1977, when he lost that election in Virginia Beach. Finchem's face would fill the screen as he argued that the PGA Tour had the right to make its own rules, and that walking was "an integral part of the competition of the game."

As theoretically valid as his arguments might have been (and there were many deep-thinking intellectuals who sided with the tour), Finchem lost the perception battle when it came to Casey Martin. The commissioner looked like an exclusionary elitist, a snob who had brushed aside this gritty kid who loved his mom, his country, and Jesus, and who had battled against all odds to compete. The Dickensian imagery made for great television: a middle-aged white guy with a penchant for political platitudes shunning this warm-hearted underdog simply because the kid had a physical disability. Technically, of course, that wasn't true, but it didn't matter. That was the picture the general public saw. Nobody cared about the legal minutiae, and the broader principle of a federal law intruding on a professional sport was difficult for people to comprehend. All the average citizen saw was Casey Martin's smiling, boyish face and atrophied leg, followed by Finchem's stoic profile, lips barely moving as he reiterated the tour's legal position.

Even the golf media sided with Martin. Columnist Bill Fields wrote a decidedly pro-Martin piece in *Golf World* where he said, "In no other sport could someone who has trouble walking have the opportunity to prove himself the way Martin has, provided he gets the opportunity to ride between shots. Right now, golfers are riding while winning Senior tour events, state opens, and club championships. Course records don't get an asterisk if a player uses a cart. Martin is disabled, not injured. He's not the able-bodied man pulling into the handicapped parking space in front of the store. As he crunches 270-yard drives and knocks down the flagstick with approaches, he is one misstep away from a fractured tibia, a complication that could hasten amputation of his leg."

As if the situation could get worse for the tour, Martin won the first Nike tour event he played. Amid a media throng unlike anything the developmental tour had ever seen, Martin shot 19-under-par for four days to win the Lakeland Classic by one shot over Steve Lamontagne, an event that wouldn't have made the back pages of most newspapers (even in Florida where the tournament was held) if it hadn't been for Martin's pending lawsuit. With camera and tape recorders rolling, a bright-eyed Martin smiled and said, "I love to play golf, and if I don't have a cart, my leg gets so painful that it's not worth it. If I break it, I could lose it. But I hope it all works out. I would love to make a career out of this."

Frank Capra couldn't have written a better script. Martin had just enough genuine "gosh, gee-whiz" in him to make every mother in America want to adopt him, and he had the kind of quiet courage that misted the most hardened men's eyes. To top it off, he finished his week by saying, "A huge weight had been lifted. All the stuff about the court and me playing in a cart, it kind of weighs on you emotionally. Just to win is an amazing relief. I'm kind of saddened, though. I need a cart, but I would do anything to be able to walk down the fairway."

It was impossible not to like Martin, and even harder to pull against him in his battle to play the tour, especially after Finchem's response to Martin's win. Before the new Lakeland Classic champion had a chance to hoist the trophy, a faxed statement from Finchem was circulated around the clubhouse. "We congratulate Casey Martin on his win, just as we do the victor in all our events," Finchem said. "The fact remains that Mr. Martin participated and won while using a golf cart under the terms of a court order. We continue to assert that everyone who plays on the PGA Tour or Nike tour should be subject to the same rules and reg-ulations and that, further, the PGA Tour should retain the right to determine the conditions of competition, including requiring all PGA Tour and Nike tour players to walk."

The only thing missing was Jimmy Stewart calling Finchem "a warped, frustrated old man." This was a drama the PGA Tour did not need.

Three weeks before the trial was to begin, Martin told reporters he would have to declare bankruptcy if he lost to keep from having to pay the tour over $1 million in legal expenses. Nothing, it seemed, was going Finchem's way when it came to this case. Editorialists across the country lined up against the tour, headed by the *New York Times,* which said, "An exception for Casey Martin will not hurt the sport. It will make the PGA Tour look wise and compassionate. It will add diversity and interest to a game that doesn't need to be any more dull or homogenous."

That was the tamest opinion. Steve Hummer of the *Atlanta Constitution* used his column to rhetorically ask, "What exactly would Martin's inclusion change about the fundamental make-up of professional golf, other than the stereotype that it is manned by constipated country-clubbers who can't comb their hair until getting an official ruling?" And Larry Guest, the controversial columnist for the *Orlando Sentinel,* opined, "Rolling out all the heavy artillery, such as anti-cart legend Arnold Palmer and a team of high-priced lawyers, to thwart young Martin, couldn't be more unpopular to the masses than if Finchem ordered all the songbirds at tournaments shot down as nuisances."

For two excruciating months Finchem and the tour endured an unending barrage of criticism. Even Fred Couples's emotional victory at the Bob Hope Chrysler Classic, after his father, Tom, had passed away on Thanksgiving Day, couldn't deflect from the Martin story. It was all-consuming, and it was just the kind of foul ball Finchem didn't want to hit. All the hard work he had put into building the tour's goodwill was being nuked before his eyes, and there seemed to be no end to the devastation. As former USGA executive director Frank Hannigan aptly put it, "Six months ago the PGA Tour was everybody's favorite sports organization. Now it's the Manson family."

When the case finally came to trial in Eugene, Oregon, in February, every media outlet from Court TV to the BBC covered it. The testimony was gripping. Doctors from the Mayo Clinic said that of the 900 worldwide patients they had seen with Klippel-Trenaunay-Weber syndrome, only a handful had as much bone deterioration as Martin. It was a marvel of nature . . . a miracle of God! . . . that Casey was able to walk at all, much less compete in a professional athletic contest. By the second week of testimony, the tour realized it was losing not only the battle of public opinion but the legal battle as well. "This isn't about Casey Martin," tour lawyer William Maledon insisted. "Anyone who focuses on Mr. Martin is wrong. Altering the rule for one competitor, for any reason, fundamentally alters the nature of the game."

Judge Thomas Coffin wasn't buying. In his ruling the 52-year-old magistrate said, "I've heard evidence from some of the witnesses—I think Mr. Palmer was one—that this would be the end of PGA Tour golf as it is known. That's clearly not the case. Granting a cart to Mr. Martin does not mean, in any way, shape, or form, that anyone else out there has some right to ride a cart. Any perception that he has an unfair advantage by riding a cart, as I've said, is simply wrong."

Casey won! For all the tour's prognostications of doom, the judge decided that professional golf would survive unscathed if Casey Martin rode in a golf cart until the day came when he stepped on a root or slipped in a bunker and lost his leg. The tour filed an appeal (much to the chagrin of many of its own members who thought the whole thing had gone way too far) and, as if he hadn't flogged himself enough, Finchem vowed to continue the fight in the appellate courts.

Tom Lehman, always a voice of simplistic reason, said, "I think the PGA Tour made a big mistake. I've told them from the beginning that they were in for a public-relations butt-whipping. The best they could do was negotiate with Casey and try to settle this out of court by saying something like, 'We make our own rules, but we will give you a cart.'"

That became the prevailing opinion. The tour hadn't said Martin's requests were reasonable and deserved consideration. They said he was jeopardizing an integral part of the game. They hadn't said Casey's courage in the face of this debilitating disease was commendable, and, even though the tour still made the rules, a special exception could be made for such an outstanding young man. They said riding would end the PGA Tour as we knew it. The organization that had become the most powerful force in golf, that prided itself on its "smoothness," and that was headed by a man with more political experience than anyone in the game, had succumbed to bombast. And Tim Finchem had just stepped on his first land mine.

By the time anyone started paying attention to tournaments again, David Duval had gone from a nonwinner with seven runner-ups and a questionable ability to finish to the hottest property in professional golf with four wins in eight starts (including the final three of the 1997 season). He still wore that scraggly goatee, however, and his long sideburns and sunglasses made him look more like a surfer or a snowboarder (both of which Duval was) than the tour's leading money winner. Finchem would consider saying something to him about his facial grooming, a subtle suggestion, maybe something like, "Hey David, need to borrow a razor?" or "David, you'd be a handsome guy if you'd shave that stubble off your face." The PGA Tour wasn't the NFL, where headbands, armbands, sweat towels, shirttails, and shoes were all regulated and monitored by the league with fines levied regularly for players who appeared out of uniform. Still, the tour had an image, one that had been built and groomed over the years. Finchem's job was to ensure that that image remained untarnished, and players like Payne Stewart never let him forget it. Stewart was a vocal critic of some of the younger players who, in Payne's view, didn't understand the importance of presenting themselves in a top-shelf manner. It seemed funny that a man who wore plaid knickers and brass-toed shoes would vent his concerns about other players' attire to Finchem, but that was Payne. Finchem, recognizing that Stewart and the others had a valid point, would smoothly and subtly "recommend" that a player tuck in a shirt or shave. Fortunately no one had worn a cap backwards or sideways, and "do rags" hadn't yet become in vogue with golfers. Finchem did have to deal with sandals and cargo pants these days, however, but that was just one of the changes in golf the commissioner was trying to balance.

Fortunately, after Duval shaved and the Martin verdict died down, Finchem's tour nestled into a routine, doing no harm and making few waves. Mickelson had won. That was always a plus. Nobody understood the value of image better than Phil Mickelson. Predictably humble and gracious in victory, just as he was in defeat, Phil always said the right things and thanked the right people. It was part of his nature. Even when he was a kid winning American Junior Golf Association events, Mickelson never missed a chance to thank the host clubs, the tournament volunteers, the sponsors, and most of all his parents for providing him with the opportunity to play golf. He would often tell the sponsors of junior golf stories of how his mom had taken on a second job so that Phil could play tournament golf in the summers. And every time he gave that speech the senior members of the crowd would say, "Wow, what a great kid that Mickelson is." Now that great kid was the owner of 13 PGA Tour titles, and rather than his parents, it was his wife, Amy, whom Phil never forgot to thank after a tournament win. Usually the effervescent Amy Mickelson was by her hubby's side, clapping for him, hugging him, and flashing a broad, ever-present smile that was as genuine as it was bright and toothy. Despite those who thought she couldn't be real, Amy Mickelson was just as perky away from the cameras as she was on the 18th green. She had been a Phoenix Suns cheerleader, and now she was Phil Mickelson's pompom brigade, a role she clearly loved. They were a solid couple, the kind of happily married romantics that were far too rare among the rich and famous. He was a solid, grounded player, and she was the most positive and supportive spouse imaginable. Together they were exactly the kind of image Finchem loved for the tour: young, attractive, gracious, polite, and always smiling. The PGA Tour would have been well served by cloning a dozen or so Phil and Amy Mickelsons.

Tiger only won once in 1998, at the BellSouth Classic in Atlanta, but he had lost in a playoff in L.A., and had the best record in the majors of anyone who didn't win on the PGA Tour. Despite struggling at times, Tiger remained the number-one player in the world on the world rankings, and he never fell out of the top 10 on the money list. It wasn't what people expected, but golf wasn't a win-every-week kind of sport. Tiger was fine. He had said he was working on some things with his coach, Butch Harmon, and when he perfected the swing adjustments he was making, he would win again and he would continue to be a huge drawing card. The pseudo-slump also appeared to be good for Tiger. He matured during the trials of 1998, waving more and scowling less, engaging more fans than in the early days of Tigermania while swearing less and slamming fewer golf clubs into the turf. He had not only grown more patient with his golf game, he had become more patient and tolerant of the ancillary aspects of his fame and celebrity. He didn't blow off reporters anymore (even when they needed it); he didn't make excuses; and he didn't take himself too seriously. At the Tour Championship in October, Tiger wore a towering Afro wig to the range on Halloween. He looked like an early '70s version of Sly Stone. Even the fans didn't know what to make of it, especially when Tiger snuck up behind a kid in the gallery and said, "Boo!" It was self-deprecating and, in hindsight, uproariously funny. It proved that despite all the hoopla he had endured

Tiger had grown up and regained his sense of humor. He was comfortable again, and when Tiger got comfortable, the rest of the golf world needed to watch out.

Ernie Els won at Bay Hill and Justin Leonard won the Players Championship, coming from five shots back in the final round to win by two over Lehman and Glen Day. In the spring it looked as though 1998 would live up to its billing as the year of the under-30 crowd. Then something unexpected happened. In one of the biggest surprises of the '90s, Mark O'Meara became the first player since Arnold Palmer in 1960 to birdie the last two holes at Augusta National to win the Masters. It was O'Meara's first professional major championship, and it caught everyone, especially David Duval, who was waiting in the Butler Cabin after finishing with a final-round 67 to tie for the lead at eight-under-par, by surprise. Duval watched on television as O'Meara stroked his 20-foot birdie putt on the 18th into the hole to win by one. "Never, ever had I felt like that at the end of a golf tournament," Duval said. "Right then I understood what the majors are all about. Really and truly understood for the first time."

So did O'Meara, who had been close on many occasions but never on top at a major.

The world had changed quite a bit in the seven months since O'Meara stood on the fringe of the 17th green at Valderrama and watched as Tiger's putt trickled off the front of the green and into the water. An intern scandal had erupted at the White House, Saddam Hussein had thumbed his nose at the United Nations, Kentucky had won its seventh NCAA basketball title, and the Windemere Blue Jays, coached by Mark O'Meara and starring 8-year-old Shaun O'Meara, were in the midst of an eight-game winning streak. Since returning from Spain, O'Meara had finished the season with a respectable showing at the 1997 Tour Championship before returning home to Orlando, where he celebrated Christmas with Alicia, Shaun, and his 11-year-old daughter Michelle. He also celebrated his 41st birthday in January while playing in what the tour called its "West Coast swing."

O'Meara was unofficially known as the "King of the West Coast swing," primarily because 8 of his 14 career victories had come in California and Hawaii. Although he didn't card any wins in the 1998 swing, O'Meara once again showed signs of brilliance, shooting a final-round 64 at La Costa Resort in California to tie Tiger for second in the

Mercedes Championships. O'Meara then shot five rounds in the '60s en route to a sixth-place finish at the Bob Hope Desert Classic. A good start . . . typical O'Meara . . . but nothing that would have indicated what was to come in the rest of 1998.

Sunday night after O'Meara's Masters victory, editors at *Sports Illustrated* gathered in the Time Warner building on Avenue of the Americas in New York and debated over the cover shot for their post-Masters issue. Prior to his win the battle cry at *SI* had been "anybody but O'Meara." After all, O'Meara was a balding 41-year-old with very little sex appeal for the magazine's Gen-X demographic. Many argued his win was an anomaly, a one-time aberration, an unrepeatable event unworthy of cover-photo coverage from the sports magazine of record. In fact, the entire 1998 Masters had been one big old-fart anomaly. Gay Brewer, 66, shot an opening-round 72, two better than O'Meara on Thursday. Gary Player, 62, became the oldest man in Masters history to make the cut, and 58-year-old Jack Nicklaus made a charge on the weekend, closing with rounds of 70 and 68 to finish tied for sixth with David Toms, ahead of Tiger, Leonard, Mickelson, Love, and Colin Montgomerie. Then O'Meara, in a cap and brown shirt that accentuated his paunch, drained a 20-footer for birdie to win on the last hole. It had to be an anomaly.

Even O'Meara seemed self-effacing in the wake of his victory. "I'm not a great player. I consider myself a good player . . . a nice player," he said in typical O'Meara-speak. *Oh, gee, don't talk about me as if I'm something great. I'd rather be underestimated.* His true feelings came through a week after his Masters victory, however, when at the MCI Heritage Classic O'Meara sought out Alan Shipnuck, the unsuspecting 24-year-old beat writer for *Sports Illustrated. SI* had chosen Pedro Martinez, the spectacular hurler for the Boston Red Sox, for the cover of its issue, relegating O'Meara and the Masters to a two-page spread in the middle of the magazine.

Shipnuck, who had nothing to do with the decision, met the real Mark O'Meara on Hilton Head. "Hey, bud," O'Meara said after tracking Shipnuck down. It was his typical greeting whether meeting friend or total stranger. "What do you have to do to get on the cover of your magazine?" He didn't wait for an answer. "I know I'm not as photogenic as some others, but Pedro Martinez? Is Pedro going to be any less amazing next week than he is this week?"

Shipnuck tried to explain the decision, but O'Meara dismissed him before he could finish. The point was made. O'Meara had revealed more of himself than he might have wanted. He walked away from that encounter as a man on a mission. If nothing else he would prove to the bozos at *Sports Illustrated* that he was more than a one-shot wonder.

Hilton Head turned out to be a bad week for Shipnuck. After the O'Meara episode, Shipnuck asked 41-year-old Payne Stewart, who shot an opening 69 at Harbour Town, "So, Payne, at forty-one, do you think your career has peaked?" Stewart's ears turned a deep crimson and his jaw twitched. "No," he finally spat, his gaze burning through Shipnuck. "I don't think that at all."

Stewart proved that point to Shipnuck and everyone else by coming within one putt of winning the U.S. Open Championship at Olympic Club in San Francisco. Then O'Meara made 1998 the Year of the Old Guys by winning the British Open and finishing fourth in the PGA Championship, coming closer than anyone in three decades had to winning three major championships in a year. O'Meara also won the Cisco World Match Play championship at Wentworth in London, defeating Tiger Woods with another dramatic final-hole putt.

In the Tour Championship at East Lake Golf Club in Atlanta, 40-year-old Hal Sutton made it one more for the old guys by beating Vijay Singh in a playoff, capping off a year full of surprises with one of the best comeback stories in golf. Sutton had fallen so far from his "Prince Hal" days that he was embarrassed to practice next to other tour players. "I couldn't have hit the ball much worse," he said. Then, after 10 years of bouncing between instructors, struggling to analyze a game that had been completely natural for most of his young life, Sutton went back to his old college coach, Floyd Horgan, in late 1996. In two years, Horgan had gotten Sutton back on his game.

"Hal had a very natural golf swing," Horgan said. "He was ahead of his time. The way he uses his body is the way golf has evolved, but he had gotten away from that. Instead of rotating his arms in a natural rotation he was taking the club back very shut [golf lingo for a closed clubface, an often devastating swing flaw]. From there, he was fighting going left. You can't play at the PGA Tour level when you're worried about going left."

Sutton had found that out, falling as low as 185th on the money list and having to use his one-time-only special exemption as an all-time top-50 money winner to keep his card. "You get a little complacent when you're not paying attention to what you should be, and then you do things that cause you to lose your confidence," he said of that time. "All of a sudden you start searching. It could happen to anybody. I told myself if I didn't play my way back on [tour] I would go do something else." With Horgan's help and the support of his wife, Ashley, Sutton did make it back on tour, and with his win at the tour championship he moved one step closer to another of his goals: another shot at the Ryder Cup.

Shortly after he returned to his Ponte Vedra office after the Tour Championship, Finchem's phone started ringing. One after another, players called asking the same question: whom should they vote for as 1998 Player of the Year? The choice was between O'Meara, who had won two majors and a match-play; and Duval, who had won four times in 1998, three times in a row at the end of 1997, and was number one in scoring and money for the year. "I told everyone that both were deserving," Finchem said in a feeble attempt at fence-straddling. "The decision wasn't mine to make."

Jim Furyk had one opinion. "If you win two major championships, you're player of the year, period," he said. Others thought four wins, a scoring and a money title deserved a nod. The intangible—the one thing no one would speculate on—was what impact O'Meara's Ryder Cup statements had on the vote. The answer should have been none, but human nature always seeped into elections, no matter how objective they might be. Players remembered what O'Meara had said about being paid to play for your country, and even after he was given several opportunities to amend his remarks at the British Open and again at the World Match Play Championships in London, O'Meara had stuck to his guns, saying, "I know I can't win this debate over here, but, look, I'm a professional golfer who makes his living playing golf. When I play, I feel I should be compensated. There are a lot of people making a lot of money on the Ryder Cup, and we're not a part of that. Do you think the PGA of America would send my kids to college if I were injured next year? This is my job."

In the closest vote in a decade, O'Meara won Player of the Year honors for 1998.

Just when it appeared as though Finchem would escape the remainder of 1998 without further incident, the tour's God and country event—the Presidents Cup, an even-year biannual event designed as a countermeasure to the Ryder Cup and featuring an "international" team of players who didn't call Europe or the United States home—turned into a glorified silly-season event with the Americans simply going through the motions. In 105-degree temperatures in Melbourne, Australia, and surrounded by swarms of gigantic horseflies, a band of professionals from Africa, South America, Japan, Fiji, Australia, and New Zealand handed a heavily favored U.S. team a defeat so lopsided it made Valderrama look close.

The problems were relatively simple: the Presidents Cup was held at an awful time (December 11–13, when most Americans were engrossed in holiday shopping and NFL playoffs), it was in an odd time zone for Americans, and, even though there were a few truly international players like Shigeki Maruyama and Naomichi Ozaki from Japan, most of the international team members lived in America and played the U.S. tour. Greg Norman's children had never lived outside South Florida, while Nick Price, Vijay Singh, and Ernie Els called the Sunshine State home. Australian Steve Elkington had been a resident of Houston for over a decade. Elkington even sounded more Texan than Australian, occasionally letting an "Ooo wee" slip out after a good shot by one of his fellow international teammates. "The problem with the Presidents Cup," Lanny Wadkins said, "is that you have a bunch of Americans flying halfway around the world to play a bunch of guys who live in Orlando."

Interest at home was weak as well. CBS chose not to send its primary golf anchor, Jim Nantz, to cover the event since the network planned to tape-delay the telecast, but even that plan backfired. On Saturday, the network interrupted its taped broadcast for 20 minutes to show the impeachment hearings of President Clinton, a cruel twist of ironic fate for an event named the Presidents Cup.

The only thing that could have made the matches interesting was an upset victory by the international team, which is exactly what happened. The internationals were led, not by Norman and Price, but by Craig Parry and Maruyama, whose English vocabulary consisted of "good shot" and "thank you very much." As partners Maruyama and Parry defeated Lee Janzen and Scott Hoch, and Tiger Woods and Fred Couples. Between them, Maruyama and Parry accounted for 6 of the 11½ points the international team accumulated in their commanding win. The final tally was 11½ points for the international team and 5½ for the U.S. As Elkington would have no doubt said had he been back home in Houston, the internationals showed 'em where the bobcat went in the bushes.

"It had an eerie feel, sort of like Spain," Davis Love said.

Duval had no memories of Spain, but he understood the significance of the defeat. "Next September the pressure will be on us again," he said. "We don't have either Cup now, Ryder or Presidents. Thank goodness the women won the Solheim Cup [the LPGA's version of the Ryder Cup, named after Ping founder Karsten Solheim and won by the Americans in 1998]. This is different than playing Europe, though," Duval continued. "Vijay Singh is my neighbor. Nick Price? How can you not be happy for him?"

That sort of "ho-hum, we lost" approach didn't bode well for the future of the Presidents Cup, and Finchem knew it. At least he had one thing going for him: Deane Beman had been insightful enough in the first Presidents Cup in 1992 to set aside $100,000 in each player's name to be donated to the charity of his choice, a tradition that continued through 1998. It was a disaster on almost every other front, but at least in the Presidents Cup there were no ugly controversies over money.

*Seven*

# GETTING IT

DAVID DUVAL SEEMED HAPPY as he drove east on Interstate 20 listening to his favorite Atlanta radio station and passing the lonely pulpwood pines of Washington and Thomson, Georgia. "Happy" was a relative term, of course, and Duval masked his feelings better than most people in general and much better than most professional athletes, but those who knew him best could see that the 27-year-old's satisfaction level was at an all-time high. As evidence they would point to the slight upturn around the edges of Duval's mouth or his dry wit. He could still deliver a joke with the same monotone intonation he used when ordering a Whopper at the Burger King drive-through. Same old David. There wasn't much more to it than that. Outside the confines of his small circle of friends, Duval had never been accused of being demonstrative.

He would never openly tell you how pleased he was with life, and you would never get a whoop or a "Yee Ha" from him, even after he did something as historic and spectacular as shooting a final round 59 to win the 1999 Bob Hope Chrysler Classic. On that Sunday afternoon in the desert Duval had come from seven shots back with what one observer described as "a pretty easy 59." It was, as ABC's Mike Tirico said in a voice at its histrionic highest, "the best final-round . . . ever!" And yet Duval's celebration after this magnificent feat consisted of a high-five with his caddie and a couple of overhand fist pumps—no screams, no emotional collapses, no spontaneous échappés, nothing approaching the emotional upper cuts Tiger Woods routinely emoted after non-59-producing birdies, and nowhere close to the cap-pitching celebrations Arnold Palmer put on in his heyday. That simply wasn't David Duval. When asked what he was thinking as he walked up the 18th fairway knowing he had a putt to shoot 59, Duval said, "My caddie and I were wondering how they got that car out in the lake." Chrysler had displayed its newest LeBaron on a platform in the middle of the pond fronting the 18th green, and, of course, that was the topic of conversation as Duval strolled headlong into the history books. Anything else would have been out of character.

So as he drove east, over the bridge at Lake Oconee and past the last Waffle House diner between Greensboro and Augusta, Duval didn't think about destiny or his place in history. He didn't suddenly transform into a gregarious extrovert, nor did he have an enlightened epiphany that turned him into an expert on everything from weather to politics to the meaning of life. He was the same person he had been the day before, the week before, and even back in the days when he drove this same stretch of highway in a dinged-up Honda Prelude with Styrofoam cups on the floorboard and a cold pizza in the seat beside him. The fact that he was now the hottest golfer in the world, and perhaps the hottest in the history of the game, hadn't changed him as a person, and he certainly wasn't going to change his makeup to satisfy the curiosities of an insatiable public. "You can't be something you're not," he would say to anyone who asked. Duval was what he was: a shy, talented, blunt, eclectic, and often egocentric golfer, period.

He just happened to be the best golfer in the world at that moment with 11 wins in his last 34 starts, including two in a row and four in 1999 before the first of April. He had overtaken Tiger for the number-one spot in the world rankings, and he was the odds-on favorite to win the Masters, which was one of the reasons his friends believed he was happy. He hadn't won a major yet, and as the first glimpses of the old Augusta cotton mills came into view, Duval thought this could be his week.

He had led the Masters by three shots in 1998, then made two bogeys in the final three holes while Mark O'Meara birdied the last two holes to win. One minute Duval had been sure of at least a playoff, and the next he was accepting a handshake and a half-hearted congratulations from Augusta National chairman Jack Stephens. "We'll look forward to seeing you again next year," the Arkansan billionaire had said to the stunned Duval. He still remembered how it had churned his stomach to lose that way. He remembered like it was yesterday.

Duval had been on a streak back then, having broken out of the second-place doldrums with three wins in a row at the end of 1997 and adding another victory in the early months of 1998 before the Masters. That didn't compare with the blistering rampage he was on in 1999, however. He had won the Mercedes the first week out, then took nine days off for a little snowboarding in Sun Valley, Idaho, before returning to the desert for his historic 59. As nonchalantly as if he had finished even-par and in 14th place, Duval drove to the Palm Springs airport, boarded his Learjet (one of the luxuries he afforded himself after becoming a mid-20s millionaire), and flew to Phoenix, where he shot an opening-round 74 and failed to contend. But the casual observer would never have known from his demeanor whether Duval was shooting 59 or 79. There were no tantrums or scowls when he hit bad shots, and no revelry when he hit good ones. He simply did his job. "The golf course is my office," he would say, and he did not engage in small talk nor succumb to emotional fluctuations while at his office. He was a professional. If you were bold enough to politely ask for an autograph at the proper time, he would quietly and promptly accommodate you. If you asked a question at the appropriate time, you were bound to get an answer. But attempt to interrupt him in the middle of a round and you would be brushed aside like an empty paper cup. Duval might have been a youngster on tour, but he was also a man who had no time for the superfluous and who did not suffer fools. On the course he was a golfing machine, a detached cyborg complete with Terminator shades and the expressionless face of an Andrew Wyeth portrait.

But off the course, his friends knew a different side of Duval, an open side where gin games and political discussions ran long into the night, and where childlike giddiness would envelop him as he anticipated the newest Elmore Leonard novel. Books, animals, and fine wines were his off-course passions, and he freely indulged all three. Stray cats that showed up on his doorstep were fed, as were foxes that found their way onto his deck in Sun Valley. Many times he connected with the animals he met faster than the people who entered and exited his life. But then, dogs, cats, and foxes never had ulterior motives.

"David wants people around who are true and honest to him, not people who kiss his butt because he's the best golfer in the world," said Tom Weber, an old friend. "The superficial relationships he's just not interested in. David hasn't changed one bit. Some of the people around him may have changed, but David hasn't."

Most of Duval's friends were old friends, friends from childhood and from his hometown of Jacksonville. He didn't make many friends at college, nor did he appear to want to. "David was not at Georgia Tech to fit in, or make friends, or have a good time, or even to get a degree," Puggy Blackmon, Duval's college coach, said. "He was there honing his golf skills trying to be the best golfer in the world. He was never truly into the team concept."

Duval alienated many of his college teammates before he even arrived by insisting that his picture be on the cover of the media guide his freshman year, even though Georgia Tech had a number of good players, including senior Charlie Rymer, who felt equally if not more deserving of the coverage. Duval also insulted his peers, once saying to a member of the squad after a loss, "If I had any teammates worth a shit we would have won this damn golf tournament." More than once, several members of the Georgia Tech golf team wanted to slug him.

"Most of the gray hairs I have are from coaching David," Blackmon said. "I would like to have more David Duvals, but I would like to have them one at a time. I don't think I could handle five of them, or three, or even two of them. I always said when David got here he was twenty-five [years old] golf-wise and fifteen socially."

It wasn't as though Duval had been a sheltered child prodigy who had been indulged every whim. He was an average kid from a middle-class family whose father happened to be the club pro at Timuquana in Jacksonville. The people in north Florida knew him, especially the Timuquanan members he beat regularly, but up until his junior year of high school, nobody outside gator country had ever heard of David Duval. When an American Junior Golf Association event was held at his home club the summer of his junior year, Duval qualified and won. It was his first national exposure, and it caught Blackmon's attention.

"Nobody knew much about David's playing skills," Blackmon said. "But I knew his dad. We had both been club pros in Jacksonville and we had played a lot of golf together. I knew Bobby Duval was a great player, and I thought if his kid had half the talent Bobby had, he could be a super player. It wasn't until the summer after his senior year, after he had already signed with us, that he had a great year and everybody knew about him."

That year included winning the U.S. Junior Amateur and three AJGA events, including the prestigious Rolex Tournament of Champions. Suddenly everybody knew about David Duval, but nobody really knew him. After he arrived on campus in Atlanta, and even after he departed four years later, Blackmon likened him to an alien, an extraterrestrial to whom everything about planet Earth and the human interaction therein was totally foreign. "David is like ET," Blackmon said. "He always said exactly what he felt, and sometimes, when he was in a bad mood, it came out bad. But David has a good spot in the middle, and as he has grown to trust more people that spot has gotten bigger."

Blackmon was a devout Christian who had been a club pro and one of the original staff members at the American Junior Golf Association before taking the coaching job at Tech. Kids were his life. He had always enjoyed the junior clinics and youth programs he ran when he was a golf pro, and he had loved watching AJGA kids like Davis Love and Billy Andrade grow up and mature into first-class citizens. Georgia Tech provided the same opportunity for him, and he had adapted well, becoming a good coach and an even better mentor. But when Duval arrived, Blackmon was faced with one of the biggest challenges of his life. As a golfer, David Duval was an exceptional talent, becoming the third man in history behind Gary Hallberg (Wake Forest) and Phil Mickelson (Arizona State) to be named First-Team All-American in each of his four collegiate years, but Duval was a social misfit, a man who would swear at perfect strangers and who felt no need to bond with the rest of his teammates, or anyone else for that matter.

"He seemed distant, constantly distracted," Duval's psychology professor, Terry Maple, said. "Once I assigned a paper to him on sports psychology, hoping that would bring him out and spark some interest. It didn't. He did the work, and he was a bright student, but he just never seemed interested in anything or anyone."

During one of his mild playing slumps, Blackmon demoted Duval to the number-two spot on the team behind Tom Shaw. Duval responded by shouting, "You've gotta be fucking kidding me!" Shaw's feelings, and even his performance, were irrelevant to Duval, and he didn't give a shit what the rest of his teammates thought. Duval knew he was the best player, not just on the Georgia Tech golf team but perhaps the best in the country. Blackmon knew he had a potential disaster on his hands.

But Puggy Blackmon was an indefatigable optimist, and Duval soon became his life-reclamation project. Gail Blackmon would cook, and the three Blackmon children would play; Puggy would do what he always did when he was home, only now he had an extra child, an older child for whom he cared like a brother. David Duval would wrestle with the children in the family room and play catch outside in the Blackmons' backyard. And he would laugh, not a snide laugh or an arrogant laugh, but a warm, good-natured, family laugh. Away from home, Blackmon would ride with Duval, often renting two cars instead of one on team trips, and the two would room together. The rest of the team just shook their heads. They couldn't grow any more resentful of Duval. At least Coach was keeping him out of their hair.

"A lot of people perceived him as Darth Vader," Blackmon said. "You just couldn't penetrate David's little bubble, but he is one of the most sincere people I've ever met. He doesn't allow a lot of people into his circle, and you have to earn his trust and respect, but when he gets around people he enjoys, he is very social."

Even after he became the hottest golfer on the planet, Duval continued to be a befuddling dichotomy, springing back and forth between acts of genuine kindness and raunchy arrogance. When he wished to silently voice his displeasure he had no problem thrusting his middle finger skyward no matter who was standing nearby, but he pulled his endorsement commitment to a cigar company after the company broke a pledge not to print the ads in magazines or newspapers read by children. When he learned that the Jacksonville chapter of Toys-for-Tots was about to lose the lease on their warehouse, he picked up the phone and anonymously paid the organization's rent, but then he refused to sign a visor for the mother of a 14-year-old fan, even though he was in the process of signing a stack of publicity photos when the request was made. "Sorry," he said. "That's just the way it is." This was the same man who spent an entire day with Jesse Peetz, a 13-year-old with a blood disease Duval had met through the Make-a-Wish Foundation. They hit balls for two hours together, putted for another 45 minutes, hung out in the locker room, and chatted about golf over lunch, a day the Make-a-Wish coordinator called "way above and beyond" what had been expected. His acts of kindness and graciousness were rarely as public as his afternoon with Jesse Peetz, however. For example, after being given backstage passes to an R.E.M. concert, Duval was the only celebrity visitor who personally contacted the band's management to offer his thanks. When he learned that a lady who worked for him had adopted a houseful of abused children, Duval emptied his closet, giving clothing and shoes to the children. Several months later, he couldn't wait to show Blackmon the stack of thank-you letters he had received from those kids. Then, at almost the next moment, he chided a photographer for taking his picture, his voice filled with contempt as he said, "What the hell was so important about that shot?"

Duval's relationship with the media had been particularly tempestuous. Naturally private and normally suspicious, his worst fears were realized during the NCAA tournament in his senior year at Tech. A reporter from the *Louisville Courier-Journal* had contacted Blackmon and requested access in order to write what Blackmon said "was supposed to be a positive piece on David." Six years later, Blackmon still seethed when remembering the incident. "You don't get a lot of big-time stories written about college golfers," he said. "This guy did a hatchet job on David. It was the most irresponsible piece of journalism I've ever seen."

The reporter focused on three incidents, all, according to Blackmon, taken out of context. "David was playing with Chris Couch," Blackmon said. "On the first hole, Couch walked up and put his bag down in front of David, so David asked him to pick it up. Later, on a hole where no one was around, David had to go to the bathroom, so he jogged across the fairway out into some trees where he took a whiz. Then on the next tee there were some bananas and apples out there and David peeled the skin off an apple with his teeth and spit it out on the side of the tee. Well, when the article came out the reporter made it sound like David had ripped into the guys he was playing with for moving in his line, that he had urinated on the fairway, and gotten angry after missing a putt and littered the golf course with chunks of an apple. I was livid.

"To make matters worse, a paper in Florida picked up the story and ran it, and suddenly this was national news. Homer Rice [Georgia Tech's athletic director] started getting calls and letters from alumni wanting to know what was going on. It really hurt David, big time. I don't think he'll ever completely get over it."

Duval continued to carry the article as a constant reminder to keep his guard up, but since making it on the PGA Tour he had developed some decent working relationships with the media. Tim Rosaforte with *Golf World* had done a couple of good features and gained a good rapport with Duval and his inner circle of friends. John Feinstein had also gotten him to open up, specifically about Duval's experiences in the 1998 majors, but also about his past and the one incident from his childhood that seemed to have everyone in the golf world mesmerized.

It occurred when Duval was 9 years old, barely into Little League baseball and in love with everything his older brother, Brent, did. Brent was the outgoing sibling in the Duval family, the one who took after his extroverted father, and who, at age 12, showed a great deal of potential in golf. But during his 12th year Brent became pale and weak, and when Bobby and Diane took their oldest son to a hematologist, the news was devastating. Brent had aplastic anemia, and his only chance of survival (a 50-50 chance at best) was a bone marrow transplant from one of his siblings. Brent's sister Deirdra was not a match. David's marrow was 90 percent perfect. He would undergo the marrow donation, an excruciatingly painful procedure David still remembered vividly. "The pain was unbelievable," he had said. "I think most of the scars are gone."

At first it appeared as though the transplant worked, but soon after the procedure, Brent developed graft-versus-host disease. A bacterial infection set in, and Brent died from internal organ damage. A distraught 9-year-old David thought he had killed his brother, and the imagery of Brent, pale and still, beneath a plastic bubble and violated by a seemingly endless array of plastic tubes connected to pitiless machines, haunted David.

David's mother, Diane, sank into depression, continuing to speak of Brent as if he were alive and becoming overprotective of her other two children. Diane also battled with alcohol abuse after the loss of her son, a problem David would later help her overcome. Bobby left the home a year after Brent's death. Although there would be many attempts at reconciliation, Bobby and Diane eventually divorced.

Now, after becoming the number-one golfer in the world, everyone seemed obsessed with every detail of Brent's death, his parents' divorce, and every other private detail in David Duval's life, and he simply didn't get it. "Why does anybody care?" Duval asked Blackmon in one of their many and frequent conversations. "I'm not a story. I'm no different now than I was three years ago, or four years ago, but it's like since I've won some golf tournaments I'm suddenly supposed to be an authority on everything."

Duval told friends he was uncomfortable with all the amateur psychoanalysis being bantered about, especially in regard to how his brother's death might or might not have shaped his personality. But while the obsession with his past continued to befuddle him, his only real concern was the truth. "Coach," he would tell Blackmon, "I don't care what they write about me as long as it's accurate."

Tiger's coach, Butch Harmon, was one of the first to utter the ultimate comparison when discussing Duval. "Whether you like him or not, he doesn't care," Harmon said of Duval. "He is what he is. That was Ben Hogan to a T."

There it was: the ultimate golf comparison! And coming from the coach and teacher of his chief rival! It was enough to send an audible gasp and a palpable pause throughout the golf community. This was golf's holy grail, the game's ultimate icon, and now someone as authoritative as Harmon, whose father had won the Masters and who was considered one of the finest swing coaches in the world, was putting Duval on the same pedestal. In golf, Jack Nicklaus certainly held the most impressive records, and Arnold Palmer was the most popular player in history, but there had been plenty of "Next Nicklauses" and "Next Palmers" throughout the years. Johnny Miller had been the "Next Nicklaus" before Tom Watson became the "Next Nicklaus," all of whom preceded Hal Sutton as the "Next Nicklaus." Even Gary Nicklaus, Jack's third son, was labeled as the "Next Nicklaus" when he was only 16 years old. Seve had been "Europe's Arnold Palmer," and the new British Amateur champion, Sergio Garcia, was being touted as "Palmeresque." But there was only one name in golf spoken in hushed tones, with reverential respect, and the kind of saintly deference reserved for icons. It was true regardless of the art form. There were plenty of "Monets" and "Picassos," but there was only one Rembrandt. In golf, every decade produced a Watson-, or a Miller-, or a Seve-wannabe. But there was only one Hogan. That name stood above all others, and in golf, a comparison to Hogan was the ultimate canonization.

"When David gets ready to play the game of golf he goes into a world not a whole lot different from the one Ben Hogan went into," Blackmon said. "If you remember the Hogan stories of how he would not remember speaking to [his wife] Valerie on the golf course, that's the way David is during a round. He's in his own world. And when he comes off the golf course it takes him a while to come down from that focus. Until he comes out of it, he generally isn't very social."

Ben Hogan's legend extended to more than just his golf simply because of his singular, obsessive devotion to golf. He was a mythological figure who actually lived and breathed and played some of the best golf anyone had ever seen. He was a man Jack Nicklaus would watch practice, a man who once said he "tried to hit the ball on the third groove." And we all believed him! But there was a reason for the veneration. The Hogan Mystique, as it was called, came about because of the man's work ethic, his devotion to craft, and his mercurial nature on and off the course. Verbal history had it that "Hogan hit balls till his hands bled," an image of martyrdom and devotion that, whether true or not, elevated Hogan to the stratosphere of his profession.

Hogan was also supposed to have played entire rounds of golf without uttering a word to his playing partners. He would become so focused that even his wife became an unrecognizable blur, a distraction to be blocked out. Hogan was a tactician, a driven competitor, and a tough man who had no time for diversions and who did not tolerate irrelevant and foolish interruptions.

"I feel sorry for the rich kids now," Hogan had said. "They're never going to have the opportunity I had because I knew tough things. I had a tough day all my life and I can handle tough things. They can't. Every day I progressed was a joy to me and I recognized it. I don't think I could have done what I've done if I hadn't had the tough days to begin with."

David Duval said, "I'm a firm believer that if you need motivation from outside sources, you're not going to go very far. You have to have inner motivation, and I understand that I have to improve and get better to keep up with all the different players. But I don't rely on that. I count on myself for that. I've learned what it takes to get where I want to go."

Hogan was the Ice Man, his hard expression never changing while in the midst of his task.

Duval was the Terminator, his eyes hidden behind dark Oakley sunglasses, his expression solemn throughout a round. "I've probably lost my cool," he said. "But to be successful out here you have to find the personality under which you best perform. For me that's not worrying about stuff."

Hogan had no patience for the inane. He once grew weary of a press conference and quipped to the assembled scribes, "Someday a deaf-mute is going to win a golf tournament, and then what are you going to write?" And when he was asked a question he didn't particularly like, he told the reporter, "That's the stupidest question I've ever heard." Yet Dan Jenkins, a sportswriter from Hogan's hometown of Fort Worth, was one of his best friends.

Duval invited Tim Rosaforte to go snowboarding, and the golfer opened his home and his life up to Gary Smith of *Sports Illustrated,* but when he was asked about a report that he hadn't spoken to his pro-am partners at the Mercedes Championships until the 16th hole, Duval sternly said, "I don't know what you're talking about."

The Hogans jealously protected their privacy. Valerie Hogan once said, "They [the press] wanted to know when he blinked. We couldn't have that. For goodness' sakes, he's not the president."

According to Duval's girlfriend, Julie McArthur, "David treasures his privacy and his time and he's lost a lot of that. It's something he's going to have to get used to. Since he shot 59, people want to speak to him no matter what."

In 1955, Valerie Hogan told *Sports Illustrated,* "I think that sometimes Ben has suffered from being such a perfectionist. In everything he does, he works so hard. I think the price he's had to pay by being a perfectionist is that he's missed out on companionship and friends." She would ask him, "Weren't there many nights when you would rather have been out with the boys going to a football game or the movies?" He simply answered, "No."

"David Duval sets goals and is his own person," Blackmon said. "He is not driven by rankings or the press or his entourage. He's also a very private person. If David had a choice between going to a cocktail party where the most important people in the world were in attendance or going home and reading a book, he'd be home reading the book. He's a brilliant kid, and he's got it a lot more together than a lot of guys out there."

Even Duval himself added credence to the comparisons when he said, "I'm not comparing myself to Nicklaus or Watson or Hogan, but all those players in the past believed that the way they were playing was the way to play. I believe the way I'm playing is the way to play."

Neither Hogan nor Duval were master conversationalists, each speaking as if he were allotted a word budget and would suffer horrible consequences if he went over his daily syllabic allotment. A question would be answered honestly but in as few words as possible. Each man also had friends who would swear he was the nicest person who ever walked the face of the earth, a perfect gentleman who was simply misunderstood, and each had detractors who would snarl while calling him a complete ass.

What Duval and Hogan shared most, however, was a deep-seated love of the game, and the solitary peace found in the hours of repetition and the perfectly logical cause-and-effect that was golf's practice tee. Duval had been 9 years old when Brent had died. Shortly afterward he started taking golf seriously, often playing in thick Florida morning fog when he himself was barely visible, and spotting the flight of a golf ball was virtually impossible. While many of his schoolmates hung out at the club pool and enjoyed the hormonal enlightenment of their teenage years, Duval practiced golf, forgoing serious female relationships and normal high-school social interactions in lieu of the solitude and self-control of the game.

When Ben Hogan was 6 years old he witnessed his father, whom many speculated suffered from manic depression, shoot himself in the bedroom of the family's Fort Worth home. According to the *Fort Worth Record* account of the incident on Valentine's Day, 1922, "No one was in the room with Hogan at the time, excepting his six-year-old son [Benny] who was playing on the floor. His wife and two other children were in an adjoining room when they heard the shot and, rushing in, found Hogan on the floor with a smoking revolver by his side." Not long afterward, Hogan began caddying, and, years later, he spent long, solitary hours practicing and mastering his craft, escaping into his own world and caring little about the opinions of others.

As Duval entered the old cotton town of Augusta, Georgia, for what would be the focus of the golf universe for the next seven days, he knew that there were two glaring differences between Ben Hogan and David Duval. In the first 12 weeks of 1999, Duval had earned $2,598,300—more than any golfer in history for a single season, and more than Hogan had earned in his entire career despite being the tour's leading money winner five times. But Hogan had nine major championships to his credit, had four Player of the Year titles, had five Vardon Trophies for low scoring average, and had never lost a match in the Ryder Cup. Duval had one Vardon Trophy and one money title, but no major wins and no Ryder Cup appearances. He still had a long way to go.

"David just wants to be David," Blackmon said. "He wants to be honest and upfront with people and he wants people to be honest with him. You always know where you stand with him, but he can't help wondering why you care about his personal life or why you think it's any of your business. He's not out there trying to create an image. That doesn't concern him a whole lot."

Nor was he trying to create a rivalry with the man he supplanted as the number-one golfer in the world, Tiger Woods. But Duval didn't have to create a rivalry where none existed: there were plenty of others willing to do that for him. Tiger had rocketed to the number-one spot in the world rankings in 1997 with a blitz similar to the one Duval was now experiencing, but the two of them had never gone head-to-head in the final round of a tournament, much less a major, so any notion of a rivalry was pure speculation. They hadn't even been paired together, for God's sake! How could anyone say there was a "rivalry"?

They could and did because golf needed rivalries, and as nice as guys like Andrew Magee and Jeff Maggert were, they didn't make for the kind of compelling drama golf needed to sustain momentum and support the every-round-every-week television coverage the PGA Tour was getting in 1999. Duval and Tiger were perfect drawing cards— young, strong, hard charging, and slightly irreverent. Tiger was an emotional wonder, his eyes sparkling and his million-dollar smile lighting up the cameras when he played well, and his stern gaze and temperamental outbursts taking viewers aback when shots didn't go his way. Duval was a dispassionate Generation-Xer, but also a throwback to the Hogan era and to Hogan himself. Together Tiger and Duval were the perfect one-two punch the tour needed. Forget that neither player considered it a rivalry. The media wanted it to exist, therefore it would exist.

The only problem was, when either Tiger or Duval was in contention the other was not. Nicklaus and Palmer had become rivals because of their head-to-head battles in major championships. The same was true of Nicklaus-Miller in the early '70s, and Nicklaus-Watson in the late '70s and early '80s. But Nicklaus was now 60 years old and hobbling with a cane after hip replacement surgery, and Tom Watson was about to turn 50 and was preparing to make his debut on the golf-cart-riding Senior tour. Golf had been left to languish with such matchups as Mark Calcavecchia versus Sandy Lyle, and Bob Tway versus Paul Azinger—nice to watch if you were an ardent golfer, but less than compelling when it came to attracting new fans to the professional game. Then Tiger came along with his prodigious length and "second place sucks" attitude and everything changed. When he destroyed the field at Augusta National for his fourth win in seven months and his first major championship, many wondered if anyone could challenge him for the top spot in professional golf. When Duval started winning in clusters in late 1997, everyone assumed the battle was joined.

But the battle, so far, had been from a distance. When Tiger won the BellSouth Classic in 1998, Duval finished tied for 14th, and the week Tiger won at Torrey Pines in 1999 Duval was carving some rad sick powder (as the snowboarders would say) on the slopes of Sun Valley. When Duval won the Mercedes, Tiger tied for fifth, and when the former shot 59, the latter was taking the week off. And so it went. Duval won the Players Championship, while Tiger finished tied for 10th. Tiger lost a playoff in L.A., where Duval finished tied for fifth, and when Duval won in Atlanta, Tiger was tuning up his putting stroke at Augusta National. Now here they were: rivals, heavyweights, *mano a mano* contenders who had never so much as smelled each other on championship Sunday. It was contrived and silly, and both Duval and Tiger knew it.

"Certainly I'd embrace it if that came to pass," Duval said. "But I think it's hard to say that we have a rivalry right now. You know, you certainly don't want to leave out an Ernie Els or Phil Mickelson or Davis or Justin. I think the big reason you can't put that rivalry label on us yet is because he and I haven't come down to the last nine holes of a major event. Until that comes to pass, it's hard to make it a comparison to Nicklaus/Palmer or Nicklaus/Watson–type rivalry."

Publicly, Duval said that being number one on the world rankings didn't mean anything to him, but privately he would bristle when people mentioned Tiger's name ahead of his own, even though Duval openly admitted that "I'm not like Tiger in the sense that Tiger is a star outside the game." He didn't believe there was a rivalry, but Duval knew whom it was he needed to continue to beat. "Tiger raised the standard out here," he said.

Tiger also publicly dismissed the whole rivalry notion, saying, "It is very difficult to get a situation where there are two guys who are far and away better than anybody else. There are so many good young players out here on the PGA Tour. I don't see how you can say David Duval and I are the two best, because anybody who plays out here knows he can win any given week. It's cyclical. Everybody's going to have his runs. I think both David and I understand what we want is to win a lot of major championships, like Mark [O'Meara did last year]. David won four times, but what would you rather have, four wins or two majors?"

Others thought Tiger was just as motivated by Duval's ascension as Duval was pushed by Tiger. Butch Harmon, the man who likened Duval to Ben Hogan, said, "Do I think Duval playing so well the last eighteen months pumps Tiger up? You bet I do. You know he's not publicly going to say that, but you know it's the case."

Duval knew that golf was not a one-on-one competition. "This is a game where failure is the norm," Duval said, and he knew that if he focused on Tiger and not on the task in front of him, that he would lose what he had worked so hard to build. He knew he had to remain within himself—true to himself and to what he was—and he had to put the thoughts of rivalries and the endless media probes behind him if he were to reach his personal nirvana. They could call him Ben Hogan all they wanted, but if he never won the big ones, the comparisons would be fleeting and futile. They could compare him to Howard Roark, his favorite literary character from Ayn Rand's 1943 novel *The Fountainhead,* but most had no idea what Roark stood for, or what the concept of Objectivism was all about. They knew nothing of the goals the Objectivist ascribed for himself. As Roark had described it, "If you want to know what it is, listen to the first phrases of Tchaikovsky's First Concerto, or the last phrases of Rachmaninoff's Second. Men have not found the words for it, nor the deed, nor the thought, but they have found the music. Let me see it made real. Let me see the answer to the promise of that music. Not servants nor those served; not altars and immolations; but the final, the fulfilled, innocent of pain. Don't help me or serve me, but let me see it once, because I need it. Don't work for my happiness; show me yours, show me that it is possible; show me your achievement; and the knowledge will give me courage for mine."

Neither Duval nor Tiger won the Masters, although Duval made a series of charges throughout the week that were ultimately thwarted by too many double-bogeys and even one triple-bogey at the par-five 15th on Friday. "This place makes you look foolish at times," Duval said. "It certainly made me look foolish at 15." He went on to make a critical double-bogey at the par-four 11th on Sunday that dropped him from contention. He would have to wait to know that thing of which men had not found words. There would be more chances—certainly Pinehurst, site of the U.S. Open, suited his game, and Carnoustie for the Open Championship would be a good test, as would the newly lengthened Medinah in Chicago at the PGA Championship—but until then Duval could only watch others, in this case José María Olazábal, who won the Masters by two shots over Davis Love. His day would come. As long as he pushed away the distractions and remained true to his purpose, he knew his day would come.

Somewhere outside the green gates at Augusta National in one of the many ranch-style homes that bordered the property, a stereo was playing. It was not the first phrases of Tchaikovsky's First Concerto, or the last phrases of Rachmaninoff's Second, but until such time as Duval arrived in North Carolina, it would have to do.

Little could David Duval have known that he not only would not win a major in 1999, he wouldn't win another event the rest of the year. And how unfathomable it would have seemed at that moment if someone had told Duval that his four-win performance wouldn't even garner Player of the Year honors, and that he would miss winning the money title by almost $3 million. "You gotta be fucking kidding me!" he would no doubt have said. For even the most faithful Objectivist—even Alan Greenspan, who studied beside the great Ayn Rand and who (it was rumored) had a crush on the advocate of egoism—even he had to base his beliefs on what was reasonable, not on what was possible. Alien invasions were possible. Stock market crashes were possible. David Duval losing the 1999 money title was possible, but not probable, not even reasonable. He had won over $2.5 million in the first three months of the year! Who was going to top that?

Tiger's maturation continued through the Masters and on into May. He had gone to Augusta a week early where he enjoyed being less than the center of attention and where he could continue the slow steady progress he had been making in his game for the past 18 months. It had been after his historic 1997 Masters win that Tiger and Butch Harmon started tinkering. Tiger had seen videos of his swing during that week, and he was shocked. "It was a perfect timing week," he had said, implying that the golf swing that won the Masters by 12 shots was flawed and needed fixing. "I couldn't believe what I saw. I knew I had to make some changes." Specifically Woods felt he needed to shallow his swing plane in order to develop a more consistent path through impact. This change wouldn't make him any longer, but as one of the longest hitters in golf Woods didn't need added length. It would, however, improve his misses, cutting down on shot dispersion and providing more distance control with his irons. Woods also began physical conditioning, lifting weights, stretching, and working on cardiovascular conditioning to increase muscle mass and stamina without hindering his flexibility and feel. He added 15 pounds of muscle in the 18 months from the middle of 1997 through the first week of 1999, and his conditioning improved tremendously over the same period.

At Augusta he was close. After enjoying the Champions' Dinner with the other winners, where O'Meara served sushi and chicken fajitas and said, "Hey, Bud, if I had one last meal that would be it," Tiger shot even par rounds on Thursday and Friday, followed by a 70 on Saturday and a 75 on Sunday. He finished tied for 18th with Bill Glasson, Scott McCarron, Brandel Chamblee, and Justin Leonard—not what he had hoped for, but every week he was getting better, inching closer and closer to a swing he knew would be his ticket for the long haul.

He certainly could have continued to win with the old swing, perhaps even winning again at Augusta in 1998 and 1999, but that would have been shortsighted, and Tiger's career plan wasn't one year, or two years, and or even three years out. To accomplish the goals he had established for himself would take decades. He needed a golf swing that would hold up for a lifetime of playing against the best.

Financially he was set. His agents had asked for and gotten an obscene amount of money from Nike, American Express, Wheaties, and Titleist, and he didn't need to worry about money. Tiger had promised his half-sister that, in return for doing his laundry when he was at Stanford, he would buy her a house when he became a famous professional golfer, and, even though his sister would have never held him to it, Tiger had followed through on that promise, buying her a home in the San Francisco area. He had also bought his mother a $750,000 home in Tustan Ranch, a gated community in Orange County, and he owned two lots at Isleworth where he would build his own lakeside chateau in due time. He had a fractional ownership in a jet, but his portfolio remained liquid enough that he never had to worry about being strapped for cash. The tour money title was important to him only in the sense that it was the barometer of how you fared against the rest of the players on tour. Tiger would have worked just as hard if they had been playing for $100 a week instead of $3 million. He wanted to be the best. He had goals to reach, things to prove; records to set, and even more records to break.

Tiger's goals weren't a secret. By the time he left Augusta in 1999 every jot and tittle in his life had been microscopically examined. There had been books, articles, parodies; he even had a Showtime Original Movie made about his life. But the goals had always been there, and they remained the same no matter how high his celebrity star rose.

They were old and yellowed by 1999, but in concept they were still there, taped above the single bed in the small bedroom across the little hallway from the kitchen in the modest middle-class tract house on a corner lot in Anaheim. The living room would have perhaps been a more appropriate place for them, but those walls, particularly the long windowless wall on the right that separated the living area from the garage, were covered with framed newspaper clippings, plaques, photos, and magazine covers. The tables were also covered. There was crystal everywhere with trophies in so many corners of the room a visitor might feel uncomfortable walking around for fear of breaking something. Everything was still clean, in a precise, military sort of way, and the room in the back, one of two bedrooms in the house, was well kept, almost preserved. That was where the goals remained. Jack Nicklaus's records, from his 18 professional majors to his tournament-record-setting scores, had been taped to the wall, not as a poster, but as a "To do." This was where Tiger had lain in bed at night and dreamed of the day when he would be the number-one player in the world, the man whose footsteps golfers heard and whose presence on the leaderboard they feared. And the goals he had set for himself as a golfer were simple: eclipse Nicklaus as the best golfer in the history of the game. That was it in a nutshell.

Tiger had come a long way in developing one of the components needed to reach his goals in that he was more patient, more mature, and more at peace with himself than he had ever been. The struggles to work through his swing changes and to become more comfortable in his celebrity continued, and he still vented occasionally, letting his temper flare after a poorly hit shot, but those episodes were less frequent than ever. He was a successful, professional man, and he had learned to behave as such.

Having a girlfriend helped. Joanna Jagoda, a beautiful and brilliant student who had accompanied him to several events, and who seemed quite at ease amid the hoopla that was Tiger Woods, had been in Tiger's life for a year, and, while his development as a golfer and an adult were certainly attributable to a lot of factors, Jagoda's presence did nothing but enhance Tiger's maturity. Now all he had to do was complete the work on his golf swing.

It happened on the back of the driving range at Isleworth, a spot where Tiger, O'Meara, John Cook, and Payne Stewart regularly practiced when they were home. It was May, and the next stop was the GTE Byron Nelson Classic. Tiger was hitting balls, working on various shots, hitting low draws and high fades, and controlling the spin and the trajectory of each shot the way he wanted when it dawned on him that the changes had finally taken. No longer did he have to worry about reverting to his old habits. The hours of tedious effort had paid off. Tiger's game had finally come around.

He propped his club against his golf bag and took out his cell phone. Harmon's number in Las Vegas was programmed into the speed dial.

"Hello," Harmon said.

"I've got it," Tiger said without preamble.

It was all he needed to say. Like his earlier understated proclamation, "Second place sucks," this was a groundbreaking declarative statement—simple, yet powerful in its implications. Golf was not a game anyone truly "got." You had moments when everything fell into place and the swing seemed so effortless and natural you wondered how you could have missed it, but those were always followed by times when you felt like an eight-armed spastic who had no idea which arms should hold the club. You didn't "get" golf; golf got you. But this was Tiger Woods, the man who had changed the old rules. When Tiger said, "I've got it," he meant it in a way most golfers could never understand.

Harmon understood. As he put away his cell phone, Tiger's coach knew that David Duval's time on top was about to come to an end. When Tiger got it, Harmon knew, nobody could stop him.

The next week Tiger traveled to the St. Leon Rot in Heidelberg, Germany, where he (along with O'Meara, Ernie Els, Nick Price, Colin Montgomerie, and Jesper Parnevik) played in the woefully overtitled

Deutsche Bank–SAP Open TPC of Europe. After "getting it" only a week before, Woods shot 69–68 to take a two-shot lead into the weekend. After Saturday, his lead was three, and as he strolled down the 18th fairway on Sunday en route to a bogey-free 68 and his second win of the year (although, because it was a European tour event, the PGA Tour didn't count it), Tiger knew he was on his way to a good year. "I'm playing much better than I did in 1997," he said after the win. "My swing is better than it ever has been. The only thing I can say about 1997 is that I made more putts from 30 to 40 feet. I wasn't as good a ball-striker as I am now. I couldn't control my trajectory as well, either."

Tiger didn't repeat the words he had uttered to Harmon the week before, but he didn't have to. Those who saw him in Germany knew they were in trouble. Tiger had gotten it, and there was nothing any of them could do but watch.

From the time he arrived in Germany after getting it, Tiger became virtually unstoppable. In his last 11 events of 1999, Tiger's record looked like this:

| | |
|---|---|
| Deutsche Bank TPC of Europe | win |
| Memorial Tournament | win |
| U.S. Open | tie for third |
| Western Open | win |
| British Open | tie for seventh |
| PGA Championship | win |
| Sprint International | tie for 37th |
| WGC-NEC Invitational | win |
| Disney World Classic | win |
| Tour Championship | win |
| WGC American Express | win |

When Jack Nicklaus won 10 out of 33 events in the 1972 and 1973 seasons it was considered a milestone. Not since Byron Nelson won 11 tournaments in a row in 1945, when most of the tour was either still away at war or just returning home from military service, had anyone manufactured such sustained dominance. Then Duval came along and won 11 of 33 from his first win in 1997 through his BellSouth victory in Atlanta the week before the Masters, a streak Fred Couples said was "so good it's almost goofy." But no one spoke of those streaks anymore, even though Duval's was less than six months old! Now there was another streak, and suddenly Nelson's 11 consecutive wins didn't seem so out of reach.

If a college football team went 8–4, they would be bound for a major New Year's Day bowl and a high national ranking. For a golfer to go 8–4 against fields that included the likes of Duval, Love, Mickelson, Els, Leonard, Montgomerie, Price, Westwood, and teenage Spanish sensation Sergio Garcia was unfathomable. It defied all logic and reason.

To his dismay, Duval fell back into second place in the world rankings, and his early-season streak that had prompted players to ask him when he planned on taking a few weeks off was all but forgotten.

Duval wasn't forgotten, however, and in August he made news again, not for winning a golf tournament but for being, as Blackmon put it, "honest and upfront." In an interview with *Golf Digest,* Duval was asked about the Ryder Cup and why the always heavily favored Americans continued losing. Duval, as he always did, said exactly what was on his mind without exceeding his daily word budget.

"To say we win because we're the best players is silly," he said. "That's not fair to the other teams. The Europeans we play at the Ryder Cup are great players. Same with the internationals in the Presidents Cup.

"But I don't spend a lot of time thinking about it, because I haven't figured out why we make such a big deal about it. The Ryder Cup is an exhibition. The whole thing has become a little overcooked, but it's probably going to stay that way until players choose not to play.

"We are professionals, and if the figures are correct, they're supposedly going to gross anywhere from $20 million to $30 million. Where's it all going? At least at the Presidents Cup last December they sent $2.9 million toward charity. Not a lot, but something. Now we can sit here and argue all day about whether players should be paid for a Ryder Cup, but that's really not the point. Speaking for myself, that's not the solution. That's not what I'm after."

Duval didn't stop there. He went on to suggest that there would come a time, perhaps in the not-too-distant future, when players would simply say "No thanks" to the PGA of America when the Ryder Cup rolled around.

"If you have twelve players on a Ryder Cup saying, 'We need to talk,' what are the alternatives? Does the PGA of America go to the next twelve guys on the list and ask them to play?" Duval asked. "Without the players they're not going to have a Ryder Cup, but all the other people who go to the Ryder Cup to work or whatever, aren't they still drawing their salaries for the week? Mark O'Meara got blasted for bringing up the compensation issue during the last Ryder Cup, and he was absolutely right. Meanwhile, the people criticizing him were paid that week. They aren't donating their services to the cause. Why don't they work for free, too? Better yet, let's take some of that big Ryder Cup pot and cut it up and give it away to charity. That's supposed to be what we're all about, isn't it?

"Something has to happen here, and the best solution will be if it's done and nobody knows about it. We do our talking privately, and it all gets done quietly."

Unfortunately for David, that was not to be. The drama of what would become known as the "Pay for Play" scandal would be played out on a world stage for everyone to see and hear, and, even though Duval had clearly stated that he wanted no money for himself and that charity "was what we're all about," his comments about the Ryder Cup being "an exhibition" were like a spit in the eye of golf fans. He hadn't said anything Tiger wasn't saying, and it was Phil Mickelson who had first suggested that the PGA of America donate a chunk of the proceeds to charity in each player's name, but Tiger and Phil would not be vilified. If anything, Tiger had been even more blunt in his observations, saying, "It's completely unfair the way it is now. I played in 1997 and didn't enjoy it at all. It's like pros on parade. They take us to a bunch of functions that raise money, yet everybody is compensated but us." Still, it was David Duval, the man behind the dark shades and expressionless face, who would bear the brunt of the public's outrage. And, just as that tattered and yellowed 6-year-old feature from the *Louisville Courier-Journal* had changed David's approach to the media, the "Pay for Play" eruption would forever tarnish his perceptions of life in the public eye. He wasn't a warm and cuddly personality, and that made him an easy target. When the criticisms started flying, it was David Duval, the man who had said the least, who wound up getting it worst of all.

# Eight

## PAY FOR PLAY

IT WASN'T THE MONEY that upset the younger players as much as the hypocrisy. When Duval made his comments he thought the PGA of America would gross "anywhere from $20 million to $30 million" on the 1999 Ryder Cup. Given the financial history of past matches, that was a pretty good guess. In 1995 at Oak Hill in Rochester, New York, the PGA of America grossed $28 million. Profits weren't disclosed, but everyone, including the players, thought it couldn't have been that expensive to run a three-day golf tournament with no purse. But profit wasn't the point. What drew the ire of the players was the fact that while the PGA of America milked its cash cow, organization CEO Jim Awtrey was saying things like, "The Ryder Cup Matches have a long and illustrious history dating back to 1927, and they have always been played solely for pride in country and possession of the Ryder Cup. That tradition remains far more important than direct financial gain."

Awtrey stood by that statement, even when reports started leaking out that the 1999 matches in Brookline would make all previous Ryder Cups look like nickel sideshows at a county fair. "I'm not going to apologize for running a successful organization," Awtrey said defiantly. No one was asking him to apologize. A simple explanation and input into the process would have mollified everyone. Then when the numbers for 1999 became public, the issue was elevated to an entirely new level.

On July 30, *Golf World* magazine broke the news that the PGA of America would gross a staggering $63 million from the 1999 Ryder Cup. Television would be responsible for $13 million of that, with corporate tents and tables accounting for $32 million. Merchandizing, ticket sales, and the food and beverage and program advertising would account for the remaining $18 million, making the Ryder Cup the most lucrative event in golf by a wide margin. The magazine also reported that the PGA of America was expected to net $23.5 million—a huge sum, but one that left many wondering how on earth you could spend $40 million running a one-week golf tournament when building a pretty nice course from the ground up rarely cost more than $10 to $15 million.

The players were astounded. Who did the PGA of America think they were dealing with, a bunch of mental midgets? They were professional athletes, sure, but they were also independent businessmen, entrepreneurs, self-promoting, merit driven, individual marketing machines. Did anyone seriously think that because they were jocks they couldn't count? It didn't take long for every player between 1 and 15 on the Ryder Cup points list to run the numbers. No matter what the outcome the Ryder Cup was still only 28 matches played over three days, which meant the PGA of America was going to gross $2.25 million per match. The whole thing was mind-boggling.

The PGA of America had even attempted to run an illegal lottery for Ryder Cup tickets. In June 1998, as it began taking ticket applications for the Ryder Cup, the PGA of America tried to capitalize on the event's popularity by charging what officials called "an application fee." The tickets would still be issued by lottery, just as Augusta National did for the Masters practice rounds, but unlike Augusta or any other organization, the PGA of America wanted a five-dollar "application fee" to accompany all requests. According to PGA officials the fee was designed to "defray the costs of mailing, telemarketing, credit card processing, and administrative expenses."

Those costs were covered in the first week as officials at the PGA of America acknowledged receiving more than 30,000 applications (netting over $150,000 in nonrefundable fees) from all 50 states and 12 different countries in the first seven days of the lottery. Extrapolating these numbers through the August 31 deadline, the PGA of America could have netted as much as $1.8 million in application fees with no guarantees for tickets.

That nifty little profit center caught the attention of investigators in the economic crimes division of the Florida Attorney General's Office. Les Garringer, head of the economic crimes division for the state, wasn't expecting the call he got on a Friday afternoon in June from a reporter investigating the PGA of America's ticket policy. "I'm not a lawyer, but I think this is an illegal lottery," the reporter said after explaining the processing fee to Garringer.

"Let's see," Garringer said as he opened his statute book. "According to Florida law there are three elements that make up a lottery: a chance, a prize, and a consideration, or money put at risk. This appears to fit all three. I don't know how you could distinguish this from any other lottery. It's something we'll definitely look into."

Three days later the PGA of America issued a written statement declaring its discontinuance of the "application fee" policy. Within a month, all the five-dollar checks had been refunded.

Once the $63 million revenue number was revealed, the whole "honor and privilege" argument was a little tougher to swallow, especially for some of the younger players who weren't around back when the PGA had to beg networks to televise the matches and everybody lost money on the deal. One player asked aloud, "I wonder how much money they would generate without us?" The player who said that didn't realize it at the time, but his statement typified the degeneration of the Ryder Cup, not because of its financial implication but because of two words the player used: "they" and "us." This wasn't the United States and the Europeans he was referring to as "us" and "they," nor was it the PGA of America and the European PGA Tour who were at odds. This was the PGA of America being referred to as "they" and an American player from the PGA Tour who was calling himself and his peers "us." The growing malignancy between the two sides, both American but each representing disparate interests, had finally metastasized. Before it was over, one side would wrap itself in the flag and accuse the other of being driven solely by money, a charge that, while untrue, left a lingering stench over the whole squalid affair.

Tom Kite had seen it coming for two years. He had warned Jim Awtrey of the impending dissatisfaction building among players who felt the dog-and-pony show had gone a bit too far. Awtrey thanked Kite and put the concerns in a file for discussion at a future meeting at a future date among future officers.

"They knew this was coming for years," Deane Beman, who structured the Presidents Cup charity package before the first match was ever played, said of the PGA of America's predicament. "They had been warned and they could have nipped it in the bud by simply doing what we did with the Presidents Cup."

Phil Mickelson had approached Awtrey after Valderrama with just that sort of request. Mickelson asked why a portion of the Ryder Cup proceeds weren't donated to charities of the players' choosing, just as the

PGA Tour did with the Presidents Cup. Awtrey told Mickelson that it would never happen. The PGA of America, through its "grass-roots programs," gave money to charity and "promoted the good of the game," and "made golf fun." The PGA of America knew best how to spend its money, thank you. That was why they had a board of directors. If the players had any questions they should take them up with their player representative on the board.

Awtrey did not intend to alienate the players, and he was befuddled by the predicament he found himself in after the $60-million number was made public. What he didn't see was the culture clash that had been coming for years, and that simply collided before the Brookline Ryder Cup. This wasn't just about money. It was about respect. It was about having the decency to fly the players' caddies over in the same comfort that PGA of America officers and staffers enjoyed. It was about booting PGA of America corporate hacks out of the players' locker room after the rounds, and it was about asking players for their opinions on charitable disbursements, involving them in decisions, and keeping them in the loop. It was about priorities, and understanding that this was a competition, not a corporate outing with golf thrown in as afternoon entertainment. But most of all it was about control.

The PGA Tour was the ultimate meritocracy. Independent contracted players were compensated based on their performance, and the tour was in place to facilitate events for them to practice their craft. The PGA of America was the ultimate bureaucracy, with 24,000 dues-paying members feeding an ever-expanding corporate beast. Tour players were paid to wear golf shirts. PGA of America golf pros sold golf shirts to 18-handicappers. PGA Tour players earned their way on tour either through a qualifying tournament or through the Nike tour. PGA of America members worked as apprentices, giving lessons, booking tee times, and schmoozing club members. To earn a PGA of America membership you had to go to a series of business schools—weeklong seminar-type sessions where you were taught that cabretta leather (the material of choice for most golf gloves) came from the underbelly of Ethiopian hair sheep. Then you took tests (like the CPA exam, only with different questions) to make sure you fit the PGA of America mold. Tour players didn't get it, and they didn't appreciate being treated like half-baked apprentices who had missed the cabretta-leather question. Some of them had, quite simply, had enough.

David Duval was not the first to cry foul, but because he had never participated in a Ryder Cup, his criticism was met with particular hostility. Many of his fellow teammates, including red-white-and-blue-bleeding Payne Stewart, thought Duval should at least go through the opening ceremonies and experience a match or two before spouting off about what should and should not be changed regarding the Ryder Cup. Most didn't realize that Duval had an insight many of the other players did not. His father, his grandfather, his uncle, and his college coach were all dues-paying PGA of America golf professionals. And, like Larry Nelson, who had also been a sweater-selling club pro before qualifying for the tour, Duval's closest mentors had harsh opinions about their own organization.

"As a PGA of America member, and this is almost universally true, we always have wondered for years where all the money went," Puggy Blackmon said. "I mean, they raise millions ostensibly for junior golf and other programs, and if you look at the work the PGA supposedly does out in the communities, it's the club pros, volunteering their time and resources, who end up doing all the work for free! So where does the money go? We're paying membership fees. We're doing the work for free. Where's it going?"

Blackmon wasn't the only prominent and influential PGA of America member who raised such questions. Al Chandler, a former director of the PGA, said, "The organization has lost its heart and soul. Sixty-three million dollars is a lot of money, yet the prize money at some of our club pro events is less now than it was in 1976. How do you explain that?"

Awtrey didn't, nor did he believe he needed to. "When someone says to me, 'What are you doing with your money?' I say, Look at the bottom line," Awtrey said. "About two percent is what we would call profit: maybe in the $1 million to $2 million range on a $100 million budget. We are driving everything back into programs that grow the game. The faster the game grows in health, the better our members will do in the job market. Today I would hope you would look at us and say the PGA is doing more for the game."

Blackmon believed Awtrey was engaging in what Northern Ireland's Darren Clarke would call "some good ole fashioned blarney." "We're like a bunch of farmers," Blackmon said. "We're out busting our butts, working around the clock at clubs around the country, paying our dues every year, and the PGA of America talks about all the educational opportunities and good-of-the-game programs they've got going on. Well, where are they? Is there anything on a national level you can point to and say, There's a PGA of America program that made a real difference in growing the game? I can't. There's only so much money you can put into The First Tee program [which was a PGA Tour initiative]. David Duval was simply asking where the money was going. He wanted accountability."

So did other non-tour-player members like Chandler, who said with a sense of despair, "I don't know why the officers don't realize the discontent that exists among a large part of the organization. It used to be we were great teachers but didn't know anything about running a business. Now look at what we are. We're a totally business-oriented organization making millions of dollars, but at the same time we've gotten away from what we should be."

Even players who were ardent Ryder Cup supporters thought the players should, at the very least, be in the loop when it came to disbursing the $23 million in profits. Jim Furyk, one of the least controversial and fiercely patriotic competitors in golf, said, "Let us make a donation to the charity of our choice. It's an honor to play for your country, but the flip side is that a lot of guys wonder where all the money is going."

Out loud and in public none of the Ryder Cup qualifiers and no one who was close to qualifying used the word "boycott," but behind closed doors there were a number of players who thought opting out was becoming quite reasonable. "Imagine the outcry if Tiger Woods chose not to play a Ryder Cup, or David Duval," Duval said. "I think it could happen."

To everyone's surprise, the player who started it all, Mark O'Meara, said he had "changed his tune" when it came to the Ryder Cup. O'Meara, sometimes called "The Godfather" on tour because of his intimate friendship with Tiger, had put up with enough criticism in the previous 24 months to continue carrying the torch for Ryder Cup reform. It seemed O'Meara couldn't go abroad without someone saying, "Nice playing, Mark. Now, you didn't really mean what you said about being paid to compete in the Ryder Cup, did you?" He had finally had his fill at Carnoustie, where he ripped into the press, saying, "Why don't you all donate your salaries that week?" To which one of the witty scribes in the back of the room responded, "We don't make $50,000 for covering a corporate outing." Neither argument was well crafted, but by then the debate had deteriorated to quibbling snips and mud slinging. No one was going to win, and O'Meara thought it high time he had a change of heart. "I'm not going to boycott," he firmly stated.

No one was going to boycott, not because of any noble leanings or any sense of duty or honor to God and country. They were far beyond that. No one would boycott because none of them would do anything to hurt Ben Crenshaw. The Ryder Cup meant too much to Ben and Ben meant too much to all of them for anyone to walk away. The "honor and privilege" of playing in the now-lucrative Ryder Cup might have lost its luster, but the honor and privilege of playing for Captain Ben Crenshaw certainly had not.

He was from Lone Star–loving, Hook-'em-Horns Austin, Texas, and his name was Ben Daniel Crenshaw—Ben, not Benjamin, just like another noted Texas golfer, William Ben Hogan. But home state, golf, and the same three-letter name were where the similarities between Crenshaw and Hogan stopped. If Hogan was the Ice Man on a word budget, Crenshaw was the Good Humor Man, a kind soul who earned the nickname Gentle Ben and who was considered one of the world's greatest ramblers. He might talk for 20 to 30 minutes without ever completing a thought or even a sentence, but somehow he still captivated the listener. It wasn't so much what Gentle Ben said, but the warm, rich way in which he said it that drew people to him. He was a feel-good presence, with an emotional radiance that made everyone around him feel good. Crenshaw was a man who, at age 47, still saw pictures in the clouds. He coached kickball for his 7-year-old daughter's team, and loved speaking at St. Andrews parochial school where the students (including his daughters) didn't mind his ramblings. No matter where he spoke or to whom he was speaking, Crenshaw couldn't hide his emotions, nor did he try to. Even watching the *Beauty and the Beast* video with Katherine (12) or Claire (7) brought Gentle Ben to tears. "He's pitiful, just pitiful," Crenshaw's wife, Julie, said of her husband. "When he goes to a movie, he just cries. That's one thing I love about him; he's not afraid to show his emotions. That's one reason the public likes him, because he lets them in."

He had always been that way, even when he was being touted as the next great talent in professional golf in the early '70s. Crenshaw would sheepishly grin at the accolades being heaped on him and choke back tears every time he received an award. He had been the first man in history to win the NCAA title in his freshman year, and when he arrived on tour in 1973, back when Fred Couples was a skinny 14-year-old trying to fit in at O'Dea High School in Seattle and Jean Van de Velde was an 8-year-old kid playing tag with his older brothers, Ben Crenshaw was golf's sex symbol, a long-haired, smiling heartthrob who attracted as many squealing teenyboppers as David Cassidy. If *Tiger Beat* had been looking to put a golfer on its cover in 1973, Crenshaw would have been the hands-down choice.

Whether it was flashing a smile at Ben's Wrens (the contrived nickname given to Crenshaw's teenage female following) or bearing down in a match against his boyhood rival Tom Kite, Crenshaw's feelings were never far from the surface. He played the game on instinct. Ask him to analyze his own golf swing and he would chuckle, look at the ground, kick a little grass, and say, "Well . . . you know . . . golf's a funny thing like that sometimes . . . you know . . . I've played a lot of good golf over the years and I've played some sorry golf, too, and . . . well . . . ha, ha . . . that's just golf." But ask him about the feel of the game, the essence of the game, and he could expound on that for hours. Crenshaw played the way he lived, by feel. When he needed a birdie on the final hole of the 1972 NCAA Championship to share medallist honors with Kite, Crenshaw thought nothing of making a 30-foot putt. It was expected. He could feel it.

He won the first professional event he played, the 1973 San Antonio–Texas Open, where he picked up a whopping $25,000 first-place check and earned praise from tour stalwarts like Lee Trevino, who said, "Oooooh, boy, wait until he understands just how good he is. When he does you couldn't beat him off with a baseball bat. He's got the best setup, the best grip, the best swing I've ever seen. His personality is too good to be true. He's as nice as he seems. If he catches on to just how talented he is the rest of us may be getting food stamps to eat."

When Crenshaw found himself in contention for his first major, the 1983 Masters, he stood over a 60-foot putt on the 10th green not thinking about lagging or worrying about three-putting, but expecting to make it. When he did, Kite, who had been tied for the lead at that point, was stunned, but Crenshaw wasn't. He had felt it. It was expected. Golf was a metaphysical experience for Crenshaw. The mechanics of the game were secondary to the Oneness a player needed to have with the game and with his surroundings.

Crenshaw made you believe in ghosts—not spooky ghosts, but ghosts of golfers past, like Harvey Penick, who had been a mentor for many of golf's best players, including Crenshaw, Kite, Davis Love, and Hal Sutton. Penick had passed away before the 1995 Masters, and the Tuesday before play was to begin, Crenshaw acted as a pallbearer at Penick's funeral. On Sunday, with thousands of people who had never heard of Harvey Penick, and feeling the spirit and presence of the late nonagenarian, Crenshaw made a two-foot bogey putt on the 18th to win his second Masters by a shot over Davis Love. When the putt went in, Crenshaw collapsed, putting his hands over his face and weeping like a child, with his caddie, Carl Jackson, consoling him and congratulating him at the same time. On that day, Ben Crenshaw became golf's mystic champion.

He was also the game's reigning historian, collecting obscure first-edition books on the numbing nuances of golf architecture and the history of the hickory shaft, and tediously studying tournaments and players from past centuries. Crenshaw did more than learn facts about the past. Like all good historians he brought the history of golf to life, propelling himself and those who listened to him back in time. "When I first started in my career, I talked to Ben Crenshaw about the history of architecture," former U.S. Open champion Jerry Pate said. "He taught me a lot about the history of design and gave me a lot of confidence in my [architectural] career."

Labels for Crenshaw included "teacher," "designer," "conciliator," and "ambassador"—all the traits that would normally qualify a player as a great Ryder Cup captain. But this wasn't a normal Ryder Cup, and Crenshaw's appointment had come under fire from the moment he was announced in late 1997. Many critics thought the PGA Tour needed a warrior, a Bobby Knight personality who could fire up the young Americans and intimidate the opposition. Crenshaw was a buy-you-a-beer-and-tell-you-a-story kind of guy. Cracking the whip and slamming his opponents were not part of his style. The integrity of the game was too important to him for something like that.

However, anyone who assumed Crenshaw didn't care about winning didn't understand the man. In 1987 when the U.S. lost the Ryder Cup at Muirfield Village, a frustrated Crenshaw broke his putter in anger during the middle of a match and had to putt with a one-iron the rest of the round. A stunned Captain Jack Nicklaus had turned to Crenshaw and incredulously said, "You broke what?" Tom Kite, a man who played against Crenshaw for over 30 years, said, "He's a tough, tough competitor."

But was he tough enough to lead America to victory in what was shaping up to be the most contentious and controversial Ryder Cup in history? Even he couldn't definitively answer. "Am I tough enough?" Crenshaw said. "That's a fair question. Given my reputation it's understandable. Hopefully, it won't have to be a question of my being too hard or too soft.

"But you can book it; [the Europeans] will be united. More than us? I can't say that. I hope not. But I know in the past, you could almost feel that it meant more to them. They want [the Ryder Cup] terribly. One reason is the flag. The Ryder Cup has become so huge, because of patriotism."

That was what rankled Crenshaw most about the skirmish between the PGA of America and the players. This wasn't supposed to be about money or control; this was about America! They played "The Star-Spangled Banner" and raised the American flag during the opening and closing ceremonies at the Ryder Cup. The National Anthem! Crenshaw cried at baseball games when they played the National Anthem. He would no doubt be a blubbering mess when the band struck Francis Scott Key's opening chords in Boston.

"Boston, Boston, Boston," Crenshaw chanted as if leading a cheer. "That's all our players should be thinking of now. All the other stuff, like talk about money, can wait."

It was his flag, his country, and his game that had led Crenshaw to pour himself into the captaincy like no other captain in history, ignoring his own golf game and, at times, his family, to plan every detail; read every book, every article, every tidbit of history; and immerse himself in a job that paid him nothing and that would likely cause him nothing but grief. He knew the conundrum: if they won, it was because the U.S. players were too talented; if they lost it was the captain's fault.

Crenshaw also knew he was from a different generation from the players he would coach, but they were all from the same country, for goodness' sake. He had been on Ryder Cup teams and played for his country. He knew what it was all about. Crenshaw had been baptized by fire, literally, during his first trip abroad as a member of a U.S. team. He knew what it meant to be under siege. And it was from that first experience, almost three decades ago, that Crenshaw had learned what it meant to represent America.

It had been 27 years since a 20-year-old Ben Crenshaw, fresh off an All-American season with the University of Texas, packed his bags and boarded an airliner bound for South America, representing his country for the first time with three other top amateurs: Vinny Giles, Mark Hayes, and Martin West. Together they were Team USA, headed for Buenos Aires, Argentina, for the World Amateur Team Championship, commonly known as the Eisenhower Cup, an international amateur team stroke-play competition coordinated by the USGA and designed "to promote unity and goodwill" through competition, much like the goals Samuel Ryder had set for the Ryder Cup in the 1920s. It was the first time Crenshaw had been to South America so he was more than a little nervous as he checked his luggage. This was a chance to play the game he loved for the Stars and Stripes, and for Crenshaw there was no greater honor.

It was October 17, 1972, only five short weeks after terrorists stormed the Olympic Village in Munich killing 11 Israeli athletes, and this contingent of U.S. golfers, which included both the men's and women's teams along with a dozen delegates from the USGA, had been in Buenos Aires for just under a week. The women's team, which consisted of Jane Booth, Laura Baugh, and Mary Budke, had played the week before the men and won the Espirito Santo Cup, defeating a strong Canadian and Argentinean team. Mrs. Robert M. Monsted, the non-playing captain of the women's team, had given the players the option of staying an extra day to watch the men, but as much as they wanted to support their friends, a week in South America was enough and the women had voted unanimously to leave.

After getting settled into the Sheraton and playing a morning practice round with his team, Crenshaw congratulated the women in the hotel lobby, gave them all goodbye hugs, then adjourned to the fifth floor for a shower and a little putting practice on the newly installed hotel carpet before dinner.

Up until then the trip had been remarkably uneventful. In three days of practice the 128 players from 38 countries had seen nothing but cloudless 75-degree days. Crenshaw had adapted well to Argentina. The golf course suited his game, the food had been great, and the people were friendly. There were vague rumors of political unrest, but since no one on the U.S. team spoke enough Spanish to hail a cab or order a Coke the Americans hadn't had any substantive conversations on the subject. The only anxious moments had come on the 45-minute bus ride between the Sheraton and the Olivos Golf Club. The roads in Buenos Aires were narrow and winding, which added some unnecessary excitement to the trip. Opening ceremonies were scheduled for October 18, and since the Americans were defending champions USGA president and team captain Ward Foshay had prepped everyone on the pomp and circumstance that was to follow.

Vinny Giles, the only returning player from the 1970 World Amateur team, understood that things were about to get busy, so that afternoon he and his wife Key walked into downtown Buenos Aires for lunch and a leisurely afternoon of shopping. The rest of the team stayed at the hotel, Mark Hayes resting in his room while Crenshaw and Marty West were chatting (or flirting, depending on your definition) with the daughter of a USGA delegate in the hallway. A minute later golf was the last thing on any of their minds.

At 4:13 P.M. on that sunny Monday afternoon the hammer of a cheap alarm clock struck a bell closing a circuit and detonating a neatly wrapped bundle of dynamite hidden in a canvas bag on the 22nd floor of the Sheraton. The explosion shook buildings a mile away, and the top two floors of the hotel disappeared in a plume of smoke while chunks of concrete, wood, and plaster were blown as far as 1,000 feet away.

"It shook everything," Hayes said. "I ran to the window, and there were mattresses, sheets, towels, wallboard, all sorts of debris falling onto the awning and the circular driveway outside."

After a surreal moment of watching drywall falling from above Hayes ran into the hallway, where Crenshaw and West were staring at each other with "What the hell was that?" looks. By that time fire alarms were blaring and flames were visible from the windows. "I thought it was a sonic boom," Crenshaw remembered. "We didn't know anything at that point, but it was chaotic."

"There wasn't mass hysteria because we really didn't know what had happened," West said. "My biggest concern was the roads. They were so narrow and busy I wasn't sure the fire trucks and ambulances could get through to the hotel."

The 23-year-old Hayes had another concern. "We couldn't get out," he said. "Obviously the elevators didn't work, but the doors to the emergency stairways were locked." For a few moments Crenshaw and his teammates didn't know if the lockdown was by accident or design. According to Hayes, "We didn't know what was in store for us."

Nick Weslock from Ontario, a member of the Canadian team, thought he was in the midst of an earthquake. "I was in the shower," Weslock remembered. "I jumped out and saw that my rear window was gone."

Another Canadian, Lois Crozier from West Vancouver, who was in Argentina with her husband Gerard, wasn't as fortunate. Her room on the 21st floor was directly below the blast. The explosion blew a layer of concrete separating the floors into Crozier's room, killing her instantly and critically injuring her husband and Patricia Traka, a friend of the Croziers from Massachusetts.

Bedlam erupted outside the hotel. Giles and his wife had just walked out of the Botticelli Leather Goods store where he had spent $16 for a pair of low-cut tasseled loafers. "We weren't more than four or five blocks away," Giles remembered. "At first we didn't know what it was, but there was smoke and sirens everywhere. It was like the whole world was on fire. My most vivid memory is coming back down the hill toward the hotel and seeing a convoy of military trucks cordoning off the area. Soldiers were piling out and prodding people back. We were already getting reports that at least one person was dead and a dozen or more were injured. With executive committee members and wives we had at least a dozen [Americans] down there in addition to the team."

After several anxious attempts, three of those Americans—Crenshaw, Hayes, and West—finally discovered a fire escape and quickly exited the building. Hayes, an active-duty Specialist Fourth Class in the U.S. Army, who had been given a one-week leave to play in Argentina, immediately recognized the AK-47 assault rifles being brandished by the militia along the sidewalk. The 18-inch bayonets attached to the ends of the barrels didn't require identification.

"There were soldiers and stretchers and all sorts of stuff," Crenshaw said.

Doug Roxburgh, another member of the Canadian team who took an eight-millimeter movie camera to the 22nd floor the day after the bombing and filmed the damage, described the scene as "scary. Essentially the army had control of the country and it didn't take long for armed guards to take over the hotel."

The hotel bombing was only one example of the political tensions in Argentina at the time. In addition to imprisoning political dissenters and journalists like publisher Jacobo Timerman of the newspaper *La Opinión,* the Argentinean government was dealing with triple-digit inflation, Marxist insurrections, and the imminent return of exiled former president Juan Perón. According to Able Dimont, who was the Buenos Aires bureau chief for UPI in the 1970s, "Argentina was in the beginning stages of civil war. Members of the Perónista Revolutionary Vanguard regularly targeted golf courses because golf was considered a symbol of the aristocracy. Other groups like the Marxist ERPs and the Perónista group Montoneros consistently attacked American interests in Buenos Aires because America was seen as a suppressing capitalist interest."

In fact the Sheraton had been bombed before. In July 1971 the hotel was the target of a terrorist attack by the Perónista Revolutionary Vanguard, which issued a statement calling the Sheraton a "monopolist international interest that exploits Argentinean workers."

As if the tensions were not high enough, the World Amateur Council had selected the most inappropriate week imaginable for the championship. "October 17th is Juan Perón Day," Dimont said. "It was the [27th] anniversary of Perón's ascension to power. Perón was preparing to return to Argentina after being exiled in Spain, so his supporters were attacking anything and everything American. The Sheraton bombing was part of an organized terrorist campaign against American targets."

Despite all that the USGA failed to contact the State Department or any other government agency about security in Argentina prior to the trip, and according to the players, security was never discussed. "I don't think any of us had any idea who Juan Perón was," West said. "We certainly didn't go over there with any fear that there would be a problem. I guess it was the naïveté of youth."

Crenshaw agreed. "We didn't know anything about Perónistas. It was certainly out of the blue."

According to State Department officials travel advisories for Americans weren't formalized in the early 1970s. "There have always been services available to assist U.S. citizens traveling abroad," according to Christopher Lamora of the Bureau of Consulate Affairs at the State Department. "But there was no formalized program for travel advisories or warnings until the late 1970s. Before that time advisories were issued on an ad hoc basis." Which meant the USGA or one of the players would have had to contact the State Department about safety in Argentina prior to departing—a phone call no one chose to make.

"The World Amateur Council picked the sites two years in advance," said retired USGA executive director Frank Hannigan, who served on the USGA staff at the time. "Buenos Aires was chosen for the 1972 event in 1970, so there was no way anyone could have known about the Olympic bombing or the other things. P. J. [Boatwright] called afterward and said [the bombing] had nothing to do with the golfers, so that was that."

Once the hotel was evacuated the Argentinean military swept the building and found four more explosive devices that had been set to go off at the same time as the bomb on the 22nd floor. According to police reports, the first blast disrupted the other devices and prevented their detonation. "They wanted to bring down the entire hotel," Weslock said. "If those other devices had gone off none of us would be here."

By 8:00 P.M. the fires had been extinguished, the other bombs had been disarmed, and guests were allowed to return to their rooms. But for the four members of the U.S. squad, tensions didn't subside. "I wanted to go home," Giles said. "Ward Foshay met with us and said the Argentineans assured them the matter was under control. It was something of a political issue with the USGA."

According to Crenshaw, the U.S. team was advised to leave Argentina after the incident. "We got a cable from the State Department afterward saying it was up to us, but that we should probably leave. Obviously we chose to stay."

Throughout the night, combat-ready militiamen patrolled the halls of the Sheraton and machine-gun-armed guards were stationed at every entrance and on every elevator. Tuesday, as the players prepared to depart for the golf course, soldiers searched golf bags and stood guard on the buses. Militiamen also surrounded the perimeter of the Olivos Golf Club during opening ceremonies on Tuesday, October 18th. According to Giles tensions during the official flag raising were palpable. "That's when I was the most scared," Giles said. "Because we were the defending champions they put us on a pedestal during the ceremony. All I could think about was some crazy fool out in the bushes with a machine gun who could mow us down at any minute."

Fortunately for everyone, there were no further incidents, and within a few days things died down. The USGA, while in no way covering up the incident, wasn't eager to acknowledge the fact that a terrorist bombing had taken place during an event designed to promote international harmony. Boatwright made no mention of it in his official account of the tournament for *The Golf Journal,* nor was there any mention in the 1972 *World Amateur Golf Council Record Book.* In fact the first sentence of the USGA's official history of the event reads, "In a world fraught with tension and uneasiness, amateur golf, drawn together in 1958 by the World Amateur Golf Council, is fulfilling its purpose of fostering friendships and sportsmanship among all peoples through the World Amateur Team Championship."

The only oblique reference to any problems came in Boatwright's notes from the 1972 World Golf Council meeting. The notes read, "On motion, the council has decided that all future competitions shall be staged in countries that are free of serious political problems."

While none of the American team members can recall any details of the tournament itself (which the United States won by five shots over Australia), each had vivid recollections of the bombing and the tensions it generated. "Looking back on it now and knowing about the other bombs, we're very lucky to be here," Crenshaw says.

Other than the players, most of the principals involved in the 1972 bombing had passed away by 1999. Perón died in 1976 having never reclaimed the presidency of Argentina. Most historians believed the subsequent military government assassinated as many as 10,000 dissenters in what became known in Argentinean history as the Dirty War. USGA executive director P. J. Boatwright died in 1991, and past USGA president Ward Foshay passed away in 1992.

Vinny Giles was a renowned sports agent, founder of Pros Incorporated, which represented Davis Love, Justin Leonard, and Tom Kite, among others. Mark Hayes was a senior tour player, and Marty West had gotten out of golf and was a broker with Paine Webber. Crenshaw, of course, was the most famous veteran of that, the only terrorist incident ever involving golfers. And it was that experience—that frame of reference, of standing on that podium looking into the eyes of bearded soldiers in camouflage fatigues with AK-47s at the ready, that history of putting it on the line for American golf—that raised Crenshaw's ire when he considered the current crop of professional malcontents. How dare they inject money into the Ryder Cup! Nobody was trying to shoot them. Nobody was trying to blow up their hotel! The world was at peace and American golfers were experiencing riches beyond their wildest expectations, and yet the U.S. team—his team—was rumbling about boycotts over money. It was almost too much for the emotional Crenshaw. He had virtually given up golf, making only two cuts in 1998 and shooting more rounds in the '80s than at any time in his career. Taking this job as captain had cost him many thousands if not millions of dollars, but the Ryder Cup wasn't about money.

When Crenshaw arrived in Chicago for the PGA Championship at Medinah, where he and Awtrey had arranged a "clearing the air" meeting with those who had qualified for the Ryder Cup team on points, he didn't look healthy. His skin was ashen and his face twitched more than it ever had before. He also smoked more than normal. Crenshaw had always smoked, but the blue cloud from the Marlboro Lights seemed to envelop him more fully now, as if sucking more carcinogens into his system would somehow resolve the controversy. The meeting was set for Tuesday. It was hoped the "pay for play" issue could be put to rest before the end of the week.

Davis Love came into the meeting at Medinah's recently renovated Arabic-styled clubhouse ready for a confrontation. Love was the player representative on the PGA of America board and he continued to be a company man. His father had been a PGA of America club professional, and any slap at the institution was a slap at the profession to which his father had devoted his life. There was nothing more rancorous in Love's mind than these players, some of whom had never won a Ryder Cup and one of whom had never played in one, disrupting this storied event. It was Love who set the tone of the meeting, saying to his fellow tour players, "This isn't about charity. This is about putting money in your pockets."

The meeting was testy at times, even though Tim Finchem was in attendance as an arbiter, a politician, and a conciliator who had once been considered a master at "putting hands on troubled waters." But this controversy would test all his skills.

"No matter which side you come down on, we should all be ashamed of ourselves for bringing this up now," Tom Lehman, perched in the 11th spot on the points list and on Crenshaw's short list of picks, said. "This all could have been handled privately, behind closed doors."

The meeting took place behind closed doors, but it wasn't long before details began to leak out. Phil Mickelson asked several pointed questions about the financial decisions the PGA of America had made, including the sale of the organization's two merchandise shows for a reported $120 million and the payment of $6 million to The Country Club. Mickelson's logic was simple. If Sherwood Country Club in Sherman Oaks, California, had paid $1 million to host a made-for-TV event (the Showdown at Sherwood, a made-up rivalry between Woods and Duval), then there must be plenty of golf course owners willing to pay for the Ryder Cup. In fact, the $7 million difference between what Sherwood paid for one 18-hole match and what the PGA paid The Country Club in Brookline was enough money for the PGA of America to build its own golf course! "They've got courses beating down the door to host the Ryder Cup, yet they're giving the club all that money," said Mickelson, a savvy investor who stayed abreast of the stock market and was known for his business acumen. "Who negotiated that deal?"

That was one of many questions Awtrey failed to answer in the one-hour meeting. Afterward, Awtrey and Finchem held a joint press conference intended to put the issue to rest. It didn't. "Basically, where we are is . . . that it is not an issue with the players and the PGA," Awtrey said to the befuddled looks of reporters. "We're going to be working together to look at basically how we can continue to grow the game of golf, support the Ryder Cup, and the players would like to look at how we can involve them in the charitable input. That's basically it. There is no issue between us and the players, and we're going to talk, cooperate, and work together."

When asked whether the PGA would designate a specific dollar amount to charity in each player's name, Awtrey obfuscated and became tongue-tied. "Well, there's details to work out," he said. "What we've agreed to do is sit down and . . . ah . . . work toward making sure that as we go forward with charitable contributions . . . that we seek input from the players. And that's basically what this was about. We didn't sit down and try to decide any immediate answers . . . but an agreement on what our objectives were . . . and that's what we did in the meeting."

Reporters looked at Awtrey as if he had two heads. Then, in an attempt to paint the entire episode as a media-driven nonevent, "No big deal," as he was prone to say, Awtrey said, "I really believe that this issue started this summer with the media, and as a result of all the discussions, we're now talking about it and we're finding that we've all got the same objectives; that the players do not want to be paid, but the players are looking at how the Ryder Cup can be supportive of growth of the game . . . and charities . . . and that's where we are. Players understand where the money is going. That's not something that's hidden. We've talked about that. We've shared with them where the money is going, and what the PGA is all about, and they're supportive of that."

This was news to many of the players who walked away from Tuesday's meeting with absolutely no idea where the Ryder Cup money was going. That wasn't the point, however. The press conference was designed to sooth tensions and put forth a unified front. Awtrey looked pleased as he left the podium.

Twenty-four hours later, all that goodwill and camaraderie fell to the bottom of Lake Kadijah, the man-made body of water surrounding Medinah's championship layout. Ben Crenshaw, pale and a little jumpier than usual, sat before the assembled scribes and, after rambling for several minutes about everything from captain's picks to the relative merits of match play, smiling and throwing in an occasional chuckle, he had a moment of laconic lucidity. When asked about the previous day's meeting, Crenshaw said, "It was a good meeting. The philosophies that were discussed from some people . . . they've agreed to . . . Jim Awtrey has spoken . . . and so has Tim [Finchem] . . . They have to take it down the road." Typical Crenshaw-speak. Everybody smiled and assumed he had actually said something.

Then it happened. Crenshaw's gaze hardened, and his normally jovial mannerisms changed. His smile slipped away and he became still and intense, gripping the base of the microphone before speaking again. "I want to say one thing," he said, leaning closer to the table. "I'm personally disappointed in a couple of people in that meeting. I mean that. They know who they are. And whether some players like it or not, there are some people who came before them who mean a hell of a lot to this game. It burns the hell out of me to listen to some of their viewpoints. The meeting was good because it cleared the air. Those players knew how I stood before I went in there. And that's all I'm going to say about that."

But it wasn't all he would say. Afterward Crenshaw named names, singling out Tiger, Duval, O'Meara, and Mickelson as the players with whom he was "personally disappointed." He went on to condemn Tiger for calling the Ryder Cup an "exhibition," and he showed particular contempt for Duval, saying, with no small measure of incredulity, "He hasn't even played in one yet!"

Players were stunned by the captain's remarks. "I'm sorry he feels that way," O'Meara said. "I thought when we left that meeting everybody was on the same page. I'm disappointed because I thought it was a dead issue." In an attempt at self-defense O'Meara rhetorically asked, "If I'm so unpatriotic, how come I'm the only player who did a clinic for the U.S. troops?" He was referring to a May trip to Ramstead Air Force Base in Germany in May where O'Meara gave an extensive clinic, signed autographs, and mingled with U.S. troops.

O'Meara was penalized in more subtle ways for his role in the insurrection. Although he denied any knowledge or involvement, Jim Awtrey seemed to be the only person who wasn't surprised by Mark O'Meara's tee time in Friday's second round. Just like the USGA, the PGA of America set the pairings and times for the first two rounds of the PGA Championship considering numerous factors, including television coverage, speed of play, and where the players fell in the world rankings. Tiger Woods would not be placed in the final group of the day since the later groups were forced to contend with spiked greens, sun-baked conditions, and slow play; since Tiger was obviously a marquee player whose television presence drove up ratings, he could be assured of times that coincided with the network's early-round coverage. So imagine O'Meara's surprise when he saw that he was in the third from the last group on Friday with Loren Roberts and Joe Ozaki. It was a slap in the face for a two-time major champion, and it didn't go unnoticed.

"I bet twenty guys must have come up to me this week and said, 'Nice tee time,'" O'Meara said. "I was warming up and the club pros [the only players playing behind me] were saying, 'What are you doing here?' I saw some guys in the locker room and they said, 'How'd you do?' I told them, 'I'm just going out.' I was out there picking up flag sticks."

Awtrey denied that O'Meara's tee time had anything to do with the fact that he was the first player to go on record with the issue of player compensation, but when O'Meara confronted Awtrey about the tee time, the CEO of the PGA of America averted eye contact and gave O'Meara the same kind of nonanswer he had been shoveling out in his press conferences the entire week. The message from the PGA was clear: we take care of guys who are on our side. "I must be in the penalty box," O'Meara said.

"I'm disappointed names were leaked," Mickelson said of the post-meeting fallout. "The meeting was designed for the players to ask questions." Mickelson had obviously asked the wrong questions, and he was branded as a greedy miscreant for daring to ask how an organization grossing $63 million could be netting only $23 million. He was no management guru, but $40 million in expenses seemed a little steep. But to ask the question was to be named as a greedy troublemaker, and that didn't sit well with Mickelson.

Nor did Tiger particularly care for being singled out. "I was told he mentioned names and I was one of those names," Tiger said. "I don't know what that means, but I've been talking about this since the last Ryder Cup. The Ryder Cup is an enormous money maker. Because of that, I think it's our right to give funds to help our communities."

Tiger didn't take controversial positions lightly, but when he took a stand he remained unrepentant and unwavering. At the Showdown at Sherwood, which was a TV show disguised as a golf tournament, not unlike the old Challenge Golf matches Arnold Palmer used to host, Tiger's caddie, Steve Williams (who had taken over in early 1999 after Tiger fired Fluff Cowan) showed up at the golf course in shorts. Caddies weren't allowed to wear shorts on the PGA Tour, but this wasn't an official PGA Tour event. Still, someone from the tour confronted Williams, telling him that if he didn't put on long pants he would never caddie again on the PGA Tour. When Tiger heard this, he calmly told the tour official to lay off his man, or "you can tell Tim Finchem I'll be playing my golf in Europe." The issue was dropped. Williams wore shorts. Now, Tiger was taking another stand, and while it might ruffle some feathers, he knew that standing up for what he believed would earn him a great deal of respect. It was what leaders did. And as the number-one player in the world, Tiger had assumed the role of tour leader.

Crenshaw called all of the players on Wednesday night to apologize, then went on television Thursday afternoon to apologize again. According to Larry Nelson, who watched the events from a distance, "Ben got caught up in something he shouldn't have gotten caught up in, but he's such an emotional guy and he wants to win so badly that he couldn't help himself."

Awtrey also appeared on CBS later in the week and said, "We'll have a final plan by the end of the year." But the damage was already done. Players left Chicago more confused and befuddled than when they arrived. Awtrey had thrown gasoline on a PR brushfire, and Captain Crenshaw had raised all sorts of questions about his diplomatic skills six weeks before he was to lead the U.S. team to Boston to try to reclaim the Ryder Cup.

Fortunately, Tiger and 19-year-old Sergio Garcia provided some of the best golf drama of the year, deflecting the public's attention away from the pay-for-play scandal and back to the most exciting PGA Championship in recent memory. Their combined age wouldn't have qualified for the senior tour, yet they were two of the most dynamic players in history, providing just the kind of top-notch duel everyone hoped would come from Tiger and Duval. Energized by the prospect of a real-live rivalry, the Chicago galleries flocked to the final two groups on Sunday.

"Boy, this is just great," Crenshaw (who shot 77–74 and missed the cut) said as he watched the unfolding drama. Crenshaw had stayed to watch his team and make the final decisions on his captain's picks. On that front he had plenty of help. When he showed up in the locker room on Sunday, Crenshaw found a note on his locker that said, "Pick Me," with an arrow pointing to the left. Fred Couples had the locker immediately next to Crenshaw's, and the captain couldn't help but smile. Fred was a friend, and under any other circumstances he would have been on Crenshaw's short list, but Couples had skipped the British Open and, in Crenshaw's words, "just hadn't played enough." Plus, Couples had married Thais, whose cancer was in remission, and she had two wonderful children whom Fred adored. His life was happy, and his golf had suffered as a result. He was always a good Ryder Cup player, but not this time.

Crenshaw had other ideas about whom he would choose, but, unlike Kite, he didn't pore over the statistics. He would make his picks as he did everything else: by feel. He put those thoughts aside for a few moments, however, as he watched the final moments of the 81st PGA Championship, and saw what would go down in history as one of the most memorable golf shots of the decade.

Garcia didn't want to be called Garcia, even by newspaper writers who, by rule, called everybody by their last name. "Just call me Sergio," he had said. "Garcia is so formal. Sergio, I think, is better." It was with that same sort of boyish naiveté that "Just call me Sergio" Garcia seduced America during the final major of the 1900s. His polite demeanor, sparkling smile, and youthful exuberance captured the imagination and the support of the majority of fans in Chicago, and the rivalry that the media had longed for was finally upon them.

Andalusians believed the eyes were sexual organs. By that standard, Sergio had lost his virginity at Medinah with Michael Jordan, Ben Crenshaw, and 7.7 percent of American households witnessing the act. "He is really a special person," tour veteran Jay Haas said of the 19-year-old. "Not just a golfer. He's got something that a lot of people are missing."

Like all seductions, this one started innocently enough by the blue waters of Lake Kadijah. On the 13th green, a serene but demanding par-three over the lake, Sergio, playing just ahead of Tiger, hit a six-iron to within 18 feet of the hole. It was a good shot, but one that appeared academic. Tiger had reached 15-under for the week through 11 holes on Sunday and had a five-shot lead. Any of the top 10 to 20 players in the game should have been able to protect a five-shot lead with eight holes to play, but with Tiger it was considered a fait accompli. Tiger had some doubts, however. "A five-shot lead can evaporate pretty quickly," he said. "If I make a couple of mistakes; they make a couple of birdies, and, boom, we're tied. That's exactly what happened. I made a couple of mistakes."

The first mistake came at the 12th where Woods reached the green in regulation, but three-putted for a bogey to drop one shot. Then, at the 13th tee, Woods watched as Sergio examined his putt from every angle, his crowd base growing with each smile and wave. When he rolled the left-to-right breaking putt into the hole to reach 11-under, Sergio looked back at the tee, his fist in the air and his twinkling eyes locked on Tiger. "I wanted him to know that I was still there and to show him that he had to finish well to win," Sergio said of his look. "But it wasn't a bad thing. I mean, I did it with good feelings, not hoping he would make a triple-bogey or whatever. I was kind of telling him: if you want to win, you have to play well."

Oh, the breathless seduction! More than ever, girls wanted to marry him, and men wanted to take him under their wing and tell him in quiet whispers what a gift he had been given. "We love you, Sergio," the best of Chicago's teenage female sect screamed on Sunday. Sergio's caddie, Jerry Higginbotham, could do nothing but shake his head. "The vibes out there today were insane," Higginbotham said. "I've been out here a long time and I've never heard anything like it."

The vibes got better for Sergio when things started going bad for Tiger. A five-iron shot at the 13th flew into the long rough behind the green. From there, Tiger had to guard against blading his chip over the green and into the water. He hit his shot too firm and it rolled off the front edge. He then hit a poor third shot and two-putted for a double-bogey five. The lead was down to one. Sergio bogeyed the 15th, which left the door open for Tiger, who parred the 15th and opened the lead back to two.

Then at 16, the shot that consummated Sergio's seductive relationship occurred with such explosive fervor it shook the assembled golf fans down to their Nikes. Sergio hit a three-wood from the tee, but he drove his ball through the fairway. To the anguished cries of the masses, the ball nestled between two roots at the base of a large tree. Sergio was, according to every analyst who saw his predicament, dead. The only option was to punch his ball back out onto the fairway and try to get up-and-down. But Sergio grew up (if you consider a 19-year-old to have grown up) playing golf in Spain with Seve Ballesteros, the master of the inventive shot, and Sergio knew that being two down with three holes to play called for drastic measures. "I had a shot, but I had to hit a big slice," he said. "The problem was that on the downswing I could hit part of the tree. If I aimed right, I might hit the second part of the tree."

Higginbotham took issue with the "I had a shot" statement his boss made. "Nine out of ten guys on the PGA Tour chip out sideways," Higginbotham said. "Nine out of ten don't even think about hitting that shot."

Armed with a six-iron Sergio took a vicious swing, closing his eyes and falling backward on one foot. The ball shot out from the brush and curved 25 yards toward the green. "I opened the clubface, made a full swing, closed my eyes and hit the ball, and went backwards in case it hit the tree," Sergio said. "Then I opened my eyes and saw the ball was going at the green and I was pretty excited." So excited in fact that he ran down the fairway, leaping into the air to watch the ball come to rest 25 feet from the flag. "I'll put it in my top-five shots," he said with a smile and an alluring wink. The deflowering of Chicago was complete.

The ecstasy was tempered with a dose of reality, however. Sergio missed his birdie putt at 16, settling for the most memorable par of the year. When Tiger bogeyed the 16th, the lead had dwindled back to one, but that was where it would remain. Sergio parred the 17th and 18th, and Tiger made a clutch 8-footer for par on the 17th, then two-putted for par on 18 where he dropped his eyes, clenched his fist, and collected the second major title of his career. Tiger won, but Sergio scored.

Even Captain Crenshaw was impressed. "Unbelievable," he said. "I don't think anybody has ever seen a shot like that." There was a new rivalry, and a new hero in golf. Sergio wasn't even old enough to rent a car or drink a beer, but as Jay Haas had said, he was really special.

"I've always said this kid is a better person than he is a golfer," Sergio's agent, Robert Getterriez, said. "This won't make him a brat. He is special."

Crenshaw made his captain's picks on Monday: one by the book and one classic Crenshaw. Tom Lehman finished 11th on the Ryder Cup points list and was an obvious pick. He was 2–0 in Ryder Cup singles, having beaten Seve at Oak Hill in 1995 and Ignacio Garrido on comeback Sunday at Valderrama. "He exudes leadership," Crenshaw said. Lehman was in with ease.

The second pick came from feel. Steve Pate had been on tour 15 years where he had accumulated six wins and earned the nickname "Volcano" for his fiery temper. His only other Ryder Cup appearance had been in 1991 when he was one of Captain Dave Stockton's picks, but that debut had ended badly. The night before the Gala Dinner, Pate was in an auto accident, where he suffered a broken rib. While he was with the team throughout the week, he played only one match, which he lost. By Sunday it was obvious he couldn't go on, so Pate pulled out of the singles competition. That sort of selflessness was what Crenshaw needed. Plus Pate was always good for a joke or two in the clubhouse. He would add some much-needed levity to a tense team and that, along with his ability to drive the ball with the best in the game, was why Crenshaw went with his gut and picked Steve Pate to round out his team.

It was a good squad: the 12 best golfers in the world, as some would say. But then someone always said that before the Ryder Cup.

# Nine

# OH, LOOK, MUFFY . . .

LEE WESTWOOD WAS THE first to say it. "Europe is far inferior to the U.S.," the Englishman said without a trace of a smile. "We are massive underdogs." Oh, how they laughed at that one as they boarded the Concorde in London, Ryder Cup in hand! It would be the running joke for most of the four-hour supersonic flight to Boston.

On paper, they were inferior. The lowest-ranked player on the U.S. team was Steve Pate at 31st in the world. Half the European team fell below that. America had one Ryder Cup rookie, and he was ranked number two in the world (David Duval) while Europe had seven rookies and three more players whose only experience had been at Valderrama. The United States had seven players with two or more Ryder Cups under their belts. Only José María Olazábal with five appearances and Colin Montgomerie with four could be considered European veterans. Still, there was an air of confidence among the European players as they waved to whooping fans gathered in the airport to see them off. They were always underdogs, no more so than at Valderrama, and they always seemed to do quite well once the starting gun went off. The Ryder Cup wasn't played on paper. If it were, Payne Stewart's comments wouldn't have been so ironic. Stewart had said, "On paper, they shouldn't be caddying for us." That elicited another hearty chuckle from the Euros as they caressed the two-and-a-half-foot gold cup they had kept in the European PGA offices for four years now. The matches were contested on grass, not paper. And on grass, the "massive underdog" Europeans were 2–2 in the nineties and 2–0 since 1995.

No smile was any broader than the toothy, ear-to-ear grin beneath the bushy mustache of captain Mark James. Most players would readily admit that the European's lighthearted confidence trickled down from their captain. James, a bald man with only a 3-inch swath of salt-and-pepper hair curving around the back and sides of his tanned head, was a seven-time Ryder Cup veteran who was one month shy of his 45th birthday. He had worn his thick mustache longer than any member of his current team had been shaving, and he had played in Ryder Cups back when the United States fielded such stalwarts as Don January and Dave Hill. But one look into James's baby blue eyes and you knew this was not a tired man. He sparkled, and according to those who had been around him during the run-up to the matches, he had added levity to the proceedings since the day he had been named European captain. When asked what it might mean to have four Swedes on his team, James had deadpanned, "I guess I would have to lay in some more dried herring." Or when asked how pressure would affect him, James never missed a beat when he said, "It doesn't bother me. I'm very bad without pressure, and very bad under pressure." He was no John Cleese, but as Ryder Cup captains went, James was about as funny as they came.

He was certainly more affable in that regard than Ian Woosnam, who had openly campaigned for the job of captain by claiming he was the one man with enough moxie to beat back the Americans on their home soil. In the post-Seve European Ryder Cup era, that was exactly the kind of bravado nobody wanted. James didn't take himself or his role too seriously; something all Europeans could agree was a good thing this time around.

James had also played so well in 1999 that, up until August 22, when the final roster was set at the BMW International Open in Munich, it looked as though he might qualify for the team. If that was the case, he had said he would step down and turn the reins over to his assistant, Ken Brown. It was a prospect no one in Europe wanted to consider. They called James "Jesse" because of his maverick, gunslinger approach to life, but having a playing captain or having him hand off the captaincy to an assistant at such a late date was a little too maverick, even for the Europeans. No one openly pulled against James, but there was a palpable sigh of relief when he failed to make the top 10 in Ryder Cup points.

The relief was even greater when James's captain's picks were announced. Despite some predictions to the contrary, he went conservative, choosing Jesper Parnevik, who played the majority of his golf on the U.S. PGA Tour, and Andrew Coltart, another rookie who had finished 12th on the points list. Most thought James would choose Bernhard Langer, but Coltart and Parnevik were fine. Nothing too radical.

The picks did mark the end of an era, however. For the first time since the matches were opened up to Europe, the Ryder Cup would be

contested without Langer, Nick Faldo, Ian Woosnam, or Seve Ballesteros, all men who had made the Ryder Cup the most anticipated golf
event in the world. Without Europe's "Big Four," the Ryder Cup would
have remained a late-season ho-hum American rout. Europe started
winning and the Ryder Cup became interesting because of those men,
all of whom had hit a mid-40s career slump.

Most of them bowed out gracefully, recognizing that their time had
passed. Faldo, however, wasn't prepared to go, and when James said to
him, "You're not a member of the side," the all-time leading Ryder Cup
point winner took the news badly. "When he told me that even winning
[in Munich] wasn't enough I was knocked over," Faldo said. "That was
the real killer. I'm gutted. If I'd known the state of affairs I wouldn't
have come here."

Few sympathized with Faldo's plight since he had played some of
the worst golf of his life in 1998 and 1999, and since his personal shenani-
gans continued to provide fodder for the tabloids. After leaving his wife
Gill for American college student Brenna Cepelak, Faldo became a
Fleet Street regular, donning the cover of every lowbrow rag in Europe
whenever he and Brenna went out. When he broke up with Brenna by
phoning her from Florida and saying, "It's over, love," the press had a
field day. During those times of personal turmoil and then when his
game abandoned him, Faldo didn't get a lot of support from his fellow
European players. He had stepped on far too many toes over the years
with his rude and dismissive temper to garner much support when
things turned south. As for his cries of indignation at not being considered by James, Ian Woosnam summed it up for everyone when he said,
"What's Faldo done? Nothing! I haven't done enough, and I've played
better than him all year."

Even though his team had the most rookies of any European squad
in a quarter-century, James felt good about his chances. "I think it's an
excellent team," he said. "I'm confident we can win, because it doesn't
matter who was there before. It's the standard of players we have this
time that matters."

Those were exactly the words of encouragement Jean Van de Velde had
hoped to hear from his captain. Jean was one of the seven rookies, having
locked up the ninth spot in the points total fairly early with his second-
place finish at the Open Championship. Now, as he and Brigitte were

nestling into their seats on the Concorde, it was good to know the captain had confidence in the team. The Van de Veldes sat near their friends Padraig and Caroline Harrington, who were also making their maiden Ryder Cup voyage. Padraig had finished second to Colin Montgomerie in Munich to lock up the 10th and final automatic berth. At the time he had said, "This hasn't sunk in yet and probably won't for a while." As they fastened their seat belts in preparation for takeoff, Jean wondered if it had finally sunk in for his friend from Dublin.

He also wondered what the Coltarts were feeling. Andrew and his wife Emma had made the decision to induce labor so their first child, Bonnie, would be born before the Ryder Cup, thus eliminating any distractions that could have been caused by Emma's water breaking while Andrew was in the middle of a four-ball match. Talk about devotion! Rookie or not, Coltart was a man any captain would want on his team.

Paul and Marian Lawrie took seats behind Jean and Brigitte for their first Ryder Cup flight, and Jean got the sense that Paul Lawrie was just as confident in his debut on this team as he had been in that fateful playoff at Carnoustie. He hadn't won again after the Open, and he was still ranked 49th in the world, but Jean knew Lawrie would be a factor.

The rookie no one questioned was Sergio Garcia. He was the X-factor for Europe. If Sergio could get on a roll, he could woo many of the fans to his side and take away much of the Americans' home-course advantage. He could also play with anyone, regardless of age. The only reason Sergio stood no better than 28th in the world rankings was that he had been playing professionally for only a little more than five months. He was one of the best, even at 19, and while he might technically have been a Ryder Cup rookie, no one thought of him in those terms.

The other Spanish rookie no one thought of in those terms was Miguel Angel Jiménez, who, at 35, was technically old enough to be Sergio's father. He had also been one of the steadiest players on the European tour for the past two seasons. This was a man who had grown up on the outskirts of Malaga and who had worked in a garage trying to earn enough to feed himself and his family. That career stint had earned him the nickname "Mechanic," but it had also earned him a great deal of respect among those on board that plane. Jiménez had lived through some tough times. He appreciated every moment of this experience.

Finally there was Jarmo Sandelin, the "mad Swede": the only man in the history of the PGA European Tour to wear a fishnet shirt during a tournament, prompting the tour to write a "no nipple" rule into the dress code; the only man in golf who wore crocodile cowboy boots as golf shoes; and the only man on either Ryder Cup team to have to decide between having his girlfriend accompany him to the matches or having his regular caddie on his bag. Jarmo's girlfriend, Linda Lundberg, was also his caddie, and, given the choice between lugging the bag around during the week or partaking in the festivities with the other wives and girlfriends, Lundberg chose the latter.

Sandelin would be the wild card. A strikingly handsome man with thick wavy hair and classic Nordic features, he had played his way onto the team with victories at the Spanish and German Opens earlier in the season, but since then his game had deteriorated. In his last seven starts before the Ryder Cup, he missed three cuts and finished 65th, 30th, 43rd, and 30th, not the kind of peak performances Captain James and his teammates were looking for. But golf was perhaps the least worrisome aspect of having Jarmo as a teammate. He was a lightning rod of controversy, even among his own players. During the 1998 Trophée Lancome in Paris, Sandelin accused winner Mark O'Meara of cheating, claiming that O'Meara had improperly replaced his ball after it had been marked on the green. Sandelin went so far as to produce videotape of the questionable incident. He then challenged O'Meara to return the trophy and the winner's check as the proceeds were, in Sandelin's words, "fraudulently obtained." An impartial committee from the European tour met on the incident and determined that O'Meara had won the event under the rules. No further action was taken. But Sandelin wouldn't let it die, which angered many players from both sides of the pond. He was an unseemly troublemaker who reveled in mischief.

It was amusingly ironic to many when, at the 1999 Trophée Lancome, Sandelin found himself on the receiving end of a cheating allegation. Lee Westwood insisted that Sandelin's ball had moved after he had addressed it (a one-shot penalty under the rules). Sandelin disagreed and the discussion became heated. It wasn't until noted rules official John Paramour stepped in and determined there was insufficient evidence to penalize Sandelin that play resumed. Westwood was just as dogmatic in his charge as Sandelin had been the year before, and before the night was over, the two men had engaged in a shouting match outside their hotel in full view of a number of other players including Mark O'Meara (who did his best to keep a straight face).

As outrageous as those stories were, they weren't the worst examples of Sandelin's personality. For that you had to go back to the 1996 Dunhill Cup, a combination match-play, stroke-play format played at St. Andrews. It started on Saturday of that week when Sandelin took Nick Price to a playoff in their match. In addition to being the nicest man in golf, Price was dealing with the terminal illness of his caddie, Jeff "Squeaky" Medlin. Everyone was sensitive to the tough times Price was having, except Sandelin. For some inexplicable reason, after holing a 30-foot putt to beat Price, Sandelin held his putter up to his shoulder like a machine gun and pretended to rattle off shots at Price. Sandelin did the same thing the following day in his match against Phil Mickelson after holing a 15-foot birdie putt. But Mickelson was having none of it. As they walked off the green, Phil put his nose within a centimeter of Sandelin's forehead and explained to the eccentric Swede in unambiguous terms that his behavior needed to improve. In a friendly country club two-dollar game Sandelin's antics might slip under the radar, but at the professional level it crossed the line. On top of all that, Sandelin chose to put on his machine-gun display in Scotland six months after the Dunblane Primary School massacre, where a deranged gunman shot up a kindergarten class. Because of the timing, many thought Sandelin either suffered from some mental defects of his own or he was simply an insensitive Neanderthal.

Whatever he was, he was a teammate this week, and all of them, including Montgomerie, Coltart, and Lawrie (all Scots), were going to have to work with him.

The flight was short and comfortable. Olazábal putted down the center aisle of the plane, and Mark James kept everyone in stitches with his dry humor. Sergio listened to music over some headphones with his eyes closed, and the Van de Veldes and Harringtons chatted about their upcoming week. This was the first time many of them, including Jean and Brigitte, had been to Boston, and many of the wives were as excited about getting to see the new city as they were about the matches.

It was also the first time in over two decades the Concorde had landed at Logan Airport in Boston. After several months of broken windows and rattled shingles, residents of East Boston had successfully lobbied to ban the supersonic jet from coming in or out of the area, but an obscure exception was written into the law allowing diplomatic personnel to fly in on supersonic aircraft (something no one ever expected to happen). This time it did. Prince Andrew flew in with the European Ryder Cup team so the Concorde would qualify under the diplomatic exception, and East Bostonians and Winthrop residents were none too pleased. The plane rumbled in with an apocalyptic thunder, setting off car alarms and scaring several elderly Winthrop residents out of their wits. The Europeans had made a grand entry. It was time for the matches to begin.

It had been 62 years since a visiting Ryder Cup team had arrived in Boston. The first time, in 1927, the British team quietly arrived in town the same day Babe Ruth hit his 15th and 16th home runs of what would become a record-setting 60-home-run season, and stories were still circulating about Charles Lindbergh's fantastic transatlantic flight two weeks before. This time around, as European players and wives were gathering their garment bags and deplaning onto the ramp, Boston officials were asking federal investigators to look into corruption and abuse charges relating to an infrastructure project called "the big dig," affectionately nicknamed "the big ditch" by some witty locals. The area surrounding Logan Airport looked like Baghdad after a bombing raid with roads, bridges, and walkways torn to shreds in the name of progress. Fortunately an army of Boston's finest escorted the Ryder Cuppers through the construction maze to the Four Seasons Hotel, where they had the fifth floor to themselves. If they hadn't realized it before, on Monday, September 20, 1999, when they arrived in Boston to more hoopla and fanfare than any of them had ever seen, the European Ryder Cup team realized this was going to be something very different.

On the American side, all was forgiven (or at least forgotten) for the week, and Captain Crenshaw was doing everything in his power to bring his team together and prepare them to win. "This issue is behind us," he continually said, over and over as if he were trying to convince himself as much as anyone. Then, with a faraway look, he said, "Pulling this team together is something I'll cherish the rest of my life. No captain could look at this team and say these are not the best."

Not long after the PGA Championship players started noticing where the $40 million was being spent. Right after the conclusion of the WGC-NEC Invitational, a small group of Gulfstream-IVs picked up the Ryder Cup team and their caddies and flew them from Akron to Boston for a quick practice round at The Country Club. G-IVs didn't come cheap, and these were fully loaded with all the plush appointments and freshly catered food and drink a self-respecting golfer could want on a one-hour flight. Crenshaw and the PGA of America also put the caddies up in the Four Seasons during the practice-round trip, a little atonement for past indelicacies where caddies were concerned. It went a long way toward soothing tensions. Then Ben gave out specially labeled bottles of wine to the players and caddies with the Ryder Cup logo and each person's name embossed on the label. He kept saying things like "These moments are going to stay with you for a lifetime" and "Just remember how you feel during all of this."

Crenshaw had done more than take over as leader of the team. He had become the Ryder Cup, embodying the very essence of what he thought the event was supposed to be. "It's extremely important that people know what we're playing for," he said with unwavering conviction. "We're playing for our *souls*." Walking through the clubhouse at The Country Club, he would point to old photos of Francis Ouimet, a 20-year-old kid who became the first American amateur to win the U.S. Open Championship right there in Brookline, and he would speak of the event as though he, Ben Crenshaw, had been in the gallery that day back in 1913. He re-created events in the present tense, saying things like "No one thinks Ouimet has a chance, but he knows he can pull this thing off."

Now it was Crenshaw's turn to pull something off—to jell a team that was as fractured as any in recent Ryder Cup memory, to overcome all the controversy and the pressure, and lead his team. Part of that, he realized, meant indulging a few idiosyncratic requests. When Payne Stewart ran up to him and said, "Ben, I've got the secret that's going to win us the Ryder Cup," Crenshaw had said, "Well, quick, tell me what it is."

Stewart paused for a moment to let the suspense build before saying, "A Ping-Pong table."

Crenshaw tried not to blink. "A Ping-Pong table?"

"Yep," Stewart said, his Ozark tenor getting louder and higher by the second. "Everybody's going to be uptight, you know, nervous, full of nervous energy. They need some way to let that out. A Ping-Pong table is perfect. It'll get their minds off being nervous and give them something to do in the hotel rather than sit around thinking too much."

Crenshaw nodded. "Okay, Payne. I'll get us a Ping-Pong table."

And he did. Crenshaw had a table placed in the team room on the sixth floor and Stewart used it almost every night. The most interesting match involved Stewart and Aerosmith lead singer Steven Tyler (who brought his kids to the Four Seasons to meet the U.S. players), who played a doubles match against Mark O'Meara and Rose Lietzke, wife of Crenshaw's assistant captain, Bruce Lietzke. O'Meara and Lietzke won, but according to O'Meara, "Payne came back and beat Jeff Maggert playing on his knees. That tells me Jeff needs to work on his Ping-Pong."

Tyler wasn't the only celebrity who paid a visit to the players. Michael Jordan, John Elway, Mario Lemieux, and, of course, President and Mrs. Bush all came by. The Bushes had known the Crenshaws for years, just as they had known the Kites for years, and Mrs. Bush hosted a luncheon on Wednesday for the wives at the Harvard Club. Celine Dion was a constant fixture in the hotel and in the galleries throughout the week, as was former Eagle Glenn Frey. O. J. Simpson never visited with anyone but he strolled along the gallery ropes throughout the matches, watching the action from beneath a Callaway golf cap and behind a pair of dark glasses. Baseball legend George Brett was denied access to one of the shuttle buses because he didn't have the right credentials—three thousand career hits got you nowhere at Brookline.

Celebrity visits notwithstanding, Crenshaw tried to insulate the players from what he could see was shaping up as a very different golf environment from anything they had ever experienced. Boston was abuzz with Ryder Cup fever. People on the street wanted to talk about it, even though many of them wouldn't have known a golf ball from a goose egg. But the Ryder Cup had become like the Olympics. It attracted everybody.

On Tuesday night, after a full day of practice, Crenshaw put the players on a bus outside the hotel. He had hoped to slip out to the Oyster House, one of Boston's more famous eateries, for a quiet team dinner. When they arrived, however, no fewer than 500 people waited outside the restaurant to greet them. "I wasn't used to that," Hal Sutton said. "I mean, Tiger probably was, but the rest of us weren't used to that sort of rock star celebrity treatment. It just proved to me how special the Ryder Cup had become for everybody."

After the entrees were served (which included a special sea bass the chef prepared especially for the players) Crenshaw handed out rings to all 12 members of his team. "In the Super Bowl or the World Series you have to wait until you win to get a ring," Crenshaw said. "But I'm so confident that I'm giving out your rings now."

Not all of Boston was as confident as Crenshaw, nor was everyone as patriotic as the fans who lined up outside the Oyster House on Tuesday night. Many of the comments on talk radio and local television still centered on the pay-for-play controversy, with many Bostonians branding the players as pampered and greedy. Similar comments resonated throughout the town, even though most of those voicing their opinions were doing so without the facts. "They just want more money so they can put gas in their private jets," one caller to a local sports show said. Another said, "They should all go home and let twelve guys who know what this country is all about have a crack at it." Impassioned but blithely ignorant, these opinions littered the airwaves for much of the week. Once again, Duval was the central target for the critics. One caller from Quincy (a middle-class suburb south of Boston) said, "Duval should take his millions and buy a personality. I don't care. I'm pulling for the Europeans. I hope they beat those crybabies like a drum."

These were not typical golf fans, but then again the Boston area had lost its only PGA Tour event, the CVS Charity Classic at Pleasant Valley, and the professional game had never appealed to the masses in New England the way it did in Florida, California, Georgia, and Arizona. The fans for this Ryder Cup were not what you would find in Augusta, or Pinehurst, or even Chicago. This was Boston, a town where a young female reporter had her tires slashed, received death threats, and was ultimately run out of town for complaining about harassment she had received in the New England Patriots' locker room. This was the same town where fans continued to obsess over Bill Buckner's ninth-inning error in the 1986 World Series, and where a night at Fenway Park was never complete without at least one obscenity-laced diatribe from an incensed Red Sox fan within earshot of several small children.

Crenshaw certainly sensed it. Rowdiness was in the air, and it wasn't confined to the fringe few. A large segment of people shared the sentiments of the talk-radio callers. The Americans were spoiled brats. Some said it out loud; others simply shrugged or snarled. Crenshaw knew there was an uncomfortable edge to the opinions being presented in the early days of this Ryder Cup week, but there was little he or anyone else could do about it.

Perhaps the most telling line—printed or spoken—typifying the chasm between this Ryder Cup and all other golf events came from the *Boston Herald,* a Rupert Murdoch–owned tabloid. The *Herald* ran a special Ryder Cup section every day during the week of the matches, and, as was its style, the tone was irreverent and often glib. Caricatures of players replaced photos, and Colin Montgomerie was referred to as "a Bill Parcells lookalike." It was light and harmless, not your typical golf read, but it appealed to the *Herald*'s mass audience. Then, in one of the early-week issues, the paper printed a section entitled "Things You Are Likely to Hear at the Ryder Cup," a funny spoof on the sights and sounds at The Country Club. The number-one quote on the *Herald*'s list: "Oh, look, Muffy, a Negro. It must be Tiger Woods."

It was the sort of thing that caused the reader to shout, "Oh my God!" at the breakfast table. Not only had a writer written this line, an editor had approved it, a typesetter had set it, and millions of eyes were seeing it. It was unbelievable. After the initial shock wore off, and as the week wore on, it became apparent that, beyond its race and class implications, that single line in a tabloid paper spoke volumes, not just for the way things would turn out at the 33rd Ryder Cup Matches but also for the most alarming trend in golf. People who found that humor acceptable—even normal—were in golf galleries now. The same guy who heckled the Yankees every time they visited Fenway had become part of golf's expanding tapestry. The game had grown, and new fans were a part of that. It was the price you paid for entering the arena of big-time sports. Before the week was out, the Ryder Cup would illustrate exactly what that price entailed.

When Friday's opening-match pairings were announced Thursday evening, Crenshaw sat down for his press conference, chuckled, winked, and said, "Mark James and I met down by the skating pond on number three and worked this out for ya'll." He was joking, of course. The pairings were blind. Crenshaw listed his players in the slots he wanted them to play—one through four—and James did the same. It just worked out that the second match of the first day pitted Tiger Woods and Tom Lehman against Sergio Garcia and Jesper Parnevik. The match everyone wanted to see: Tiger versus Sergio was happening early. It wasn't as dramatic as a Sunday singles matchup, but it was still an event. Golf fans would get another look at the rivalry they desperately wanted.

The other matches of the day were interesting, but none evoked the breathless anticipation of the Tiger-Sergio matchup. Lawrie and Montgomerie would team up against Mickelson and Duval in the first match of the day, while Payne Stewart and Davis Love, who had a combined seven Ryder Cups between them, would take on rookies Harrington and Jiménez in the third match. That match would prove to be interesting for a number of reasons, not the least of which was the language barrier. Jiménez's English was poor at best, and he didn't know a word of Gaelic, while Harrington's Spanish was less than fluent. Not that they needed to chat a great deal, but in an alternate-shot format (which the first matches were, going back to the original order after Seve's shift at Valderrama) a little conversation was always a help. Neither player seemed to mind, though. They would communicate just fine when it mattered. The final pairing appeared on paper to be the dullest. Jeff Maggert and Hal Sutton, nice enough guys but no Tiger or Sergio, were paired against Darren Clarke and Lee Westwood, two men who struck a blow against diet and exercise when it came to golf. Between them Clarke and Westwood carried an extra 30 pounds more than most doctors would recommend, but the extra weight did not impede their ability to play. They had proved that at Valderrama.

Phil Mickelson struck the first shot of the 1999 Ryder Cup Matches, a slight fade that found the corner of the rough. His partner Duval promptly missed the green and Europe took an early 1-up lead. The heckling began early, only it wasn't Montgomerie and the Europeans who bore the brunt of the verbal abuse in the opening match; it was Duval. "Nice shot, you prick," one fan shouted as Duval struggled to find the fairway with his tee shots. Another quipped, "Let's see an exhibition shot, rich boy." Duval never flinched, but his play never recovered, either. He and Mickelson found themselves down late in the match.

Montgomerie's evil demons went to work on the back side, however. On the 13th tee, as Lawrie was preparing to hit his tee shot, a marshal 200 yards down the fairway made a mistake and allowed a spectator to run across the fairway after the player had reached the tee. After two waggles, Lawrie backed away. Monty, not paying particularly close attention to what was going on on the fairway, assumed his partner had been distracted by a female marshal behind the tee who had moved less than 18 inches from left to right during Lawrie's routine. Monty went nuts, berating the woman and insisting that she remain perfectly still. "Pay attention to what you're doing," he demanded. "You're distracting my partner."

Mickelson just shook his head and looked at the ground. Typical Monty. He didn't even realize what had happened, but that didn't stop him from picking a fight. Mickelson had seen it before. When they had been paired together the first two days of the 1997 U.S. Open at Congressional, after shooting a spectacular opening-round 65 to take the lead, Monty grew rabbit ears and came into the second round expecting to be distracted. The beer-guzzling crowds at Congressional didn't disappoint him. On the 16th tee, when Phil hit his tee shot, a gallery member shouted, "You da' man!", prompting Monty to run across the tee shouting, "Who said that?" "I did," answered a large, well-built African-American gentleman who looked as though he could have ripped Monty's head off with no more effort than it took to open his next beer. Montgomerie became a bit more subdued. "Well, you might want to tone it down a bit," was all he could muster. Mickelson had laughed at that one for weeks. Granted, the crowds at Congressional and at golf venues everywhere were ruder and louder than they had ever been, but confrontations on the course weren't the answer. But that was Monty. Next week he would be the perfect Scottish gentleman again, but for the next three days he might say or do anything.

What he did that Friday morning was hand the United States its first defeat of the matches. Montgomerie and Lawrie defeated Duval and Mickleson 3 and 2 in a match that was never really close.

It was a sign of bad things to come for the Americans, and everyone in the gallery got the eerie sense that they had been there before. When Sergio hit his approach to 14 feet on the 14th hole and Parnevik made the putt for a halve to keep a 1-up advantage in their match against

Tiger and Lehman, one spectator, a six-foot, six-inch black man with a shaved head and an earring, puffed his Cohiba cigar and said, "I'm worried." Leave it to Michael Jordan to make one of the most prophetic early statements of the week.

As predicted, Sergio electrified the crowd. People wrapped in blue European flags with face paint and goofy hats started chanting, "Olé, olé, olé." The entire scene was surreal. What was very real, however, was the final score of the match. Sergio and Parnevik defeated Lehman and Tiger 2 and 1. The matchup everyone wanted to see was over. Sergio had beaten Tiger, and Europe was up by two.

Maggert and Sutton beat Clarke and Westwood for America's first points of the day. Davis Love and Payne Stewart, two of the red-white-and-blue brigade that was supposed to anchor this U.S. team, barely squeezed out a halve against Padraig Harrington and Miguel Angel Jiménez. Europe led 2½ to 1½ after the morning. Then things got really ugly.

The Americans looked out of synch, as if all the preparation and anticipation of this event had worn them down. They appeared nervous, unsure of themselves, uncomfortable with what they were doing. The worst victim of this apparent lethargy was Duval, who had been paired with Tiger in the afternoon matches. Numbers one and two in the world were resoundingly thumped by Westwood and Clarke. The final tally was a 1-up win for Europe, but it was never that close. Duval made only one birdie on the back nine, and even though he left the driver in the bag most of the day, he had trouble finding the fairway. After Clarke birdied the 17th, Woods and Duval missed the 18th fairway. Five minutes later the match was conceded. Two players who, in Westwood's words, "were far inferior" had beaten the number-one and number-two players in the world.

Boston fans mercilessly abused Duval. Throughout the afternoon, he was peppered with comments like "What do you think of this exhibition now?" and "Go home." He was also hammered in the press for a lack of emotion. Chris Elsberry of the *Connecticut Post* wrote, "Duval's emotions never seemed to change, and that was the sad thing. He never cracked a smile, furrowed a brow, pounded a club, pumped a fist, or issued an expletive." C. W. Nevius of the *San Francisco Chronicle* was equally brutal when he wrote, "This is starting to look less and less like a coincidence and more and more like the wrong guys are doing all the commercials."

"I told David long ago that the media, by design, was going to put him on a pedestal, lift him higher and higher, then try to knock him down," Puggy Blackmon said. "That's what happened with the whole Ryder Cup thing, and that was what was so frustrating about it. David got brutalized in the press, and a lot of the fans picked up on that, but throughout the whole Ryder Cup incident, David Duval never wanted one penny for his own pocket. Not one. He just wanted accountability."

The most demoralizing loss of the day for the Americans came, again, at the hands of the cartwheel-turning 19-year-old and his partner, Jesper Parnevik. The two Europeans made birdies from everywhere, whipping their fans into a frenzy and keeping Mickelson and Jim Furyk on the ropes throughout the round. Sergio chipped in for an eagle on the par-five 14th and the sound of his fans cheering echoed through the trees. There was a palpable sense of doom around The Country Club.

But it was Mickelson's performance that deflated the United States. Despite the fact that he made seven birdies, Mickelson missed a 5-foot putt on the 18th that would have halved the match. Behind the 18th green, Mickelson was inconsolable, openly weeping with his head in his hands while his wife, Amy, provided what little comfort she could. The birdies would be forgotten, Mickelson knew. Just as it had been in the 1999 U.S. Open when he had battled Payne Stewart to the final hole of the final round, the only putts anyone would remember were the ones he missed. None, it seemed, was bigger than that 5-footer at the 18th that Friday.

"I really felt for Phil on the 18th," Parnevik said. "I was one hundred percent sure he was going to make that putt. I was kind of hoping he would make it because nobody deserved to lose a match like that."

But lose the Americans did, and even though Love and Leonard eked out a halve in their afternoon match against Montgomerie and Lawrie, the damage was already done. The Europeans led 6 to 2 after the opening day, and many were writing the Americans off. George Willis of the *New York Post* wrote, "You might as well take down the corporate tents and park all the shuttle buses. The overrated, overconfident American team has shockingly played itself out after only one day."

Crenshaw was stunned. Looking as though he had been hit in the head with a five-iron, the captain said, "I can't believe we're looking at a four-point differential. The Europeans played some wonderful golf, I'll say that." He went on to say, "My team thought they played very well. I thought we saw, obviously, some great scoring out of both teams. I think that . . . 6 to 2 . . . Is that right? . . . 6 to 2 . . . what's the . . . 6 to 2. I just don't think from my position at least, that indicates how people played out there. This is the first day. We all know tomorrow has a lot to do with a lot of things. A lot of our guys felt wonderful about the way they played. There's a slight strain there in knowing that they're four points down. They can look at the board and see how they stand, but still they know it's infinitesimally close."

By the time the sun set on Friday, the first person uttered what would become Crenshaw's new nickname for the next 48 hours: Mental Ben. He was losing it, and if the Americans didn't figure out a way to get things back in order, they might well be carrying their captain back home on a stretcher.

In the locker room after the last putt fell on Friday, Payne Stewart was livid. "They're slow playing us," he ranted. "They're putting on the stall, and it's not right! We can't let them get away with it."

The Euros were playing slower than anyone could have dreamed possible, and everyone thought that it was a planned strategy. Mark James later admitted that he told all his guys to walk off the greens last, not, as he contended, to slow up play, but to avoid being caught in the cheers and hoopla of the crowd. Most of the Americans thought that was bunk. "They definitely put the four-corners on us," said Love, a graduate of North Carolina who grew up watching Dean Smith and Phil Ford stall college basketball.

Hal Sutton didn't like hearing that kind of talk, and he didn't like the mood he was sensing in the locker room. It was time for someone to step forward and assume the leadership role on this team. Sutton had waited 10 years to get back here. He wasn't going to wait another minute. "I wasn't going to make an issue out of the slow play," Sutton said. "I'm not suggesting that Payne shouldn't have said what he said, but the reason I didn't say anything was because I knew you could always build an excuse for not getting the job done. I didn't want us building any excuses. No matter what they pulled, we had to go out there and beat them."

Sutton rallied his teammates, speaking to them about the positives of the day and giving advice on how the weekend should proceed. "I kept emphasizing that we couldn't go out there and try to keep something bad from happening," he said. "I knew that pars were not going to beat these guys. It was going to take birdies. In my first Ryder Cup experience, I was passive; trying to keep bad things from happening. I didn't want to hurt my team, and that's exactly what I ended up doing by not being aggressive enough."

He passed that experience on to all his teammates in the locker room after Friday's round, at dinner that night, and later in the team meeting. Sutton pounded home the same message. "Your contribution to the team is being aggressive," he told them all. "If you make a mistake being aggressive, that's positive, not negative. It takes birdies to win. You've got to go out and try to make birdies."

Sutton was well aware of the slow-play tactics and all the other tactics Mark James was likely to throw their way, but he also knew that if the Americans focused on the opposition's tactics and not on their own games, the matches were as good as over. Mark James would do everything in his power to throw off the rhythm of the U.S. team. As of Friday evening, he had done a pretty good job.

One part of James's strategy wasn't known at the time, but when Jean Van de Velde, Andrew Coltart, and Jarmo Sandelin saw the pairings for Saturday morning they were all a little surprised. It wasn't unusual for a player or two to sit out the first day. After all there were only eight matches, and if one paring was particularly hot (like Sergio and Parnevik) you didn't want to break them up just to insert a new player into the mix. The three rookies thought it a little unusual that all of them would sit out on Friday, but it was tough to argue with a 6–2 lead. Mark James had done a great job so far. Friday night, however, as they looked at the pairings for Saturday morning, Jean and his two rookie teammates were bemused to find that they wouldn't be playing again. Eight of the nine European players who had competed on Friday would be back out on Saturday morning. Van de Velde, Coltart, and Sandelin would have to wait and watch.

What they saw was a morning split. On a soggy and slightly chilly morning, Sutton and Maggert, the two most unlikely heroes coming into the Ryder Cup, beat Lawrie and Montgomerie 1-up in of the most contentious matches so far. It began on the sixth hole when Montgomerie had a 6-foot birdie putt to halve the hole. Someone in the gallery shouted, "Miss it," as Montgomerie was lining up his putt. Predictably, Monty backed away and glared at the offender.

"It was before he even took his practice stroke," Sutton said of the incident. "He made a big deal out of it and pointed to the crowd. You know, it's those kinds of gestures that egg people into doing it more. I wish it hadn't happened. It wasn't happening to me, so I'm not sure how I would have felt, but I don't think he should have egged those people on."

Monty made the birdie putt and thrust a defiant fist at the crowd. As he walked off the green he said to Sutton, "These people are too stupid. They don't understand that it just makes me more determined."

Then on the 14th fairway Sutton did a little egging of his own. With the match all-square, Sutton heard a number of gallery members rooting for Montgomerie. He raised his arms to the crowd, enticing them to cheer for the Americans, an act Monty labeled as "geeing up" the hostile natives. "I didn't want them to call out to Colin," Sutton said. "What I wanted them to do was get behind us a little bit more. I want the best for the European team. I don't want anyone to treat them negatively in any way. But this is the U.S.A. and I guarantee you the crowds would be cheering for them over there. It's not going to hurt for them to do it for us over here."

Lawrie, who had never experienced an event where people actually cheered a missed putt and good shots were met with deafening silence, thought the crowd had gone over the top. "Their behavior was ridiculous," he said. "If it means that much to them, then all the best to them."

Maggert, the quietest member of the group, made a 25-foot birdie putt on the 17th to put the Americans 1-up, then stiffed an eight-iron approach to the 18th to close out the match in favor of the United States. It was a hard-fought match, but Sutton and Maggert had made a statement to the Europeans. Nobody on Team U.S.A. was going to quit.

Steve Pate made his debut with Tiger on Saturday morning, and the two of them defeated Harrington and Jiménez 1-up for the Americans' second point. The other two American teams weren't so fortunate. Mark O'Meara played for the first time on Saturday morning with Jim

Furyk, and the two of them were promptly trounced 3 and 2 by Clarke and Westwood, while Sergio and Parnevik continued to roll, beating Justin Leonard and Payne Stewart 3 and 2 as well.

The afternoon seemed to be working in Ben Crenshaw's favor. His big guns—Love, Duval, Mickelson, and Lehman—were all rested and ready after taking Saturday morning off, and to the dismay of everyone (especially the Europeans), Mark James continued to go with the same players who had taken him to an 8–4 lead. Van de Velde, Coltart, and Sandelin were benched. They wouldn't play until the Sunday singles matches.

"I came here with the object of getting one hundred percent out of this team and the most points I could," James said. "I feel I've gone about it the right way. Time may prove me wrong, but that's how it's been."

Hiding Sandelin was understandable. In addition to being the pro from outer space, Jarmo hadn't played well enough in two months to justify disrupting the chemistry James had on the golf course. Even Van de Velde, with the lingering memories of the Open Championship still fresh in everyone's mind, was questionable. But if James hadn't planned on playing Andrew Coltart, why had he wasted one of his captain's picks on him? It defied logic, but then again, the Europeans were four points up with only Saturday-afternoon four-balls and singles remaining. So far the strategy was hard to rebut.

"I think it will be tough to come here, prepare to play, and for two days sit here and watch," Justin Leonard said.

Tom Lehman agreed with that assessment. "It will be beneficial for us," Lehman said. "But these are good players. They're not bums. They'll be fresh and motivated, but it helps to have experience and knowing what it's all about."

Van de Velde wasn't happy about flying to America for a week to play one 18-hole match, but this was not the time to express this view. He was a member of the team and he would support his coach. During the afternoon matches he walked around and supported his friends. On the 15th green Jean ran into Michael Jordan and had the Hall of Famer sign a cap for him. He was a regular tourist, but he would do what he had to do to support his team.

Sutton also thought James's strategy might backfire. "[The three rookies] have no feel for the action," he said. "I think it's going to be tough for them. We've rested most everyone. They've gone with their horses, so I think fatigue will have a bearing."

The Europeans showed no signs of fatigue on Saturday afternoon. Even though Lehman and Mickelson came out strong and beat Clarke and Westwood 2 and 1, the feisty duo of Lawrie and Montgomerie, angered by their morning loss, soundly defeated Tiger and Steve Pate 2 and 1 to keep the Europeans' four-point lead intact. That left any ground-gaining up to Duval, Love, Sutton (who hadn't rested a single match), and Leonard.

Love and Duval were put in charge of stopping the Sergio Express, and for a while it looked as though they might accomplish that task. But then Parnevik holed a 50-yard wedge shot from the rough for a par and a halve on the 12th, and Love missed two crucial putts from 6 and 15 feet to let the Europeans steal another crucial half-point. "We gave them an out and they took it," a dejected Love said.

The final match befuddled everybody. Just when it looked as though Hal Sutton and Jeff Maggert were unstoppable, Captain Crenshaw stepped in and stopped them. For his Saturday-afternoon pairing, Crenshaw split up the tandem, benching Maggert and putting Justin Leonard out with Sutton instead.

"I have a hunch," Crenshaw said with that twinkle in his eye he usually got after adjourning to his spiritual happy place. "It's just a feeling, but I have a hunch that Justin Leonard is due to make some putts."

That prompted NBC analyst Johnny Miller to make one of the most provocative statements of the week. "I have a hunch, too," Miller said. "My hunch is that Justin should go home and watch on television."

"I get along fine with Johnny, but what he said about Justin was absolutely wrong," Furyk said, offering what would turn out to be the mildest criticism of Miller. "That kind of stuff upsets me. There's no room for that. The flip side is, he's very popular with the viewers. He's honest with his views and he gives them what they want. People love hearing stuff like that, but people love going to NASCAR to watch wrecks, too. I don't know what that says about us."

Love, who was one of Leonard's closest friends on tour, had a few more choice words for Miller. "It mystifies me that he is supposed to be a reporter and an analyst and he becomes a critic," Love said. "There's a difference. He can say, 'Justin hasn't made a whole lot of putts, and maybe Crenshaw ought to think about sitting him out,' but there's a difference between saying that and saying, 'Justin should go home, sit on the couch, and watch it on television.' That's critical, and mean.

"If he continues talking about us like that, I'm going to have to talk to Tommy Roy, his producer, who is a helluva nice guy, and just say, 'Tom, I'm not talking to you guys anymore if you're going to treat us like that.' I mean, they're supposed to be our home network. It's not like this was the BBC or Sky Sport. This was NBC! I know they're supposed to be nonpartisan, but they at least ought not be overly critical. I don't think [Miller] said any of their guys should go home and watch it on the couch. It's out of line, and I'm not putting up with it.

"What really made me mad was that Johnny said, after all that, that he represents the game. He doesn't represent the game. Ben Crenshaw represents the game. Johnny Miller doesn't represent the game. I have not heard one person say anything but bad things about the way he does what he does. Now obviously it's biased. It's my friends on tour and people who watch golf saying this, but we have lots of guys in the locker room who say, 'I hope somebody mentions Johnny Miller out there so you guys can rip him again.' The guys on tour just don't like the way he does it. If he can say he doesn't like the way we play golf, we can say we don't like the way he analyzes. That's what it boils down to."

Miller's comments aside, Crenshaw's decision to bench Maggert on a "hunch" had a lot of people wondering if "Mental Ben" had finally lost it. Even Texas governor and presidential candidate George W. Bush came out to give Captain Crenshaw a little late-afternoon encouragement after his hunch proved incorrect. "We're close buddies," Bush said of Crenshaw. "We're from the same town and we go to the same church. I'm looking to pick him up a little bit. He's a good guy. He can handle it."

Governor Bush was in Boston with his parents and his brother, Governor Jeb Bush of Florida, but even two governors and a former president couldn't pull Team USA out of its hole. Leonard and Sutton halved their match, and the United States split the entire day. They started Saturday four points down and they ended Saturday four points down. Europe led 10–6 with only the singles matches remaining. *Los Angeles Times* correspondent Tommy Bonk said of the day, "The situation for the U.S. is, well, just what is it exactly? Hopeless? Encouraging? Embarrassing? Familiar?"

He left out "insulting" and "injurious." But as if the day needed more insult or injury, First Lady Barbara Bush experienced one of her most surreal moments late Saturday afternoon when she tried to peek into the media center to say hello to *Golf Digest* editor and fellow Texan Dan Jenkins. As Mrs. Bush stuck her head into the media center a 340-pound Pinkerton security guard nicknamed "Tiny" stopped her.

"Excuse me, ma'am. You don't have the proper credentials to be in here," Tiny said without removing the unlit five-dollar cigar from his mouth.

"Oh," the First Lady said, somewhat startled. "I . . . I'm sorry. I was just trying to speak to Dan Jenkins."

"No, ma'am," Tiny said, gaining confidence by the moment. "This is for media only."

Mrs. Bush cocked her head for a moment, then, in an almost pleading tone said, "But, I'm with the president."

Tiny still didn't get it. John Feinstein, who had witnessed the entire encounter with more than a passing sense of amusement, finally leaned and whispered into the guard's ear, "Tiny, that's the First Lady."

If there was any recognition, the guard didn't show it. Fortunately, Mrs. Bush's husband rescued her. Wearing a windbreaker with the presidential seal and his name embroidered on the front, the president shook Tiny's hand and said, "Hey there, young fellow, George Bush. Hope we don't have any trouble getting in here." The Bushes and their Secret Service detail entered the media center without further incident.

When Crenshaw entered the media center on Saturday, the only incident people worried about was whether or not he would make it through the questioning without having a nervous breakdown. He certainly looked and sounded like a man on the verge of cracking up. There were numerous palpable pauses during his oration, and his eyes seemed to wander as if he were hearing voices no one else could hear.

"Well, everyone, I know we've reached a long and exciting day," Crenshaw said as if talking to a group of children on a field trip to Disney World. "I'll just say this right now. I've never been so proud of a bunch of guys in all my life. They played their hearts out, and they'll continue to play their hearts out. I saw a lot of wonderful things today on both sides. I think that the viewing audience will certainly say that the

Ryder Cup is the most exciting kind of golf that you can ever see. That atmosphere was palpable today. It's a heck of a contest. It's a contest that . . . It's a game that we all love and we're proud of. And it was played hard, competitive, and fair. That's . . . Continuing on that note, that's why both these teams continue to be proud of golf. It's great to be a part of, I can tell you."

As Crenshaw continued to ramble, Peter Kessler, the Golf Channel's most recognized anchor, shot his producer a questioning look. Was Crenshaw having a stroke? Kessler rivaled Crenshaw in terms of his knowledge of history, and he knew that no team in history had ever come back from more than two points down with one round to play. So, what was Crenshaw babbling about?

"The matches are tremendously close," he said. "Tremendously close. Anyone can speculate whether points can go either way, but it's still . . . there it is. The outcome will hinge on tomorrow. It will take a . . ." His voice trailed off and the muscles of his face twitched with an almost imperceptible spasm. Those close enough to see it knew he was cracking up. The next words would certainly be nonsensical.

"I think we did a hell of a job of having people on our team and our players and the people . . . They felt that. It was wonderful."

No doubt about it, he had definitely wigged out. Crenshaw was a shadow of himself, a living testament to the dangers of pouring one's soul into a single venture. "Maybe golf in America has changed a little bit over the last eight or ten years," he continued to prattle. "There's vast distances to cover. It is . . . economics, maybe. There's a lot to play for each week." He stared into space again before saying, "Boy, we're just so close. I mean, unbelievably close. I think everyone knows that, and everybody feels it on both sides. There are just some tremendously hard-fought matches out there, some superlative golf. Gosh, we're seeing some unbelievable golf this week. Their side has played very well. The horses he had put in have stayed in, and they've produced. They've done wonderful things."

Then, as if he had been snapped back to the present by a flash of lucidity, Crenshaw's gaze turned serious, and he leaned forward—the exact pose he had struck in Chicago before his "It burns the hell out of me to listen to some of their viewpoints" comment. This time he paused, his back straighter, even straighter than it had been at Medinah, and with the microphone firmly grasped in his left hand, he wagged his right index finger at his audience and said, "I'm going to leave y'all with one thought, and I'm going to leave."

Everyone perched on the edges of their seats. This was Crenshaw's Gettysburg, his defining moment. Despite his incoherent ramblings, everyone thought he would finally offer something profound, energizing, and inspirational.

"I'm a big believer in fate," he said. Then another pause, as everyone leaned closer hoping to catch the words first. "I have a good feeling about this. That's all I'm going to tell you."

That was it? Kessler cut his eyes back at his producer in a what-the-hell-was-that gaze, and there were even a few audible snickers from the back of the packed room. Yes, yes, everyone walked out thinking Crenshaw had, indeed, lost all semblance of sanity. At any moment two white-clad caregivers would arrive, pat him on the arm, and say, "There, there, Mr. Crenshaw. There, there."

The Ryder Cup had claimed its first casualty. Ben Crenshaw had gone completely nuts.

*Ten*

# THE COMEBACK

DAVIS AND ROBIN LOVE had a courtesy-car driver who knew his way around Boston better than most, so they arrived back at the Four Seasons on Saturday night before any of the other couples. Once back on the sixth floor Robin went to the room to freshen up while Davis meandered down to the team room to see who might be hanging out. The room was empty except for a hotel waiter who had put out a fresh buffet of Chinese food. Never one to let good *moo goo gai pan* go to waste, Love sat down with a plate of food and the television remote. He turned on the Golf Channel just in time to see Crenshaw wagging his finger at reporters. When he heard the "I've got a good feeling about this" line, Love almost choked on his food.

"I got chills," Love said. "I couldn't eat any more. I said to myself, 'My God, he actually believes what he's saying. He's not just blowing smoke.' Nobody would have had enough nerve to guess we might win, but he went further than that. He wasn't thinking, 'Oh, they might win, so I'll say this to fire them up.' I was the only one at the hotel. He didn't think we were watching! He didn't think, 'They'll see this and it will fire them up.' He actually believed that we were going to win."

It was a sobering moment for Love, who had played on previous Ryder Cup teams for Tom Watson, Lanny Wadkins, and Tom Kite. None of those captains had ever been so brazen as to make a statement like the one he had just heard from Ben Crenshaw. Then again, nobody Love knew had ever become as engrossed in the captaincy as Crenshaw. "He thought about every little thing that was going to happen all during the week," Love said. "The things he did and said . . . I can't say it enough, Ben brought this team together. He should run for president or something."

Crenshaw would later support his friend George W. Bush for that post. Besides, Ryder Cup captain was the highest office in the land in his book and he already had that job. And as he rode in his courtesy car back into Boston, he couldn't wait to share what he knew with the rest of the team. It turned out that the "good feeling" Crenshaw had spoken about wasn't based solely on vibes from the golf gods. He had seen the Sunday pairings, and he had played through the scenarios in his mind. Crenshaw not only knew his team was going to win but he also knew how they were going to do it. When the rest of the team saw the pairings they would know, too. "We can whitewash 'em," he had said out loud to himself. Crenshaw had more than a feeling; he had fate on his side.

Tom Kite had pointed it out to him earlier in the day, but it didn't sink in until he saw the pairings. Kite, the numbers cruncher, had run the statistics. He knew that a player who played in all four matches prior to singles was almost twice as likely to lose on Sunday as a player who had rested for a match or two. Montgomerie, Lawrie, Westwood, Clarke, Jiménez, Parnevik, and Sergio had all played in every match. Sutton and Tiger were the only Americans to have played in all four matches. But Kite also knew that any player who hadn't played at all before singles stood an 80 percent chance of losing his singles match. Van de Velde, Coltart, and Sandelin would be making their debuts on Sunday while all of the Americans had one or more matches under their belts. It was tough for Crenshaw to digest what Kite was saying at the time, but once he had a chance to see it, to visualize it with the matchups on paper in front of him, he understood that not only was a U.S. win possible, it was mathematically probable. The statistics were in their favor. Of course they had been in their favor all week, but this was different. Crenshaw had the matchups he wanted.

Mark James's strategy of hiding his weakest players had finally caught up with him. On Sunday, when everybody played head-to-head in singles, there was nowhere for them to hide. So James had done what he thought was the next best thing: he had sacrificed his three non-starters early, lumping Sandelin, Van de Velde, and Coltart in the three, four, and five spots. Only Westwood and Clarke were ahead of them, the logic being that if two of his stalwarts could get a couple of early points, there wouldn't be a huge momentum shift, even if all three rookies lost. Then James loaded the guns, sending out Parnevik, Harrington, Jiménez, Olazábal, Montgomerie, Garcia, and Lawrie. They needed only four points to retain the cup, four and a half to win it outright. If Westwood and Clarke could pull a point and a half between them, he had Parnevik, Olazábal, Montgomerie, and Garcia in line to pick up the other three.

But because the Americans were so far down, Crenshaw had been forced to put his big guns out early in the hopes of creating some momentum. Tom Lehman was first out against Lee Westwood. That one could be close, but nobody wanted to win more than Lehman. Good money was on Lehman to win. Second out was Hal Sutton, who had been the man of the matches so far. Anything was possible, but Sutton looked good against Darren Clarke.

The third match made even Crenshaw chortle. Poor Jarmo Sandelin, in his first Ryder Cup match ever, had drawn Phil Mickelson, the man who came within a nanosecond of kicking Jarmo's ass into the Firth of Tay during the 1996 Dunhill Cup. Crenshaw wondered what kind of sleep Sandelin would get that night. Chalk up another one for America.

Four and five should go to the United States as well. Davis Love would take on Jean Van de Velde, while Tiger got the privilege of introducing Mr. Coltart to the Ryder Cup. Things tightened up after that. Duval drew Parnevik, and O'Meara, who had continued to struggle with his game, had Padraig Harrington. Steve Pate would take on Miguel Angel Jiménez, which made for the best-nicknamed match: The Mechanic versus The Volcano. If golf didn't work out, maybe they could strike a deal with the World Wrestling Federation. After that, Justin Leonard would take on José María Olazábal, Payne Stewart would play Colin Montgomerie, Jim Furyk got to try his game against Sergio, and Jeff Maggert brought up the rear against Paul Lawrie.

Momentum was a key, Crenshaw knew. Scoreboards were everywhere on the course, with blue flags appearing when the Europeans were up; and red, white, and blue flags going up for a U.S. lead. From a distance the U.S. flags looked solid red, and Crenshaw understood that if he could put enough red on the boards early, the crowd would become a major factor. There was no more helpless feeling than hearing a lead evaporate ahead of you. If the United States could jump on them early and often, players might begin to think of things other than their won matches. Once Crenshaw's team got their opponents board-watching, it would be over.

At the Four Seasons they methodically began to stream into the team room. Robin joined Davis, and Phil and Amy Mickelson were close behind. Duval and Julie McArthur came. Hal and Ashley Sutton. Soon every team member, every wife and every girlfriend, assembled. Some had met George W. Bush and others hadn't, but when the Texas governor came in with the Crenshaws those who met for the first time were struck by how quickly he engaged you. For a few brief moments they were spellbound.

Governor Bush thanked Ben and Julie Crenshaw for inviting him, and he spoke for a few minutes about pride, virtue, and courage. Then he pulled out a sheet of paper and began reading.

*Commandancy of the Alamo, Bexar, February 24, 1836. To the people of Texas and all Americans in the world: Fellow Citizens and Compatriots, I am besieged by a thousand or more Mexicans under Santa Anna. I have sustained a continual bombardment and cannonade for 24 hours and have not lost a man. The enemy has demanded a surrender at discretion, otherwise the garrison are to be put to the sword if the fort is taken. I have answered the demand with a cannon shot, and our flag still waves proudly from the walls. I shall never surrender nor retreat.*

*Then I call on you in the name of Liberty, of patriotism, and of everything dear to the American character, to come to our aid with all dispatch. The enemy is receiving reinforcements daily and will no doubt increase.*

*If this call is neglected, I am determined to sustain myself as long as possible and die like a soldier who never forgets what is due to his own honor and that of his country—Victory or Death. Lt. Col. William Barrett Travis.*

Santa Anna's advancing army massacred Travis, Davy Crockett, and the rest of the defenders of the Alamo, but as all good Texans knew, six weeks later, amid cries of "Remember the Alamo," charging American forces beat back Santa Anna and Texas gained independence from Mexico.

When Bush finished speaking there wasn't a dry eye in the house.

After the governor excused himself, Crenshaw showed a video that included highlight shots from each player's career set to the Queen song "We Are the Champions," followed by a personalized cheer from each player's college's cheerleaders. There was even a clip from the movie *Animal House,* the 1978 classic in which John Belushi asked the question of the ages, "Was it over when the Germans bombed Pearl Harbor? Hell, no!"

With emotions swinging between tears and laughter, Crenshaw went around the room and asked everyone to share what the Ryder Cup experience had meant. Mickelson echoed the earlier themes of pride and honor, virtue and courage. He had been painted with a brush he didn't deserve, labeled a greedy malcontent, and called an uncaring golf whore. Nothing could have been farther from the truth. At that moment everyone knew what Phil Mickelson was all about.

When it came time for Duval to speak, he had tears in his eyes. Tears! The man who had been labeled emotionless, who had been demonized, and who had been heckled by American fans steadied his quivering voice and told everyone how happy he was to be a part of this team. "I'm sick and tired of everyone saying we're not a team," he said. Duval, the man whose college coach had said, "David never really got into the team concept," had finally gotten it. He spoke to them about how his views had been mischaracterized and how he had suffered mightily as a result. But he also said, "We're better than them, so let's go show it. Let's go out there and kill 'em."

Those who were not moved before Duval spoke were profoundly moved afterward. Duval was not a man who shared his feelings with anyone. Yet here he was, overcome with emotion and talking about the spirit of the team. His words were simple—he didn't exceed his budget—but they had a huge impact on the mood of the room. Crenshaw's team had finally come together.

"You could tell everybody came together at that moment," Sutton said. "Most especially David. The comments he made were strong. He felt like he'd been chewed up and spit out, and he got very emotional about it. He knew that individual performances meant nothing. We all knew it. We were all just spokes in the wheel. David was a team player at that point."

Sutton picked up on that theme, reiterating the need to be aggressive and take the game to them. "We've got to play with more emotion," he told the team. "Raise your fists. Get the crowd into it. One of the most important things we have on our side is the crowd. If we can send enough firepower out early . . ."

Crenshaw interrupted him at that point and said, "*When* we send fire-power out. Not if, when."

Sutton nodded and continued, the intensity of his face and the punch in his voice raising the emotions of everyone who saw and heard him. "We don't want to just beat these guys; we want to beat the *hell* out of them. We want to demoralize them. We do that and the crowd will get into it, and the momentum will shift to our side."

Sutton had just summarized Crenshaw's strategy in terms everyone could understand. If (or as Crenshaw insisted, "when") the United States won the first four matches, everything would be all-square, but the momentum would clearly be with the Americans. Then it was up to everyone to support everyone else, close out matches quickly so you could get back out on the course and rev up your teammates.

At that moment, not a soul in the room thought the United States was going to lose.

Payne Stewart openly wept, as he always did in emotional settings like this, and when his turn came to speak, he invoked the memory of his father. "It would mean so much for him to be here," Stewart said.

Bill Stewart had worn canary-yellow jackets in his travels, often telling his young son, "It's better to be remembered for something than not remembered at all." In 1982 Payne began wearing knickers to be remembered. At that moment, however, Stewart wanted to be remembered only as a member of the team that won the 1999 Ryder Cup.

"We have to win this for Ben," Davis Love had said. But when Robin Love spoke, last among those who were there, she invoked another name. "I know this is going to make you cry," she said to her husband, "and it's going to make Ben cry, but I want everyone to think about what Harvey would say." She was right. The mere mention of Penick's name was like turning on a spigot. Then she invoked the words of the long-dead teacher. "Harvey would say, 'Take dead aim.'"

Even Sutton was moved. He too had once been a student of Harvey Penick—once, as in one golf lesson when Sutton was 17 years old. "My dad took me down to see him," Sutton remembered. "We started out to the range and he told my dad, 'Mr. Sutton, you just hang around the clubhouse. We don't need you down there.' So we went down to the range and he asked me if I wore a glove. I said, 'Yes, sir.' So he said, 'I want you to hit your driver with no glove and I don't want you to practice, and don't warm up.' I did what he said. I hit the first two or three not too good, and I hit the last two pretty good.

"Then he said, 'Now put your glove on and go through your normal routine.' I did that and hit about fifty balls without him saying a word. After that he said, 'Come over here and sit on the cart and I want to show you a couple of things.' He stood up and said, 'There will be people who tell you your grip is too strong, but it's not. Don't worry about that.' Then he took a club and looked backward and said, 'That's the perfect backswing.' He looked the other way and said, 'That's the perfect follow-through.' That's all he said. That was the whole lesson.

"Back at the clubhouse, he told my dad, 'You know, your son is going to be a good player and the best thing you can do for him is stay out of his way.' Those are the kind of lessons you like, because they make you feel pretty good. When you take a lesson and people tell you all the things you're doing wrong, that can be pretty demoralizing. Harvey wasn't that way. He was a good teacher and a great psychologist. He made me believe in me, and once a guy reaches a certain level, that's what it's all about."

Sutton had taken thousands of lessons from dozens of teachers since that day on the range in Austin with Harvey Penick, but of all the lessons he had taken in his life, Harvey's was the one he remembered word for word. It had been over 20 years ago, yet he remembered how many balls he hit, the wind direction, and exactly what Harvey Penick told him. Sutton would listen to too many other people over the next 20 years, and his mind would become too cluttered with swing thoughts that had no basis in Hal Sutton's reality. "Stinkin' thinkin,'" as his current teacher, Floyd Horgan, called it. He hoped all that was behind him. Now he would recall the simplest swing thought of all from the man who once made him believe in himself. Like the rest of them, Hal Sutton would "take dead aim."

Lehman was the first out, and he took control early with birdies at the fourth, fifth, and sixth, leaving Westwood stunned. Two bogeys at nine and 10 by Westwood and the first match was all but over. Lehman didn't just win; he had won decisively.

Sutton was right behind him, taking Clarke down 4 and 2 in a trouncing. Sutton hadn't just won, he had "beaten the hell out of his man," and it was time to get out there and cheer on the rest of his teammates. "This was awesome," Sutton said. "It's the greatest feeling I've ever had in golf. This is the best."

Lehman agreed. "The Ryder Cup brings it out in you," he said. "People who are normally laid back and kind of placid can get really emotional. I wanted the fans to know that I appreciated them and I recognized they were there for us. The fans all week have wanted us to smile and acknowledge them and give them something to cheer about. Well, I didn't miss a shot all day. I gave myself a chance at birdie on every hole."

Everyone watched the third match closely to see if any fireworks might erupt between Mickelson and Sandelin. None did, but the match did provide one of the funnier moments of the day. On the par-three second, an uphill 190-yard hole that is a short par-four for the members but shortened to a par-three for tournament play, Mickelson hit his shot 6 feet from the hole, and Jarmo hit a brilliant shot to within 3 feet.

As they walked up the green, Jarmo stood over his ball without moving. His hands were in his pockets, but he made no move toward his ball. Mark Ralfing, who was covering the match for NBC, said, "I think Sandelin is waiting for Mickelson to concede the putt, and it doesn't look like Mickelson is going to do it."

That wasn't it at all. Jarmo didn't realize until he reached the green that he had a hole in his pocket, and the coin he used to mark his ball had fallen out. His caddie didn't have a coin, and he certainly wasn't going to ask Mickelson for one. After fumbling around for a couple of minutes, a man in the gallery with a heavy South Boston accent said, "Hey, Jaaaamo, ya need a coin?"

"As a matter of fact, yes," Sandelin said. Seconds later the green was showered with coins from the gallery.

Sandelin picked an unlucky one, though. He missed the birdie putt on two, and Mickelson cruised to a 4 and 3 trouncing. The tide had clearly turned.

When Love made short work of Van de Velde 6 and 5, the United States had tied things up. It was up to the remaining eight players to come in with at least four and a half points for the United States to win.

Bruce Lietzke had called three of the first five matches "automatic points" for the United States, and he had turned out to be correct. The Americans were four-for-four in the early going, and Tiger was 3-up on Andrew Coltart. The boards were bleeding red, and everyone could sense a U.S. comeback.

The sixth match was critical. If Duval could beat Parnevik the streak would continue. Throughout the match, Duval had been more animated than he had ever been on a golf course. He pumped his fists; he engaged the crowd; he showed emotion; he did all the things no one had ever seen David Duval do before. The mood surrounding him became electric. If Duval was showing this kind of emotion, there had to be something special going on.

On the par-five 14th, Duval hit his second shot into the right bunker, blasted out, and made an 8-foot putt for birdie to close out Parnevik 5 and 4. But rather than shake Parnevik's hand and wave politely to the crowd, Duval put on a display. The overhand fist pumps were well intentioned, but a little weak. He looked like the cartoon dog Scooby Doo. Still the emotion was there. Duval ran around the green "geeing up the crowd" like a Boston College cheerleader. As the cheers intensified, Duval put a hand to his ear, cupping it in a mock "I can't hear you" gesture. This was the same man who never cracked a smile after shooting 59, who rifled his way to the number-one spot in the world rankings but claimed the rankings didn't matter to him, and who admitted to being reserved and quiet. Now he was leading the "U.S.A." chant on the 14th green while Padraig Harrington and Mark O'Meara waited to hit their approach shots. It was a turning point in both the Ryder Cup and the life and career of David Duval.

"My frame of reference for this event was based on two Presidents Cups," Duval said. "No offense to that event and what it stands for, but it pales in comparison to this. I love it. Winning the Players Championship was a special day for me. The final round when I shot 59 . . . If this isn't ahead of those it's at least tied."

Word of Duval's histrionic display filtered through the gallery like whispers of a revolution. The United States had the lead for the first time all week. It was fitting that David Duval would be the player to put them over the top for the first time. Tiger added to the lead with a 3 and 2 win over Coltart.

There were still matches that were too close to call, however. Maggert lost to Lawrie 4 and 3, and Justin Leonard was 4-down to José María Olazábal through 11. Montgomerie had gotten as many as 3-up on Stewart, but the tenacious U.S. Open winner kept battling back, cutting the lead to one, then losing another hole to give Monty another 2-up lead. When he wasn't trying to hold off Monty, Stewart was trying to defend him against the vicious hecklers whose insults become so vile that Colin's father James walked off the course.

On the 11th a spectator called Monty "a limey fat fuck," the vulgarian being obviously unaware that Montgomerie was Scottish.

At that Stewart stepped in. "That is enough!" he shouted. "That . . . is . . . eeeeenough." Had it been 1991 instead of 1999, a pre-Christian Stewart would have no doubt thrown an expletive or two of his own between the "eeee" and the "nough," but, while this was a kinder, gentler Stewart, he was still a man who held no quarter for those who disrespected his game.

Once the heckling was minimized (with Monty it was never eliminated) Stewart clawed his way back to all-square with four holes to play. But by then the group in front of Stewart had become the pivotal match.

Justin Leonard wasn't in good spirits when Davis Love found him on the 11th hole. At 4-down and having already been humiliated on national television by a mid-50s NBC analyst who couldn't make a 3-foot putt anymore if his life depended on it, Leonard needed a friend to cheer him up. "I'll leave if you want me to," Love had said to him.

"No, stay," Leonard said. On the 12th hole, Love provided some unintentional levity when he inadvertently walked in front of the tee as Justin was preparing to hit his tee shot. Leonard backed off and chuckled. If it wasn't the gallery or the marshals it was your own players getting in your way. Love's presence didn't necessarily help Leonard, but it had a temporary jinxing effect on Olazábal, who reeled off two straight bogeys to let Justin pull to within two holes of squaring the match. Another errant tee shot by Olazábal on the par-five 14th kept him from making birdie, and when Leonard drained a birdie putt there, he was only 1-down. Another birdie at the 15th and Leonard had overcome a 4-down deficit to pull back to all-square.

Furyk handily defeated Sergio 4 and 3, while Steve Pate defeated Jiménez 2 and 1. O'Meara had hooked his tee shot into the left rough on the last hole and it appeared as though he would lose his match to Harrington.

Leonard was the man. His was the match that would determine the Ryder Cup. After halving the 16th to remain all-square, Leonard hit his approach to the 17th 50 feet from the hole. Groans permeated the gallery. Even though Leonard was one of the best putters in the world, a 50-footer was potential three-putt range. When Olazábal's approach stopped 20 feet away, things didn't look good for the home team.

All his teammates were gathered around the 17th green, along with a few thousand interested and slightly intoxicated fans. Justin could do nothing but go through his routine. It was a 50-footer. All Leonard could do was take dead aim.

Crenshaw felt oddly at peace before Leonard hit his putt. It was on this very green, he knew, almost this very spot, where Francis Ouimet had won the 1913 U.S. Open and ushered in the era of American golf. Ouimet's old house was just across the road at 246 Clyde Street. If the grandstands hadn't been in the way he might have been able to see it from where he stood.

Leonard went through his normal procedure, keeping his head perfectly still after the stroke, allowing only the eyes to follow the ball for the first several feet. As it got closer to the hole, Leonard's eyes widened. When the ball trickled over the front edge of the hole, he raised his arms to the sky and let out a cathartic yell. The man who should have stayed home and watched on television had just made a 50-footer to win the Ryder Cup.

Or had he? Olazábal still had a 20-foot putt that would have halved the hole and extended the match, but when Leonard's putt fell in, everyone got caught up in the moment and bedlam ensued. Tom Lehman led the charge onto the green, leaping three feet into the air and charging Leonard. Davis and Justin's caddie, Bob Reifke, were close behind. Crenshaw fell to his knees and kissed the ground, while Mickelson twirled around and kissed his wife. All seemed to forget that there was still a player left to putt.

"It was unfortunate, but there was certainly no ill will," Sutton said of the celebration. He was a late joiner in the hugfest that took place on and around Olazábal's ball. According to Sutton, "I was in a catch-22. I knew Olazábal still had a chance to make that putt and tie that hole. At first I said, 'I'm not going to run out there,' but after everybody else got out there, I thought if somebody saw me they would say, 'What's wrong with Hal? Why isn't he celebrating with them?' I was in a no-win situation." Hal and Ashley reluctantly joined the fray. Five minutes later, Olazábal's putt slipped past the hole, and the Americans had officially won the Ryder Cup.

With the cup already secured, Payne Stewart conceded the 18th hole and his match to Colin Montgomerie, saying afterward, "I was disgusted with some of the actions and some of the name-calling and heckling that goes on with Colin. He doesn't deserve that. That is not what this event is about. I don't know if he's got a big bull's-eye on his back or what it is, but it's not fair. And when we got to the eighteenth hole and I got up on the green, I looked at my caddie and said, 'I'm not going to make him putt this putt. He doesn't deserve to have to stand over this putt.' We had already won the Ryder Cup, and that's what it's all about. My individual statistics don't mean crap out here, and I wasn't going to put him through that." It was a class act on Stewart's part, one that would be remembered for a long time.

Another image that would be remembered was that of the U.S. team, drenched in champagne, standing on the balcony after having climbed out a storage room window in the locker room building and singing the National Anthem at the tops of their lungs. Duval was there, glasses off, hat off, a huge smile on his face, with his arms around his teammates . . . HIS teammates . . . singing away as if he were a karaoke regular. It was a moment few of them could put into words.

Sutton tried when he said, "This is the greatest display of golf ever, right here. We knew we could do it, and we reached deep inside and brought it out. We all believed. We believed in ourselves, and in our cause, and in our team. We knew what we had to do and we did it, as a team."

When he came back into the media center, Crenshaw had regained all his color, and all his wits, and he gave the assembled reporters a wry smile and a silent nod as if to say, "I told you so." By then, they all believed. "You've got to believe in fate," Crenshaw repeated for the umpteenth time. "I said to all of you that the matches were marked by razor-thin margins with some outstanding play that we continue to see year after year, meeting after meeting. What transpired from these guys is a moving experience . . . moving. I never stopped believing. I never stopped believing in these guys. They're the greatest I've ever seen in my life. To see this day unfurl like this is absolutely something . . . It's just something to see."

*Eleven*

# YANK YOBS AND CHINAMEN

WHEN HE STOOD AT the podium during the closing ceremonies, on a stage that looked like it had been designed for an outdoor Rolling Stones concert, PGA of America president Will Mann said, "We are privileged in that we have been able to witness one of the most compelling competitions in all of sports, devoid of commercialism and resplendent in its honor."

Hundreds of assembled spectators broke out in hearty spontaneous laughter, an uproar that seemed to take Mann aback. Certainly the "privileged" and "honor" part of his comments were to be expected, even though a fair number of those who witnessed the matches found the behavior of some of the fans far less than honorable. It was the "devoid of commercialism" statement the crowd found mirthful, and rightfully so. In addition to the conspicuous plethora of corporate tents in the Samuel Ryder and Francis Ouimet Villages, everyone sitting in the closing ceremonies had just walked past the mahogany-laden Ryder Cup Superstore to get to the grandstands. For three days fans had been shelling out C-notes for logoed shirts, $55 for periscopes (a product designed by Phil Mickelson, Sr., and a must-purchase given the magnitude of the galleries), $28 for hats, $1,175 for Ryder Cup cuff links, $10 for a single shot glass, $12 for a kid's golf glove, and $4.75 for a plastic cup of beer. To say the Ryder Cup lacked a commercial component was laugh-out-loud funny, and that was exactly what the spectators at the closing ceremonies did.

On the whole, the ceremony was, indeed, honorable and it was a privilege to attend, especially if you had just witnessed the greatest comeback in golf history and one of the most dramatic moments in all of sports. Both teams put on jackets for the closing festivities, even though members of the U.S. team still smelled like champagne. Davis Love tried to balance his personal fragrances by lighting a Robusto cigar, which he smoked as he marched down past the grandstands and onto the stage. Like the rest of the team, Love couldn't stop smiling, even with the cigar in his mouth.

The Europeans were remarkably gracious at the ceremonies. Mark

James joked about Sergio finishing his homework, and he had nothing but praise for Crenshaw, the American team, the PGA of America, and the city of Brookline. It was a classy moment. Too bad it didn't last.

After the closing ceremonies the European team answered questions, and José María Olazábal gave a reasonable, thoughtful, and well-deserved scolding to the American players and fans who ran out onto the 17th green before he putted. "I think that kind of behavior is not what anybody expects," Olazábal said. "It was very sad to see. It was an ugly picture, and it shouldn't have happened. We're playing a match, we're trying to show respect to each other, and I don't think that it was the right thing to do. I understand there was a lot of emotion, but at the same time you have to keep your feet on the ground and realize what the situation is. I understand that sometimes you are carried by your emotions, and there's nothing wrong with that. But just show some respect for the opponents. That's what I think we all do out there.

"That goes for the crowds also. They were very nice, but from time to time you have some clever people who do certain things that we all know are not right. Those things don't have any place at all at a golf tournament or on a golf course. I think every one of you would agree with that. It doesn't matter where you play, just show respect. You can cheer your own team as much as you want, but show some respect for your opponent. It's as simple as that."

Everyone, even the Americans, agreed with Olazábal's assessment. The U.S. players realized they had gotten caught up in the emotions of the moment, and within minutes of Olazábal's comments, Ben Crenshaw was in front of a microphone saying, "We know what happened, and we do apologize sincerely. There really wasn't any call for that. The celebration started spilling over and it really was not something that we need to be proud of and we've apologized. For that, we're truly sorry."

By all rights that should have been the end of it. No one on the European team suggested that the celebration at the 17th in any way altered the outcome of the Ryder Cup. In fact, Mark James said, "I think we were outplayed. The way they played and with the stuff that was flowing into the hole from all angles, I don't think tactics would have made much difference. They holed a lot more shots. It was quite remarkable. That's what you've got to do in this game—ride the streak—and they rode the streak tremendously well today."

There were certainly some crowd-control issues that needed to be discussed, as everyone was well aware, but those problems were not unique to the Ryder Cup or to Boston. The nationalistic nature of the competition made for louder, more obnoxious fans, but that was nothing new. The PGA of America and the PGA Tour had been grappling with the issue of fan behavior for over two years. Monty being heckled wasn't a new thing, either. It happened every time he teed off in America. That didn't make it right, but it didn't make it unique. "It was horrible conduct, there's no question about it," Jim Awtrey said afterward. "We'll be addressing the problem with European officials when we meet in Augusta in April. We've got to work together to take those people out of the crowd and out the gate."

According to James the Europeans knew the crowds would be vocal, and as long as Europe was sporting a 10–6 lead, nobody in James's camp had any problems. "I think overall the crowds have been very fair," James said on Saturday night. "We were perfectly aware there would be big crowds, and that most of them were going to support the U.S.A. There have been a few heckles, but there have also been heckles for the American players. I wouldn't say they were ill-mannered or anything like that."

At the time those comments seemed reasonable, as did the ones Colin Montgomerie made after he endured a barrage of personal attacks on Sunday. "I use it now as a motivating factor," Monty said. "I treat it as a compliment because I must be good at this game, and it does motivate me to perform. I have a lot of ambition and that tends to bring it out. It has been difficult, not just for me, but for my colleagues as well, especially when I watched the scene on the seventeenth green. I just couldn't believe that. It was very, very difficult for everyone concerned. But I think we should take great heart in our performance. It just wasn't enough at the end of the day."

There was no hysterical indignation in those comments. They seemed quite reasonable. Monty was rightfully upset at the American players' celebration on the 17th green, and he was none too pleased about the verbal abuse of the hecklers. But he was composed and thoughtful in his admonishment. After Crenshaw apologized, everyone thought it would be over.

The next morning, Davis Love couldn't wait to get out of bed, even though, like most of the team (with the noted exception of Mark

O'Meara, who flew home on Sunday night) Love had celebrated at the Four Seasons into the wee hours of Monday morning. He spent much of that time reliving stories and watching replays of Justin's putt at the 17th. "People kept coming to my room saying, 'What are you doing sitting in here?' I said, 'I wanted to watch Justin's putt over and over again.' I couldn't get enough of it. I watched it live, then watched it all night Sunday night." On Monday morning as he prepared to fly from Boston to Orlando, Love bought every newspaper he could find and read every story on the matches. Between takeoff and landing, he had read the *Boston Globe,* the *Boston Herald,* the *New York Times,* the *Providence Journal,* the *Wall Street Journal,* and *USA Today.* In Orlando he read the *Orlando Sentinel* and the *Tampa Tribune,* and when he'd finished reading everything he could find, he started all over again rereading each paper and reliving each moment. "It was a week we'll remember for the rest of our lives," he said.

The first British headline Love saw was from the *Daily Mirror,* and it sent his blood pressure soaring. "United Slobs of America," read the half-page headline with an equally bold subheading quoting Sam Torrence as saying, "This behaviour was the most disgusting I have ever seen." At first Love thought this was the British tabloid press doing what they did best—sensationalizing the mundane to sell papers. But then he saw the quotes, and as the day progressed he heard and saw video footage of the European team saying things Love couldn't believe. "They wanted to win at all costs, and that cost was their dignity," Miguel Angel Jiménez said. "Thank God we were playing for pride and not money or it might have come to blows."

The assaults continued. Mark James, after making his eloquent remarks at the closing ceremonies and congratulating the Americans in his press conference, was now claiming that a member of the gallery spat at his wife (a charge that was never substantiated by a single independent eyewitness). But the truth didn't matter at that point, as James's picture appeared beneath a headline reading, "Yank Yob Spat at My Wife! . . . Now James Plans Ryder Snub." He was talking about a boycott! The captain of the European Ryder Cup team was suggesting the Europeans consider passing on future trips to America to contest the Ryder Cup.

Love thought it was outrageous. What the hell did they have to do? For months they had been abused for being spoiled millionaires, a

12-men-12-private-jets kind of team with no sense of comradely or
national unity. But when they did come together as a team after Saturday night's emotional group session, and when they worked as a team to
orchestrate the greatest comeback in Ryder Cup history, and when they
then celebrated that comeback with genuine, heartfelt, and spontaneous
(if not inappropriate) display of emotion, they were being ripped even
worse! The European captain was calling them "yobs," whatever the
hell that was, and players like Montgomerie, who had been gracious in
defeat on Sunday, were now saying things like, "No amount of apologies
can make amends for what they did." Ian Woosnam was even talking
about physical violence! "It's a good thing I wasn't there, or there would
have been a few metal clubheads in some people's heads," Woosnam had
said. Former boxer or not, there were a number of Americans, Love
among them, who would have taken Little Woosie up on that challenge.

"I don't blame the players as much, but they've gotten caught up in
their own press," Love said in trying to come up with a reasonable explanation for this delayed vitriolic reaction. "When they were here they
were very gracious, but then they got off by themselves and people
started telling them how bad all this was. It's sad they're whining so
much, but when you get pounded that bad, you have to find some reason
for it. They got pounded into the ground on Sunday and they're embarrassed by it, I'm sure."

Love thought the European players were doing a little "geeing up" of
their own back home, and the continuous bombardment in the European
press supported his position. According to the *Sun,* a less than always
accurate source of British news, Prime Minister Tony Blair had called the
Americans' reaction at the 17th green "disgusting." The *Daily Mail* called
it "disgraceful," in bold headlines, and columnists wrote such lines as
"American Players and Their Fans Belong in the Gutter."

The *Mirror* opined, "Football hooligans act better than the way the
Americans have treated the Ryder Cup over the last three days. Their
antics whipped the crowd into uncontrollably boorish behavior. Sporting relations between the two nations have now slipped to an all-time
low."

Love and others found the "football [soccer] hooligan" reference particularly offensive and off base. To the best of everyone's knowledge,
barbed wire had never been erected around an American golf course (or
any other sporting venue, for that matter) and riot police had never been

called in to keep order. Those were standard practices at European soccer matches. But that fact didn't stop the *Standard* from making a similar reference when it said, "A fantastic competition was sullied by a football terrace culture outside the ropes and an appalling lack of consideration from Team America inside them."

People were killed in knife fights at European soccer games. As unseemly and obnoxious as they might have been, all the Bostonian faithful did was hurl a few nonlethal expletives. In fact, it was the British who seemed intent on injecting physical violence into the mix. According to the *Daily Mail,* "Rednecks show that it may be time to start trading punches, not pleasantries."

On and on it went. The *Daily Telegraph* said the Americans "not only indulged in the worst excesses of triumphantism during and after the match, but also turned in a repulsive display of bad manners." And a headline in the *Scotsman* read, "Americans Celebrate Victory the Day Sportsmanship Died."

At least the writing was good. Most players got a chuckle out of the column Matthew Norman wrote in the *London Evening Standard.* "Let's be painfully honest about it," Norman wrote. "Yes, they are repulsive people, charmless, rude, cocky, mercenary, humorless, unpardonably ugly (that Jim Furyk shouldn't be playing golf at all; he should be playing Igor, the one who says, 'earthlings, master,' in a horror movie), full of nauseatingly fake religiosity, and as odious in victory as they are unsporting in defeat. The only thing to be said in favour of the American golfers, in fact, is that, at golf if at nothing else, they are better than the Europeans."

They were Igors and yobs who had no more in common with Europeans than did the Chinese, according to Peter Alliss, who had no qualms about consorting with his American colleagues at ABC. But at least they weren't hypocrites.

"They sure have short memories," Love said. "When we lost at Oak Hill, they celebrated and ran across the green. They celebrated like crazy in Valderrama, and their fans were no better than our fans. You ought to go back and look at the highlight videos of all their celebrations."

As for the personal insults, Love didn't condone anything that happened, but he refused to pretend that it was all one-sided. "How long have they been calling our wives flight attendants and blond bimbos?" he asked. Then he recalled a few incidents from Boston that seemed to have escaped attention. "Justin and I were playing a practice round on Thursday and European fans yelled at me, 'Oh, and four at Valderrama!' and we hadn't even started the tournament. There were people coughing when we were putting, so it was never one-sided. We weren't singing songs like that 'Olé, olé, olé' crap whenever we were up in a match. But every time we got down we heard that song. And this was Boston! We didn't have nineteen-year-old kids doing cartwheels in the fairways when we won holes. This stuff has been going on a long time on both sides. To act as though it's just happening now is not right."

Nor, according to Love, were some of the inaccurate accounts of exactly who did what during the American celebration. The *Telegraph*, for example, wrote, "The cavalry charge, led by the clear winner in the pass-the-sickbag award, Hal Sutton, was truly appalling, though, it has to be said, no more gross than most forms of American tribalism."

Tribal customs aside, Sutton was one of the last men to reluctantly join the celebration at 17. But facts be damned, Sutton wore cowboy hats and drove pickup trucks and said "ya'll" and "yes, ma'am." He was the perfect target.

Sutton couldn't have cared less. "I don't take things personally like some people do," he said. "All somebody's trying to do is divert attention away from where it should be. In defeat, whether you're American or European, whether you're a football player or a basketball player, or a tennis player or a golfer, we're all going to make an excuse as to why we didn't win. I will promise you that is exactly what they've done. If they had won they would have never noticed the crowd. If we had lost, the fact that they slow-played us would have been a bigger deal with some of the guys than it was. But you didn't hear a word about it, because we won.

"Mark James made a tragic error in the way he paired people. He put the three guys who had not yet played out there in the first few matches. To have done that was to give us the lead. In hindsight, he saw that, and so he was looking for anything to deflect attention from the fact that he made a mistake. It happens all the time. So I'm not surprised by their hostile reaction. I expected it."

Crenshaw expected it as well, but that didn't stop him from being slightly frustrated. "I apologized for the incident Sunday night in Boston and again the next day. Our players apologized. I don't know what else can be done. I feel badly about it, but the story is the comeback our guys made.

"Playing before partisan galleries has been difficult long before what happened in Boston. It is the fabric, the very essence, of team competition. If you want a perspective on that, talk to Tom Kite, who captained our Ryder Cup team in Spain. I can assure you, their fans weren't rooting for us over there."

But Crenshaw had a philosophic view on all the hoopla, just as he did on everything else. In the long run, he knew, history would remember the way his team had come together and the comeback his guys had made. "Look back at Kiawah Island [in 1991]," he said. "The same thing was said about the competition after it was over. Fans were unruly, too many breaches of etiquette, it will never be the same. Once the emotions die down, there will still be the mutual respect we have for each other. I'm sorry all this stuff has taken away from the real story. Our guys made history. We shouldn't forget that."

As usual, Crenshaw was right. By the next weekend, as Love, Leonard, Jeff Maggert, and Steve Pate took a four-round victory lap during the PGA Tour's Buick Challenge in rural Georgia, the controversy was old news, but the comeback was still fresh on everybody's mind. "I won a PGA Championship and I've been a lot of places, but I have never gotten the kind of response I have over this Ryder Cup," Love said. "People are thanking me. When it goes from people saying, 'Congratulations,' and 'Nice playing' to saying, 'Thank you,' that shows you how important it is."

Love also came to realize how important the bonding had been among team members in Boston. They had all known each other for years, but until they jelled as a team and became "the spokes in a wheel," as Sutton had called it, none of them realized what it meant to be part of something bigger than a golf tournament, something that would forever link them together as champions.

Sitting in Philips Arena in Atlanta watching an NHL hockey game with R.E.M. bassist Mike Mills one week after the Ryder Cup, Love received some unexpected congratulations from Atlanta Braves pitchers John Smoltz and Tom Glavine.

"I know what it feels like for you guys to win a World Series now," Love said to the two Cy Young Award winners.

Both men nodded, then Glavine said, "When a team comes together, there's no better feeling."

Love and his 11 teammates had learned that lesson well in Boston.

# Twelve

# BACK TO VALDERRAMA

DAVIS LOVE LOOKED BACK at the television screen as Tiger's ball rolled off the front edge of the 17th green and tumbled into the water, and he shook his head as the crowd on the hillside behind the green stood and cheered. Yank yobs and Chinamen when it happened in Boston, but in Spain what was it? Retribution? Gusto? Since the man who stood to gain most from Tiger's misfortune, Miguel Angel Jiménez, lived less than 60 miles away and had driven his Ferrari from his home to Valderrama for this World Golf Championship event, would this behavior by the crowd be considered a "spontaneous display of nationalism"? Whatever it was, it was different from anything Love had seen in the game.

Professional golf had changed more in the two years since Love had last strolled these fairways than it had in the previous decade, maybe the previous two decades. The galleries were illustrative of that. Love had been involved in several altercations with fans over the previous 24 months—drunks, mostly, who thought they knew more about golf while inebriated than Love did sober. On Hilton Head he had almost gone after a fan who called him a "pussy" when he laid up to a par-five. Mark told him to let it go, but Davis couldn't let it go. "Jack and Arnold never had to contend with this kind of thing," he had said. As a member of the tour policy board he had to deal with the issue of alcohol on the course. It wasn't getting better, but as he looked into the faces of the celebrating Spanish crowd behind the 17th green at Valderrama Love knew that banning beer wouldn't put the genie back in the bottle. The game had come too far for that.

Love would fly home on the tour's shuttle with the rest of the players, winless in 1999 but still ranked fourth in the world. But 1999 wasn't a year you could measure in wins or earnings. Love had experienced his highest moment as a golfer when the U.S. team captured the Ryder Cup, and he had gone through one of the low points in his life with the loss of Payne Stewart. This was the first week he had seen the European players since the Ryder Cup, but a lot had changed since that September

Sunday afternoon in Boston. No one was interested in rehashing that week. Payne's death had made them all realize how silly the hyperbole had become. It was, after all, just a game.

Love would play in the PGA Grand Slam (a four-player silly-season match-play event pitting the winners of the four majors against each other) in Stewart's spot. "My first instinct was to say no," he said. "I tried to talk the PGA into playing with only three, but they wanted to keep the match-play format so it was going to be four. They wanted a friend to play in his place, so I said yes. It will be difficult, but maybe by me playing I can help keep the focus on Payne. It's just another step forward."

The healing process would take time, he knew. He had been through this before. Christmas, New Year's, the start of the 2000 season, Pebble Beach, and next year's U.S. Open would all be harder because of the memories they triggered. Love couldn't help smiling as he remembered the night after the U.S. victory in Boston. Payne was in the team room, standing on a table, his hat on backward, with a bottle of champagne in his hand. The life of the party. That's the way he hoped to always remember him.

After taking a drop behind the pond, Tiger hit what appeared to be a good chip shot that stopped on top of the crest in the green, not too far from the spot where he had putted it into the water in 1997. Three putts later, Tiger had taken a triple-bogey, and his cakewalk ninth victory of the year appeared in jeopardy.

A par at the 18th left Tiger six-under for the week, five better than anyone else in the field with the lone exception of Jiménez. Tiger went to the range where he and Butch Harmon worked on a couple of swing keys in case there was a playoff. He had played almost flawless golf, but there was room for improvement. Flawless was a state of mind, and he hadn't reached that state yet.

Fifteen minutes later the practice paid off. Jiménez hit a deft chip shot that appeared destined for the hole, which would have meant an outright win for the Spaniard. (But the ball slid less than an inch by the hole, to the groans of the gallery.) The Mechanic was in a playoff with the world's number-one player, and the partisan crowd sensed the inevitable. At least they wouldn't have to play the 17th again. The play-off would start at 18 and move on to the 10th if needed.

It wasn't needed. Tiger ripped a three-wood into the center of the 18th fairway, long and straight, leaving himself a short iron into the green. Jiménez, who had been strolling around the course to thunderous applause all day, hooked his tee shot into the left rough. If he had a shot, it would be a difficult one.

Bob Combs, who had been coordinating the PGA's media efforts in Spain all week, walked out to watch the playoff and was stunned by what he saw. The Guardia Civil, soldiers who had become infamous during Franco's reign of terror, lined the fairway as makeshift marshals, standing at parade rest, their camo-pants tucked into their boots and their nine-millimeter pistols perched in their holsters within easy reach. They all wore about three days' growth of beard, and Combs couldn't help visualizing what it must have been like in the bad old days, when those guys came knocking at your door in the middle of the night. He just hoped nobody got shot before Jiménez hit his approach.

A fluttering sound overhead caught Combs's attention and he looked up to be marveled even further. An ultralight aircraft—basically a hang glider with a Briggs and Stratton lawnmower engine to keep it aloft—was cruising overhead, its pilot sitting in what looked to be a lawn chair. A large Sikorsky helicopter with military markings flew directly underneath the ultralight, its dual rotors ensuring that the rogue pilot would stay aloft or risk being chopped to pieces. Combs cautiously approached one of the soldiers who looked as though he held a reasonably high rank and asked, "What's going on up there?" He pointed casually, as if seeing an ultralight pilot within 20 or so feet of the blades of a helicopter were an everyday occurrence back home in Ponte Vedra.

"We have it under control," the officer said in broken English without hinting at a smile.

No matter how this event turned out, Combs just hoped it finished without death or injury. What a long, strange year it had been.

Jiménez missed the green with his approach and chipped poorly. It looked as though he would make bogey, but it didn't matter. Tiger hit an eight-iron to 12 feet and curled the breaking putt in for a birdie and his ninth victory of the year. The Mechanic took his bows, giving the crowd a back-of-the-hand El Presidente wave as he tapped in and walked off the green. He couldn't complain. He had beaten the best players in the world, save one.

Jiménez, and everyone else in the world, marveled at what Tiger Woods had accomplished. A streak that started in May, when Tiger "got it" on the range at Isleworth, culminated in Spain with his second $1 million victory in four months, his ninth win of the year, and a mind-boggling $6,616,585 in official earnings—more money than Jack Nicklaus had won in his entire career.

Could anybody beat Tiger Woods? Sure. He wouldn't win every time he played, no matter how good he was; golf wasn't like that. But Tiger had already redefined the game, and as his poise and maturity continued to improve, he looked more and more like a man who had his eyes set on a long-term prize no one else could fathom.

There were skeptics. Hale Irwin, from the "Show Me" state of Missouri, said, "I think we have to keep the jury out for a little while on Tiger. I'm the first to say he's the best in the world right now, but I'm also the first to say that I think there will be other players who come along who will be Tigeresque in their abilities. Tiger has certainly fueled the interest of a lot of young people, but at twenty-four years old, I'm still going to sit on the back bench and see where he is when he's thirty."

Tiger had a plan for age 30, and 40, and even 50, and as he stood on the 18th green at Valderrama and held up his second World Golf Championship trophy of the year, he was already looking ahead.

"I've had a great season," he said. "And it's nice to end it this way. Hopefully next year I'll play the same type of golf. We'll see about the number of victories . . . No doubt, my best round is still ahead of me."

He then hoisted the trophy and smiled as what seemed like a thousand flashbulbs went off around him. Five minutes later, Tiger hugged Joanna Jagoda and the two walked up the hill and into the clubhouse through a sea of shouting fans being held back by the armed soldiers of the Guardia Civil. At ease, and comfortable in his own skin, Tiger continued to blaze new trails as an athlete and a celebrity. And everyone who saw him knew he was right: the best was still ahead of him.

*Epilogue*

# NOT A FAIR FIGHT

IT WAS TOUGH to gain perspective on just how dramatically the game had changed in the two years between the Valderrama Ryder Cup and the WGC Championships, primarily because the golf season didn't allow time for reflection. As soon as the final putt fell in Spain, players headed off in different directions, some to design golf courses, others to silly-season events where truckloads of cash awaited their arrival. David Duval and Fred Couples (neither of whom had made the trip to Spain the first week of November) paired up the week after Valderrama to win the Franklin Templeton Shark Shootout, an unofficial two-man best-ball tournament hosted by Greg Norman at the same Sherwood Country Club where Duval lost to Tiger Woods in the much-ballyhooed "Showdown at Sherwood." It was a team event, and a 54-hole affair, so no one took it too seriously. But it was also Duval's first win since April. On the other side of the world Tiger jetted off to Ta Shee, Taiwan, where he looked like a road-weary business traveler as he finished sixth in the Johnnie Walker Classic. The losing streak was short-lived, however. One week later in Kuala Lumpur Tiger won individual honors by nine shots as he carried his team to victory in the World Cup of Golf. He followed that win with a handy trouncing of Paul Lawrie and Davis Love in the PGA Grand Slam, while Duval was finishing dead last in the made-for-television Skins Game. Not that these events meant much. Under normal circumstances the silly-season was a time for players to yuck it up for the cameras. Winning was secondary to the kind of show you put on. But the wave of popularity created by Tiger had changed things. Now any event, whether it was a major championship or a four-ball event in Sri Lanka, garnered the attention of fans around the world as long as Tiger was in the field.

Duval never came right out and said this bothered him. He didn't have to. The tone he took said it all. It was "the B.S. factor" that, Duval said, almost drove him over the edge. Whether it was the ripping he received in the press for the "pay for play" controversy or the "What's happened to Duval?" questions that were being raised after his six-month dry spell, the number-two player in the world clearly felt he had been wrongly vilified. "There's a lot of peripheral stuff that's absurd to my mind. It's disgusting to me that people read and believe this filth," he said, failing to specify which "filth" had set him off. "It's reckless, it's malicious, and it's unfair."

Fairly or unfairly, by the end of the 1999 season Duval was no longer viewed as a hip rebel golfer with a radical chic attitude and the best game in the world. He was just another in a long line of curmudgeonly athletes who briefly reached the top of their sports. Right or wrong, that perception wounded Duval. "I thought it was a great, great year," he said. "But no matter what happens, it's never going to be enough for everybody. That's the one thing I learned this year." He went on to make a Hoganesque admission concerning his fall from grace in the public's eye. "If I understand correctly, the criticism is really about my personality, not my game," Duval said. "People want me to be more vocal, pump my fists more, act more emotional. That's not me. I don't know how people perceive me, but I love to play, I love to compete, I speak my mind, and I won't change my approach. I'm not trying to create an image. I'm just being myself. I thought it was the scores that mattered."

Duval was right on that point; it was the scores that mattered and from the first week of April through the end of the 1999 season, he didn't post the numbers. "I played so sporadically this year that I could never get a good rhythm," he said as a means of explaining his lackluster finish. "I will try to do a better job of scheduling, which probably means playing more." He also summed up his objectives in typical Duval fashion, bluntly and unambiguously declaring, "It's my intention to do everything I can to prepare for the major championships. If this is what you want, then I'll say it: I intend to win the Masters. I intend to win the U.S. Open. I intend to win the British Open. And I intend to win the PGA Championship."

With that Duval retreated to the seclusion of his Ponte Vedra Beach home for the remainder of the year.

When he returned to the tour in January, everyone was stunned, not by Duval's play but by his appearance. David Duval had become, in the vernacular of his generation, buff. In the six weeks between the Skins Game and the Mercedes Championships in Kapalua, Hawaii, Duval's body had gone from reasonably fit to sculpted, with a body-fat percentage that dipped into the low single digits. "Look at him," Ernie Els said, pointing to Duval. "He looks like a bodybuilder."

Mr. Olympia was safe in Duval's company, but the golfer had, indeed, morphed into something extraordinary. For those who remembered the pear-shaped Duval—the college kid who wolfed down cheeseburgers and carried 25 percent body fat on his 220-pound frame—this was an alarming transformation. A high-protein, low-carbohydrate diet and daily workouts in the gym produced a trim physique, but it wasn't the kind of body that looked particularly healthy. Duval claimed to be the same weight as he had been throughout 1999, but with every vein in his forearms visible from a distance and his cheeks hollowed and taut, the new Duval earned his share of points, stares, and more than a few subtle whispers. As usual Duval didn't care what people said, and in keeping with his character, he was blunt about his motivation for trimming down. "I really feel that physical preparation will be an important piece of the puzzle," Duval said. "I need to put it together to really get beyond where I've been and improve, you know, the Masters, U.S. Open, British Open." He wasn't the only player hitting the weight room, but Duval was certainly the poster child for the new golf fitness craze. Martinis and cigarettes, long-standing staples in the clubhouses and locker rooms, had gone the way of the hickory shaft, replaced by protein drinks and traveling trainers. Tiger had raised the bar, and golfers were doing things they had never done before to keep up. "I feel like, in general, if I can be a more fit and stronger athlete, then that will translate itself into better golf," Duval said.

He was right, but it still wasn't enough. Duval started the 2000 season by shooting 12-under-par for four rounds in brutal Hawaiian winds, a score that beat 27 of the tour's best by at least five shots. But two players, Tiger and Els, played even better, shooting 16-under and lapping the field. Tiger won on the second hole of sudden death to capture his fifth consecutive PGA Tour win. No matter how good the rest of the world's best golfers played, he always seemed to be a little better. "It's awfully tough playing a guy who's driving it onto greens that are 450 yards away," Els said of Tiger. "The guy is kind of a freak. You know what I mean?" This was neither praise nor an insult, but simply a statement of fact as Els saw it. Tiger took no offense. He enjoyed it when the people he was competing against viewed him as a freak of nature.

Soon everyone would agree with Els's assessment. And no one would learn what kind of freak Tiger really was better or faster than Duval. As Tiger and Els loaded into the Kapalua courtesy van and prepared to head back to the 18th tee for the playoff, Duval stood by stoically and watched. He then said, "There's no reason why I shouldn't be going up there with them. I certainly hit the ball well enough to be as many under par as those guys."

It would be a mantra he would repeat to himself many more times throughout the 2000 season.

Tiger didn't play again until the last week in January, but when he did make it back on tour it was as if nothing had changed. Down by seven with nine holes to play at Pebble Beach in the AT&T Pro-Am, nobody gave Tiger much of a chance. Three birdies and an eagle later, Woods shot a final-round 64 to leap past Matt Gogel and Vijay Singh to win his sixth "official" event in a row, even though Tiger considered his so-called streak to be a media creation. "To do it in one year is more difficult than having it spread out from one year to the next," he said. He also took into account his loss in Asia and the fact that he had played particularly well in the Williams World Challenge, a silly-season invitational held over New Year's. Those weren't official PGA Tour events, but Tiger didn't draw that distinction. He played and did not win, therefore any "streak" he might have been on was purely fabricated. Wins were all that mattered to him anyway. He would let others dwell on the statistics.

A week later the streak no longer mattered. On the Pacific shores near Carlsbad, California, Woods's play was, in his words, "depressing," yet he still finished second to Phil Mickelson in the Buick Invitational. "To even be under par the way I was hitting [the ball] was kind of a miracle," Woods said. To finish second in a field of 155 of the best players in the world while hitting the ball that poorly was more than a miracle. It was an apocalyptic sign. The 2000 golf season was becoming the Tiger Woods Show, and no one could do anything about it.

By the time the Masters rolled around, Tiger had three wins, three seconds, and such a wide lead on the money list and in the world rankings that catching him seemed out of the question. Suddenly the modern Grand Slam of golf—winning the Masters, U.S. Open, British Open, and PGA Championship in the same season, a feat that has never been accomplished—seemed not just possible but reasonable. Tiger held the scoring record at the Masters, and he already had one win at Pebble Beach, site of the 2000 U.S. Open. St. Andrews, venue for the British Open, was perfect for Tiger's game, as was Valhalla, the Nicklaus-designed course in Louisville, Kentucky, where the PGA Championship would be played. The question wasn't whether Tiger would win a major—it was whether or not he could win them all! And if not, who would step up and challenge him? Darren Clarke and Hal Sutton had beaten Tiger head-to-head in the Andersen Consulting Match Play Championship and the Players Championship, and Mickelson had managed to win in California, but no single player seemed poised to challenge Tiger week in and week out. He was, by all admissions, in a league of his own.

Duval couldn't worry about any of that, nor could he be distracted by all the hyperbole surrounding Tiger's record. There were still four majors to be played, and Duval, the second-ranked player in the world, intended to win them. That was what he had built his schedule, body, and swing around. He was sick of being the best player never to win a major, and he was tired of being looked upon as something other than a world-class golfer because he hadn't won one of the four biggies. The Players Championship, which Duval won in 1999, had a better field and a better venue than the PGA Championship, but nobody seemed to care about that. It wasn't classified as a major, despite players like Mickelson, Sutton, and even Duval himself saying it deserved equal billing. The fact remained that Tiger had two major wins, the 1997 Masters and the 1999 PGA Championship, and Duval had none. Until that was rectified, David knew he would never be viewed on the same plane as Tiger.

He also arrived in Augusta having gone a full year without a win. Duval had won four times in the first three months of 1999, but with the lone exception of the Shark Shootout Hit-and-Giggle Classic in the off-season, he hadn't hoisted a trophy or collected a winner's check in 12 full months. A victory in a major would mean more to him than anyone would ever know.

"I have devoted the last six months to this week," Duval said. "This would be the fulfillment of a dream."

For a while it looked as though the dream might come true. Tiger, who entered the week a 2–1 favorite to win, took a triple-bogey on the par-three 12th on Thursday en route to an opening 75, his worst first-round score in the Masters since he missed the cut as a 20-year-old amateur worried about exams at Stanford. That left the door open for Duval, who seized the moment, shooting a seven-under-par 65 on Friday to take a one-shot lead into the weekend. "I feel like it's all coming together," he said. "I was most concerned I'd peaked with my golf and my strength, and I just wanted to be ready when I got here. I had no desire to be leading the tournament today. I've had one goal, and I've had it for a long time; that is to be leading when we're done on Sunday."

He had been so close the previous two years, watching in 1998 when Mark O'Meara sank an improbable birdie putt on the final hole to beat him by a single shot, and charging from the back in 1999 only to be foiled by one iffy club selection on Sunday. Now it all seemed right. Duval's time appeared to have come.

He was within one shot of the lead in the Masters through 65 holes, and stood in the 13th fairway of the final round with a chance to take command of his destiny. A birdie or an eagle at the reachable par-five would possibly move Duval into a tie with his Ponte Vedra neighbor, Vijay Singh. Head to head in a major, tied for the lead with five holes to play: that was the situation Duval had worked so hard for. It was, he thought, his time.

Ten minutes later the tournament was all but over. Duval had pondered his options from 196 yards for what seemed like an eternity. At first he chose a four-iron, and he looked and he waggled, and he looked some more. Then he went back to the bag and pulled the five-iron. Another look, another waggle, and another practice swing later, he backed off again. This one had to be right. "I was looking at Vijay's ball as the target because he hit pretty much a perfect shot," Duval said. But that target proved elusive. Duval hit a fat push, a shot much worse than the poor approach he had hit to the 16th hole in 1998 when he held the lead, or the water-bound iron he hit at the 11th in 1999. This shot was both off-line and badly struck. It never had a chance. "I just hit a bad shot," he said in perhaps the most understated quote of his career. But then, no words, no matter how eloquent, could have possibly conveyed his feelings.

Singh won the Masters by three over Els, who closed strong. Duval finished his week with another poor approach to the 18th, and in a rare display of emotion he pounded his iron into the pristine Augusta ryegrass, gritting his teeth in what, for him, was a three-year venting.

"I played perfectly well enough to win the golf tournament, but the day did not turn out like I wanted," he said in his post-tournament press conference. With a vacant stare and plenty of uncomfortable pauses, he vowed to press on, taking the fight to Pebble Beach for the U.S. Open. There was nothing else he could say or do.

Despite his poor opening round at the Masters, Tiger came back with rounds of 68 and 69 on the weekend, and had pulled to within three shots of Singh's lead before falling back. He ultimately finished alone in fifth place, one shot behind Duval. "Even though I didn't get off to a good start Thursday, I gave myself a chance," Tiger said. "I got back into the tournament and had a chance on Sunday. I knew going into this week that every time I play, this game is very fickle."

Like Duval, Tiger also turned his focus to the next major: the U.S. Open, the one professional tournament some skeptics still doubted he could win.

As a "tune-up" for the U.S. Open Tiger successfully defended his title at Jack Nicklaus's Memorial Tournament in May, giving him four victories in the first five months of the season. But the most impressive statistic wasn't the number of wins, but his winning percentage. For the 12-month period from May of 1999 through May of 2000 Tiger won 50 percent of the tournaments he entered, an unprecedented mark in the modern era of golf. Winning 10 percent of the tournaments entered was considered great, 20 percent a career year, and 30 percent an unparalleled performance. No one since the Hogan era had won half the tournaments he entered. Tiger was breaking new ground. Still, some said the U.S. Open would be his nemesis. Open fairways were too narrow for his game. He didn't have the patience to accept the inevitable bad breaks that were as much a part of the National Championship as high rough and hard greens. And Tiger was too impetuous to win an Open. Bogeys and double-bogeys were a foregone fact of life in USGA events, and many pundits believed Tiger couldn't accept that. Others quipped that the U.S. Open's par-is-a-good-score philosophy didn't jibe with Tiger's aggressive propensities. Mickelson might win the U.S. Open. Duval stood a good chance. But even though Tiger had won at Pebble Beach earlier in the year, he couldn't be considered a hands-down favorite. This was a different golf course from the one the tour visited in February, and the U.S.

Open was a different event from the AT&T Pro-Am. If Tiger expected to win, he would have to bring his "A" game.

How silly he made them look.

Butch Harmon, Tiger's long-time coach, summed it up best when he said, "I've never seen [Tiger] as focused as he is right now." He certainly carried the aura of a man on a mission. Even practice rounds were all business, no toying around with his fellow professionals and no playful engagement of the galleries. Tiger looked on Tuesday the way he looked on Sunday: intense, driven, and undistracted.

Critics pounced when Tiger chose to skip the Wednesday memorial service for defending champion Payne Stewart, calling him "insensitive" and "self-centered." The criticisms were unfair and, for the most part, wrong. Tiger made no bones about why he wasn't in attendance at the seaside service. "I felt going to the ceremony would be more of a deterrent for me during the tournament, because I don't want to be thinking about it," he said. The shrill cries of the critics echoed across the bay. How could he be so calloused, especially with Stewart's navy knickers enshrined in a museum called Payne's Place behind the 18th green, and Tracey Stewart present in the gallery? How could he not immerse himself in the collective anguish of his fellow pros like Sergio Garcia, who openly wept during the ceremony and continued to honor Stewart by wearing knickers during Thursday's opening round? For Tiger it was simple. He came to Pebble Beach to win a golf tournament. Anything and everything else was secondary. To call this an insult to Stewart's memory was shallow and inaccurate. Payne would have been the first person to tell Tiger to keep his mind on his business and minimize the distractions. Besides, Tiger was one of the few professionals who had made a six-figure donation to the Payne Stewart Foundation. He also knew that if he did show up at the service, he, not Payne, would have been the focus of the media's attention. Tiger wanted to be seen on the golf course and nowhere else. He had something to prove, and nothing was going to stand in his way.

Weather made it tough to follow the action at the 100th U.S. Open. Midway through Thursday's opening round, fog rolled in like a dry-ice mist in a cheap horror movie. Back when Tiger, Casey Martin, and Notah Begay were playing Pebble Beach as students at Stanford, the kids called this sort of weather "June Gloom," a perfectly apt description for the pea soup that halted play on Thursday, delayed it on Friday, and kept everyone in a disjointed state until late Saturday afternoon. When visibility finally returned, the tournament was all but over.

Tiger played early on Thursday, shooting an Open-record 65 and finishing before the gloom swallowed the rest of the field. "I just go out and play," he said. "If someone wants to say that I'm the favorite, so be it; the underdog, so be it. But I just focus on what I need to do. Today, I felt if I could drive the ball well, then I would score. And today I drove the ball beautifully."

Meanwhile, Duval, who had come dangerously close to breaking his winless streak the previous week but lost in a playoff at the Buick Classic in Harrison, New York, fired a 40 on his first nine holes before finishing the opening round in 75 blows. By the time the gloom settled on Thursday, Duval was 10 shots behind Tiger's lead. The second major of the season was barely under way and Duval was virtually irrelevant.

He wasn't alone, however. Friday's second round stretched into Saturday as fog delays continued, but while the weather kept a lot of things up in the air, one thing was certain: Tiger had control of this golf tournament. During the front nine on Friday Tiger hit the shot that would define the championship. At the par-five sixth he missed the fairway with his tee shot, and found his ball nestled deep in the right rough. According to NBC commentator Roger Maltby, who had to stand directly over the ball just to see it, "Eighty percent of the field would wedge it back to the fairway." But not Tiger. Staring at a cliff face in front of him with a well-guarded green out of view some 208 yards away, Tiger took out a seven-iron and thrashed a shot onto the green, stopping the ball 12 feet below the hole. Maltby could do little more than laugh. He then summed up this Open in one declarative statement: "Guys, this is just not a fair fight."

Tiger finished his second round on Saturday morning in less-stellar fashion. He reached 10-under-par through 35 holes, becoming the first man in U.S. Open history to reach double digits under par before the weekend. But just as it looked as though he would run away from the field, Tiger stood on the par-five 18th at Pebble Beach and promptly hooked his tee shot into the Pacific. He was none too pleased by that development, and let his displeasure be known by slamming his club into the turf and calling himself a "fucking prick," among other things. Little kiddies back home who were turning on their televisions to watch the latest Pokémon cartoon were treated to the swearfest, as an NBC microphone picked up and broadcast every spewing syllable. Tiger apologized profusely after the round, but a double-bogey was, after all, a double-bogey. It would be the worst score he would post on a single hole and, by all accounts, the only time he would lose his composure all week.

When he finished his day on Saturday with an even-par 71, Tiger was 10 shots ahead of Els, his nearest competitor, opening the largest 54-hole lead in U.S. Open history. Still, he wouldn't relax. "I just have to go out tomorrow and get the job done," he said.

"He's hitting every shot like his life depends on it," Thomas Björn, who played with Tiger on Saturday, said of his determination. Another European player and major championship winner, José María Olazábal, was the first to definitely throw in the towel. "He's won it already," Olazábal said late Saturday afternoon.

Before he teed off in his ceremonial coronation march on Sunday, Tiger was warming up on the range when Maltby walked by and asked if he would do a pre-round interview for NBC. As he had previously done with Chris Berman of ESPN, Tiger politely but unambiguously declined. He still had work to do, and nothing would distract him from his goal.

"His eye contact was right with his caddie and nowhere else," NHL coach Scotty Bowman, winner of eight Stanley Cups, who walked as a scorer in Tiger's group on Sunday, said of his intensity. "When he's preparing to hit a shot he's oblivious to everyone else."

Such observations weren't limited to spectators. Vijay Singh stood on the range on Sunday morning and said, "The thing is, I played with Nick Faldo [on Saturday], who made a lot of putts, but Tiger makes everything! You keep hearing 'He's young' and 'He'll learn it's not that easy' and 'Wait until he starts missing those six- and eight-footers.' Meanwhile, he keeps making them. Amazing!"

Adding insult to injury, Butch Harmon roamed the range during the pre-final-round warm-ups and in response to a question said, "Hey, I talked to Tiger last night and with a ten-shot lead he wants to know what's wrong with his swing, and why he's hitting so many loose irons."

That little anecdote sent Scott Hoch into an apoplectic fit. "What's wrong with his *what*!?" Hoch said. "It's a good thing he threw away a couple of shots or he'd *really* be running away from the rest of us."

The remaining players simply shook their heads in wonder. "He's in another dimension," Els said. " I considered squeezing Tiger in a bear hug, or arm-wrestling him, or just tackling him, but that wouldn't work because on top of everything else, Tiger is getting stronger every day. I don't know what we're going to do with him."

All Els could do on Sunday was step back and watch as he played in the final twosome with Tiger. With sunny but breezy conditions Tiger hit six out of seven fairways and eight out of nine greens en route to nine straight pars on the outward half. Nine more would have certainly preserved the victory by a substantial margin, but that wasn't good enough. Tiger wasn't simply playing against the field or the golf course; history was also a competitor, and he was determined to beat her as well.

As a child Tiger dreamed of playing in a U.S. Open where he "was usually playing against Jack and Arnold and Hogan and those guys, and it was usually neck-and-neck." This time only the records of those champions remained in Tiger's way. Nicklaus and Hogan had both been nine-under-par in U.S. Opens; Jack in 1980 at Baltusrol and Hogan in 1948 at Riviera. That had been Nicklaus's winning score, a U.S. Open record of 272, but Hogan, in 1953 at Oakmont, had led wire to wire. Woods had a chance to beat all of those records and a few more in the final nine holes at Pebble Beach.

When he two-putted for par on the 18th Tiger had secured a 15-shot victory, the largest winning margin in a major championship since Old Tom Morris took the British Open by 13 shots in 1862. He also tied Gil Morgan for the most strokes under par (12) at any point in the U.S. Open, but while Tiger finished there, Morgan, who had reached 12-under in 1992 at Pebble Beach, fell away and lost the championship to Tom Kite. The other records—largest 54-hole lead, largest 36-hole lead, and best winning score—broke or tied marks established between 1899 and 1993. Tiger was in a league of his own. As Kite put it, "Nobody else is playing up to his level. No one is scrambling the way he is. No one is pitching, chipping, putting the way he is. You need competition. Otherwise it gets boring."

Els and Jiménez tied for second at plus-three with John Huston finishing one behind them at 288, respectable scores under grueling conditions and quite a contest if Tiger had been excluded from the field. "If I played out of my mind, I probably would have lost by five, six, or seven [shots]," Els said. "It seems like we're not playing in the same ballpark right now. He's phenomenal, and that's an understatement, probably. We've been talking about him for two years, but whatever I say is going to be an understatement. He's the best player in the world, by far. He's probably ahead of Jack Nicklaus at this time in his career. He just played a perfect U.S. Open. He did nothing wrong. The guy is unbelievable. If you put Old Tom Morris with Tiger Woods, Tiger would probably beat him by eighty shots."

Tiger wasn't ready to accept such broad accolades, but he did shed some insight into his mind-set after it was over. "Well, I guess I won," he deadpanned on Sunday night to a smattering of laughter. Then, on a serious note, Tiger said, "There comes a point in time when you feel tranquil, when you feel calm; you feel at ease with yourself. And in those two weeks [the Masters week in 1997 and this week] I felt that way. I felt at ease; things just flowed. No matter what you do, good or bad, it really doesn't get to you. Even days when you wake up on the wrong side of the bed, for some reason, it doesn't feel too bad; it's just all right. To have those weeks just happen to coincide with major championships is even better.

Sir Michael Bonallack, captain of the R&A, summed up the collective feelings of everyone when he said, "If Tiger Woods does not win the Open Championship this year there ought to be a steward's inquiry."

No inquiry was necessary. Tiger won the British Open Championship at St. Andrews by eight shots and set another scoring record, finishing at 19-under-par. That gave him scoring records in the Masters, the U.S. Open, and the British Open. He also became the first man since Jack Nicklaus in 1972 to hold three major championship trophies at the same time. This time the win surprised no one. In fact, on Thursday morning before Tiger teed off, Bev Norwood of IMG was sipping coffee and chatting with Ron Sirak of *Golf World* when the subject of Tiger's chances came up. "I'll never underestimate him again," Norwood said, "because I've finally realized that Tiger is the best who ever played." Not a single person who heard that statement disagreed.

By Friday, Tiger led by three. By Saturday the lead was six. Once again, it was all but over. Before the weekend British bookies posted Tiger as a preposterous 2–11 favorite. By Sunday morning, all wagers were off. Every casino in the world took Tiger off the board.

One player wasn't ready to concede, however. With a six-under-par 66 on Saturday, David Duval moved to a 10-under and into the final pairing with Tiger, the first time the twosome had been paired together in a final round. To have it come in a major made the event more special, even it if was a major where Tiger held a six-shot lead. "I just wanted to be there," Duval said. "It will be a circus. It will be exciting, a slugfest, whatever you want to call it. You get to look him in the eye, and if I can swing the club like I have the last few days and putt like I have been, I can show him I've got a little game going right now, too."

As they warmed up side by side on the driving range before the final round the circus was in full swing with cameras, microphones, and "cheeky" Scottish youths loudly begging for autographs and memorabilia. Few in the gallery knew that Tiger and David had become reasonably close friends over the previous year, often sharing plane rides and dinners together. They were still fierce competitors, but they were also fellow professionals who enjoyed each other's company. The fact that their girlfriends got along well only added to their bond. They weren't soul mates by any means, but they weren't mortal enemies, either. On this day, however, they were combatants embroiled in a major championship duel. And it seemed that all of Fife had turned out to watch their epic battle.

For nine holes at least, the fans weren't disappointed. Duval got out with three quick birdies to cut Tiger's lead in half. For a few fleeting moments it appeared as though the contest was joined. But Tiger was steady, making no mistakes, finding every fairway and focusing on every shot. As was the case in the U.S. Open when Tiger hit his "it's not a fair fight" shot, the defining moment of the British Open came in a subtle way at a seemingly obtuse time. On the fifth tee of the final round, Duval hit what appeared to be a fine drive. The crowds up ahead confirmed the shot's position with a polite smattering of applause. Then Tiger hit, and the gasp from the spectators was audible from hundreds of yards away. When the two players arrived at their balls Tiger had driven his ball 100 yards past Duval. While there were no official measurements of the shot's length, on-course observers estimated it to be in the neighborhood of 429 yards, an obscenely long and incredibly accurate shot at just the right time. Once again, Maltby's words rang true: it really wasn't a fair fight.

Duval remained close through nine holes, but fell away in the final nine. "I accomplished everything I needed to," Duval said. "I really cut the deficit, but just as everything turned out well on the front nine, that's how bad things were on the back." By the time they reached the famous 17th—the Road Hole, as it's known—the tournament was over. The fact that Duval found himself trapped in a greenside bunker on the penultimate hole was merely a burdensome insult and a brutal metaphor for all his frustrations. After crawling into the deep, sand-filled crater and examining his options, Duval took a vicious swing. The shot looked good, but it hit the lip and came back into the sand. A second blast fared no better. For his third bunker shot, David had to hit a one-handed punch just to get the ball back to the middle of the sand, so that on his fourth attempt he could finally get the ball out of the trap and onto the green. All who witnessed the episode were wounded by it. Duval had worked so hard to finally find himself in the final group in the final round of a major, and now he had become little more than a sideshow. When he two-putted for an eight in the par-four, millions felt his anguish.

Tiger cruised in with a final-round 69. The only threat to his crown in the last hour came from an overzealous mob of fans that broke through the ropes and stormed the 18th fairway, while a well-endowed female streaker pranced around the final green in her birthday suit until two of St. Andrews's finest whisked her away. It truly was a circus. Once order was restored, Tiger calmly two-putted for par to shoot 19-under-par and break Nick Faldo's 72-hole scoring record by a single shot. He then hugged Duval and said during their embrace, "You're a true champion. Walk off like a champion."

Duval did just that, answering questions afterward with candid and almost eerie calm. "It's disappointing because I feel I'm starting to play better," he said. But, as he pointed out, he put himself in contention on the final day, just as he had done in the Masters. There were plenty of other players who hadn't had that opportunity. "It's where you want to be," he said. "That's where I'm going to work hard to get again in a couple of weeks [at the PGA Championship]. I'll give it another run."

There was little doubt whom Duval would have to beat if he expected to win that elusive first major championship.

A steady stream of apologists called or made personal pilgrimages to see Earl Woods in the final weeks following his son's historic major championship runs. Those who had thought Earl was outrageous when he said such things as "Tiger will do more than any other man in history to change the course of humanity" were coming to the realization that the

68-year-old retired Army officer wasn't so crazy after all. Comparisons to Nelson Mandela and Gandhi, which Earl had made throughout the years, were still over the top by more than a small margin, but at the rate he was going, Tiger could conceivably break Nicklaus's major championship record before his 35th birthday. He was also one of the most recognized figures on the planet, with the potential to become the first billionaire athlete in history. If anything, Earl might have sold his son a little short.

Rick Reilly, the *Sports Illustrated* columnist known for his biting wit and big ego, made the trek to Earl's abode as part of the apology tour. When Reilly asked Earl if he still thought Tiger would be a larger figure in world history than Gandhi, the elder Woods stuck to his guns. "Tiger will be a more important figure outside of golf than in it," Earl said. "He will make his mark on world history, probably through his foundation. He'll impact nations. Do you recall the impact Muhammad Ali had, even with his lack of education and his lack of communication skills? Imagine someone with the education and communication skills that Tiger has, somebody with a sense of responsibility, and purpose.

"When Tiger was one year old, I used to tell my friends what was coming. They'd all laugh at me. The other day those friends came over to the house and said, 'We came to apologize. We thought you were just ranting and raving.' Yeah, it hurt to be called pompous and a braggart, but it was only because I knew, and they didn't. Everything I've said has come true. What you're seeing now is only the tip of the iceberg. And that's still true. Tiger is going to get better, more efficient, and more effective."

This time around, no one doubted Earl's word.

# AUTHOR'S NOTE

GOOD TO HIS WORD, in December of 1999, PGA of America CEO Jim Awtrey met his self-imposed deadline and presented the players of the 1999 Ryder Cup team with a plan to share the $20 million windfall from Brookline. The PGA donated $200,000 per player to charity, half going to the player's charity of choice and the remaining $100,000 earmarked for college golf programs.

After the announcement, Phil Mickelson said, "As for standing up for what's right, using my name to such a good end has made it all worth it."

# ACKNOWLEDGMENTS

AS A GOLF WRITER I am constantly being asked what the players on the PGA Tour are really like, as if professionals golfers are rare, exotic birds and only those of us who study their nesting habits can offer profound insight into their behavior. It's an odd quirk of my profession. Total strangers at cocktail parties will say things like, "Who are the good guys on Tour?" or "Is Tiger nice?" or even better, "Who has the most phony public image?"

To date, my answers have been universally the same: professional golfers are normal people, not much different from any other group of working professionals. But as I was researching and writing this book, my opinion on that answer changed slightly. During the time it took me to pen the pages, two NFL players were arrested and charged with two separate murders; one Major League baseball superstar tested positive for cocaine for the fourth time, while a relief pitcher told us all how much he detested Asian women and "queers with AIDS." As I was reflecting on the epic changes in golf that occurred from 1997 through 1999, three high-profile NBA players were named in a ninety-page federal racketeering indictment, and an NHL player was charged with assault for whacking another player in the head with a hockey stick. In the midst of all this, it dawned on me that my perceptions of the PGA Tour were all wrong. By the standards of today's modern athlete, professional golfers are not normal: they are extraordinary.

A number of those exemplary athletes, and many others who work in and around professional golf, were kind enough to share their thoughts and memories with me as I was preparing this book, and for that I am truly grateful. A special thanks to the following: Deane and Judy Beman, Puggy Blackman, President George Bush, Bob Combs, Ben Crenshaw, Bob Duval, David Fay, John Feinstein, Tim Finchem, Jim Furyk, Vinny Giles, Mark Hayes, Scott and Sally Hoch, Hale Irwin, Alastair Johnston, Rees Jones, Tom Kite, Franklin Langham, Davis and Mark Love, Julius Mason, Mark H. McCormack, Tom Meeks, Larry Nelson, Jack Nicklaus, Bev Norwood, Jerry Pate, John Strege, Hal Sutton, Jean and Brigitte Van de Velde, Martin West, and

ACKNOWLDGEMENTS

Slugger White. To the countless other people who contributed in both small and large ways to this project, I also offer my dearest thanks.

If God is in the details, I found divine inspiration in one of the greatest researchers I've ever worked with. Mary Bishop, a freelance researcher from Connecticut who once worked for *Golf World* magazine, found everything I needed and then some. No detail was too small, and her skill at digging out the obscure was priceless.

Also I wish to thank my agent, Mark Reiter, for his persistence and belief in this project, as well as my friends at Crown Publishers, Rachel Kahan and Steve Ross, without whom this book would not exist.

# INDEX

24.00

796.352
E

Eubanks, Steve,

At the turn.

| DATE | | | |
|---|---|---|---|
| | | | |
| | | | |
| | | | |
| | | | |
| | | | |
| | | | |
| | | | |
| | | | |
| | | | |
| | | | |
| | | | |
| | | | |
| | | | |